Leicester~~ and Rutland Within Living Memory

Compiled by the Leicestershire and Rutland Federation of Women's Institutes from notes sent by Institutes in the County

Published jointly by
Countryside Books, Newbury
and the LRFWI, Leicester

COUNTRYSIDE BOOKS
3 Catherine Road
Newbury, Berkshire

ISBN 1 85306 297 9

The cover photograph shows Sylvia, Jessie and Sybil.
Supplied by Huncote WI.

Designed by Mon Mohan
Produced through MRM Associates Ltd, Reading
Printed in England by J.W. Arrowsmith Ltd, Bristol

Contents

TOWN & COUNTRY LIFE — *page 9*
> Old Leicester – Some other towns and villages remembered – Church and chapel – Getting about.

HOUSE & HOME — *page 53*
> The way we lived then – The houses we lived in – Water and washday – Shopping and callers to the door – Food in season – From the cradle to the grave.

CHILDHOOD & SCHOOLDAYS — *page 99*
> When we were young – Treats and holidays – Games and chores – Schooldays: the best years of our lives?

THE WORLD OF WORK — *page 135*
> On the land – Coal, quarries and factories – Other ways we made a living – Village trades and crafts.

WAR & PEACE — *page 181*
> The Great War 1914–18 – The Second World War 1939–45 – A child's war – Doing our bit – The Women's Land Army – Growing up in wartime.

HIGH DAYS & HOLIDAYS — *page 229*
> Making our own entertainment – Royal occasions – Celebrations through the year – Christmas past.

Foreword

Over the past 30 years, life in rural Leicestershire and Rutland has changed considerably, even in some cases beyond recognition. Industries we were once renowned for have disappeared or are fast disappearing. Agriculture too has seen many changes, with more machinery and different ways of managing the land having been introduced.

Although many railway lines have been cut, motorways have multiplied and so travel to many cities and towns has been made easier. With an airport also on our doorstep, people and places only dreamed of years ago are suddenly just a few hours away and so we are able to widen our horizons even further.

But all these changes have meant that the pace of life has increased and I am sure that we all, at times, long for a quieter, slower era. Thinking and talking of the past, remembering people and places of our childhood, seems to kindle in one a warm glow as we get older and I am sure we have all, at some time in our lives, said, 'Do you remember . . .?'

I hope that as you read this book of memories of WI members, their families and friends, you too will say, 'Yes, I remember it well.'

Barbara Gill
County Chairman

Acknowledgements

Leicestershire and Rutland Federation of Women's Institutes would like to thank all WI members who supplied written material, drawings and photographs for this project through their local Institutes. Unfortunately, we were not able to include extracts from every submission: to do so would have meant some duplication of content, and of course we had to take into account the total amount of space available in the book. All the contributions were, without exception, of value in deciding the shape and content of the book. We are grateful for them all.

We would like to thank Mr Duncan Lucas for permission to use photographs from his archives at the Wigston Magna Folk Museum. Mr Lucas, former Chairman of Leicestershire County Council, offers them as his contribution to the efforts of the LRFWI. We also thank the artist Mrs Olwen Hughes for her delightful illustrations, contributed gratis, which introduce each section of 'Within Living Memory'. Mrs Hughes, recently appointed as the Lord Mayor of Leicester's Ambassador, has forged close links with LRFWI over the years.

Finally, we would like to thank Tuxford & Tebbutt and the Long Clawson Dairy.

Dorothy Pennington
Co-ordinator

THE LEICESTERSHIRE & RUTLAND FEDERATION OF WOMEN'S INSTITUTE

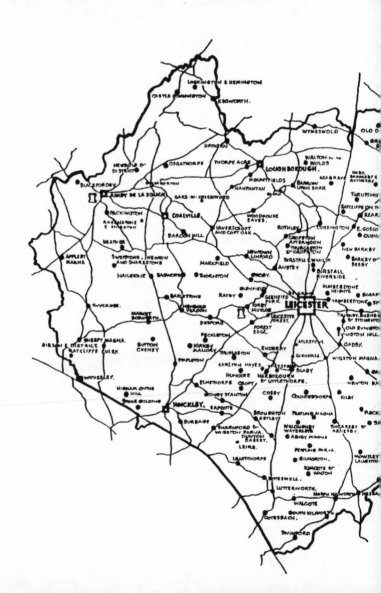

LEICESTERSHIRE & RUTLAND

HARBY

HARSTON
E KNIPTON.

NG CLAWSON   EATON   CROXTON
KERRIAL.
                                   SALTBY

B KETTLEBY   SCALFORD   WALTHAM   SPROXTON
                                  ON THE WOLDS

                                  BUCKMINSTER
                                  AND SEWSTERN.

Y   MELTON MOWBRAY.   WYMONDHAM
LARS.
          BURTON   MARKET OVERTON
          LAZARS.   E THISTLETON

                        WHISSENDINE   GREETHAM.

          GREAT DALBY.   ASHWELL   COTTESMORE   RYHALL
Y   THORPE SATCHVILLE
    TWYFORD   LANGHAM E
                              BARLEYTHORPE
Y   BURROUGH
          ON THE HILL   EMPINGHAM.
                              OAKHAM
          KNOSSINGTON.   STAMFORD.

                      BRAUNSTON.
                                                      KETTON
    TILTON ON THE HILL   MANTON.
BILLESDON
          LODDINGTON   RIDLINGTON   WING
                       E PRESTON   SOUTH
                       BELTON   MORCOTT   LUFFENHAM
TON ON THE HILL   WAKERLEY E BARROWDEN.
                              UPPINGHAM.
                              UPPINGHAM EVENING.   N
          HALLATON   LYDDINGTON

      GLOOSTON
          SLAWSTON E BLASTON.
THE LANGTONS. MEDBOURNE CUM HOLT   CALDECOTT.
                       GREAT EASTON
                       E DISTRICT
    GREAT
    BOWDEN.
HAM LITTLE BOWDEN
HAM

0 1 2 3 4 5 6 7 8 9 10 11 12
MILES

TOWN & COUNTRY LIFE

BILLESDON.

© SEAN HUGHES
'986
CHRISTMAS

OLD LEICESTER

Leicester has changed almost beyond recognition since the early years of the 20th century, but those brought up there still have vivid memories of life as it used to be.

THE LEICESTER OF MY YOUTH

'We lived in Junior Street in the early 1900s. Nearby was Cross Keys Yard. The yards had communal toilets and newspaper for toilet paper. The tap and washhouse were also communal. In winter the tap used to freeze and salt was used to melt it. In the middle of the courtyard the rubbish was piled up. "Mind the middin," people said to passers by and to children, "I'll chuck you in the middin if you're not careful!"

From the age of about five years, children used to pop in and out of friends' houses on their own. No one ever locked their doors, and nobody worried. The only thing I remember going was a pet bird belonging to my father. It was called a "roller" and was actually a cross between a canary and a linnet.

The milk was delivered from large churns in half pint cans. Old Hiram Deakin delivered the daily newspaper – *The Leicester Mercury*. It cost one penny and he collected it on Fridays or Saturdays. "Frommetie" was a kind of wheat porridge and was also delivered from door to door. Coal was twopence a bucket. It came from Levises on the corner of Long Lane and Burgess Street.

My grandmother lived in a yard up Pasture Lane. The famous boxer Len Wickerwall lived near her in Sanvey Gate. Some of the houses were very old and when a friend was asked where she lived she used to say, "Oh, you know, Agony Villas, Pains Road."

I can remember the courts being cleaned by a hose made from sheep's intestine which was attached to the tap in the yard.

Next to us in Junior Street lived a man called Mr Fisher. He roasted dandelion roots to make coffee. He also kept rabbits and grew potatoes. When he had boiled them he sometimes used to chuck them upstairs into the bedroom windows for my sisters and me.

Friday night was called "Amami night" as we all washed our hair. This was done in a tin bath placed on the table in a tiny upstairs closet. We filled the bath with a jug and had to empty it with a hose-pipe out of the window.

We made pegged rugs from old coats and tried to get a bit of red coloured cloth to make it look bright. We had sticks for furniture but nobody minded – we were all the same. We cleaned the grate with black lead and we bought a halfpenny or a penny's worth of white sand from the monumental masons on the corner of Woodgate to scrub the kitchen table and the stairs.

If there was a thunderstorm all the windows and doors were opened so the thunderbolt would pass through. Also the mirrors would be covered or turned round and all the knives, forks and scissors were put away so lightning would not strike!'

'In March 1904 my father took part in the famous "Right to Work" marches, organised by "Hoppy" White and Amo Sherry. He often told us about the march. He slept in churches and schools on the march to London and people rushed out to cheer them on and offer them shoes or food. After all that, however, the King would not see them.

During the First World War the soldiers shouted "Hurrah!" or sang *Tipperary* or *Keep the home fires burning* when they passed. If they came through Leicester station they used to chuck their letters out of the windows to be posted by us children. I remember delivering one to a soldier's mother who lived in Vine Street. We also helped the WVS ladies serve tea to the soldiers on the station.

On Armistice Day, 11th November 1918, we all watched and waited for the flag to go up on St Margaret's church spire. When it was raised we left the factories to sing and dance round the streets and even down the aisles at Woolworths!

I went to the election meetings just to hear the hecklers. I remember Churchill's wife being disgusted with the response he got at one meeting. He asked the audience, "If you are going to vote for me, put one hand up." No one did, but everyone put up two hands when asked if they were going to vote Labour!

Jennie Churchill is remembered as a very beautiful woman. She used to say, "Please vote for my husband – I shall be most upset if he is not elected." (Her husband, however, was not sympathetic to Jennie's campaign for votes for women!)

I can remember voting day when people banged on dustbin lids – mothers used rolling pins – to drum up support. One of the chants went,

"Vote for Pethwick Lawrence
Work, work, work and do your best.
If all the people he enrol –
He's sure to head the poll,
And you'll have a Labour Man for Leicester West."

Some people used to ride on a dray round the streets on voting day gathering as much support as possible. I remember singing *The Red Flag* at De Montfort Hall. My father was staunch Labour. He was also very strict, and proud that none of his four daughters "had to get married".

There were several newspapers published in Leicester. I remember the *Police News* which had pink coloured pages. My mother's brother, Fred Greaves, used to sell it in Gresham Street.

My father came out of the Pioneer Corps after the war. His Captain helped him buy a few pairs of shoes from Airborne in Northampton. At first he went round the villages, including Markfield and Stanton under Bardon, selling shoes – he was known as "Little Billy the Boot Man". Then he set up a small shop in Sanvey Gate, "Carveys". On Sermons day and Anniversary days many people came in for boots. If poor children came in he would always find something for their feet. I remember him rushing down to the cellar to find an oddment of leather to cobble a child's shoes.

He also earned a little money from gambling. He played a game called "Crown and Anchor". I am not sure what the rules were, but I know it was played on a cloth sheet from "Sports" in High Street. The banker for the game always kept the loser's money – it must have been profitable as it was very popular.

Gambling was illegal in those days and I know he used to collect bets, hidden in matchboxes, from the window sills in public toilets. He took halfpenny bets on the horses in Spittlehouse Street. If he was caught for this or playing pitch and toss, his friends would come and bail him out of Sanvey Gate police station.

The police station lock-up was also known as the "Blue Door". It was next to Gimsons timber yard. If my dad didn't come home for tea my mother knew he had been taken, ". . . can see the police have no money – they nick him for some funds!"

My grandmother kept a shop in Junior Street, near Bond Street. The shop was at the front of her house. It had shelves round the walls stocked with sweet jars and a few tins. It had a large window at the front and a gaslight mantle. Men from Inks & Saunders shoe factory used to put items like cigarettes "on the slate". If they went on the beer at the weekend they neither turned up for work nor paid their debts off on Monday. Others would simply rub their names off the slate when the shop was busy.

My mother got up at 6 am to work in the Fielding Johnson spinning factory. She came home at 8 am for breakfast and afterwards went back until 5 pm.

One of my earliest jobs was in a fish and chip shop in Sanvey Gate – The Tavern. I used to chop the potatoes with a slicing gadget. I remember during the First World War a cartoon on the wall. It showed a man putting chips into a bowler hat and saying, "Oh that's the best we can do – we've got no paper!"

An uncle of mine regularly hired a truck from Ginns and Gutteridge and bought large blocks of salt from a merchant in Belgrave Road (next to the Star Pictures or "Flea Pit"). He chopped the salt into smaller pieces and sold it door to door round the houses. We used to put it into empty jam jars and crush it when required with a rolling pin.

I left school at 14 years of age with my friends Florrie Hodgson, Gert Martin, Elsie, Angie and Flo. We went into the hosiery trade, at Beddingfields or Limekings. We made ten shillings a week.

There were many other ways of earning a little money. The "Twizzle Sisters" searched the alley and doorways round pubs to collect the empties and return them to the pubs. They went out every morning for years performing this work.

Other street jobs were digging scrap iron (from carts etc) out of the cobbles and taking this to the rag and bone man in Abbey Street. We also took rubbish wool from Gregory's factory; there the rag and bone man would not allow us much as he knew we had pinched the wool. It made us a few coppers though and we did not care.

When it snowed men queued all night for a spade from the Destructors in Grape Street, as you got paid for shovelling away the snow. If you had your own spade it was much easier to get the job.

Sometimes on Saturdays early in the morning, we went down to Smeggies in Pingle Street to get a barrow of coal. We bought it by the hundredweight. We divided the coal into penny bags and sold it up and down the streets. If anyone needed coal but had no money, we pinched a few lumps from all the bags and gave them a free bag!

Many people went gleaning, ie gathering wheat after the harvest, to make frommetie. We went mushrooming, and scrumping apples was also very popular, especially for the youngsters, who were always chased off by the farmers! From the age of 10 we went blackberrying on the Stadium estate, Sandhills. Sometimes engine drivers chucked coal out from the trains as they passed for us to collect and take home.

If people had no money on Monday for food, they took the sheets from their beds, their towels or the father's suit down to "The Crosses", a pawn shop in Sanvey Gate. The suit could be pawned for "five bob". It was usually redeemed on Friday after payment. After one month a bargain sale of non-reclaimed items was held. This was called "marking off day". If anyone especially liked an item they could give sixpence to "Mrs Layby" to lay it by until marking off day.

Anstey Nan earned her money as a prostitute. There were others too. I remember during the Second World War meeting a drunk sailor who had been to Rothley Zoo with two prostitutes. He was very much the worse for wear so I took him home, let him sleep the night, gave him breakfast and money for his bus fare home. I often wondered what happened to him!

During the Second World War we made extra money by travelling from Braunstone to the army camps in Evington where we collected the American soldiers' washing. Also during that time I remember a whole consignment of jerseys that had been sent to the factory for embroidering with pips. They were never collected so we shared them out down the street!'

MOTHER HAD A PIE SHOP

'I was born 100 years ago in a house and shop in a street where the Holiday Inn now stands. My mother had a pie shop and people came from all over and queued for her pies. I went to school at four years old. I think it was Holy Bones. I had to go four times a day by the old Jewry Wall and ran like mad. I was scared as I was told witches lived in the wall.

We wore high buttoned boots which had to be fastened with a button hook, starched white frilly pinafores, and long bloomers edged with lace, with a large ribbon bow at the back of our hair. We had desks which two sat at and if we misbehaved we got so many stripes from the teacher. We had a teacher, a Miss Stole, who said I smelled of fish and kept caning me for it, so my mother came to the school to see her and went to slap her and caught her hair and her wig fell off, much to our amusement. The culprit turned out to be the girl who sat next to me. She lived in a fish and chip shop.

My mother and father worked very long hours, 6.30 am to 8.30 pm for 16 shillings a week and I had a halfpenny on a Saturday to spend.

I started work in Wallington Street sewing baby bonnets. At the end of the week I had done 200 and spoilt the lot so I had the sack. So then I went to Wood and Sons, Fitzroy Street, Leicester, where I became a winder, which I loved. We used to go to the market on Saturday nights after eight o'clock where for a penny you could get two bananas or four apples and oranges, and a halfpennyworth of mushy peas – afterwards we went into the coffee shop, where the ground coffee smelt lovely, and had a cup for twopence.'

HARD TIMES

'I was only ten years old in 1926. I can remember my father being thrown out of work on to the dole, with most of the men from Leicester with him, and queueing at the Labour Exchange, an old wooden building. The queue stretched from Nicholas Street right down to the West Bridge and beyond, for ten shillings a week.

To know real hardship one had to live in those times. There is no comparison with today. After twelve weeks on the dole my father's money was stopped and he had to do shoe repairs in a shed in the backyard, charging two shillings and sixpence for soling and heeling men's shoes, and ladies' two shillings. There was no Social Security in those days. To help out I had to do a paper round at two shillings and sixpence for seven days before and after school, very often with no soles in my boots or shoes. We occasionally had a new pair given by the *Leicester Evening Mail*.

We lived in old slum-type houses, with one tap and one toilet in a yard to four houses and very often the tap froze in winter, also the toilet, and we had to use lighted newspapers round it to thaw it out. Also, when it snowed all the men on the dole had to report for snow clearing of the main roads, with brush and shovel into horse-drawn carts and this was then tipped into the canal.

I can remember my father being fetched out of bed by two detectives and put in Leicester Prison for a month for debt and he had to sew mail bags like a criminal, and this was only for not being able to pay his way, having no money to do so. My sister and I were put into a council children's home and separated until he was released.

Time moved on and 1930 came and I left school at 14 years of age and my father put me to being a butcher as he said, "There will always be work for butchers as people must eat." This was a job I never liked. A mechanical engineer was my first choice but as work was very scarce one had to stay put and I worked six days of twelve hours and four hours on Sundays for the princely sum of ten shillings a week, and sixpence was stopped for a National Insurance stamp.

I remember the Jarrow marchers coming through Leicester on their way to the Houses of Parliament and they stayed for the night at St Mark's church. They looked so thin and many looked ill, and their boots were worn out and had sackcloth bound round them. Things never really got good work-wise and though I enjoyed my teenage years with good pals, all too soon 1939 came along and it took a war to get the wheels of industry really buzzing again.'

POINT DUTY

'It took three policemen on point duty to control the traffic on the Clock Tower; one at the mouth of Humberstone Gate, one at Churchgate and one at Eastgate. My cousin used to do an eight hour shift on the tower, come hail, rain, sleet or snow. He did that duty for six years. Other points were at Carts Lane and the High Street, and outside Woolworths in Granby Street where the policeman stood on a box. My uncle wore a white helmet and white gloves over his uniform when he did that particular point duty. He was six foot three inches tall and when he stood on his box he was quite a big man!

Another point was at the bottom of Charles Street and Abbey Street. A very awkward corner! Another was outside the BU factory in Belgrave Road. This was when the men were leaving work and it enabled the many bicycles to get onto the road. On race days there were policemen on nearly all the major crossroads on the London Road as far as Shanklin Drive, and also one to let the traffic into the racecourse itself. Special trams used to run from the railway station to the Stoneygate terminus for racegoers only. It must have been a very tiring and quite an important job, keeping the traffic moving.'

ON AYLESTONE ROAD

'It was in 1923 that I came to live in Leicester, my first house there being on Aylestone Road, with the river Soar at the bottom of the garden. Early memories of living there were of waking up to hear "bang, bang" – the gate on the towpath of the canal going backwards and forwards, as workers going to St Mary's Mill passed through. It was possible to use the old mill bridge by paying a penny toll. Very frequently barges, laden with coal, chugged along the canal. In those days the cuckoo was very often heard, sometimes all day.

From the bottom of the garden we overlooked the skating field. By opening a sluice the field was flooded, the water freezing on very wintry, frosty days, and safe skating was possible. This attracted skaters from far and wide. Some winters the river and canal froze too and skating was possible on them.

The cattle market entrance was on Aylestone Road, and on market days it was a familiar sight to see, and hear, flocks of sheep and herds of cattle being driven along the road to market. One day we had a bullock in the back garden next door, much to the consternation of the house owner. It did no damage, just "tip-toed through the tulips". Alas, now the cattle market is closed, just the ornamental gates showing what has been.

Do you remember the Freeman's Common with its gardens and huts on lettered roads, a short cut through to Welford Road, but closed one day a year, 31st August, to show it was private land? This land has now been sold and developed and the Freemen are now living in attractive bungalows at the Freeman's Holt in Aylestone.

Further along Aylestone Road were the gasworks and I have memories of long queues for coke in the days of coal strikes. I also remember the gasworks being sand-bagged to save it from flooding from the brook which runs near. It was a fact that parents could get permission for their children, suffering from whooping cough, to walk round the gasworks for a cure.

It was a former custom in Aylestone church on Rogation Sunday for the evening congregation to walk round the village, halting at various points for a hymn and prayers, the service ending at the farm on Marsden Lane. "Blessing the crops" it was called.'

THROUGH THE GENERATIONS

'My grandmother came to Leicester from Great Glen in 1895 when she was nine years old. She told me many stories of old Leicester. One was about the Pavilion Theatre (later to become The Palace) where plays were performed. She saw Lon Chaney Snr there and was very impressed by his artistry in making himself look deformed, and wearing make-up to set the audience gasping with horror. After the theatre, supper was then the thing to have in one of the many supper houses in Edwardian Leicester. Usual dishes were pie and chips, peas, fish, black pudding and potatoes. There was a Leicester character named by the regulars the "Egg King": he would have six raw eggs (in their shells) set before him with a glass and one by one he would crack them into the glass, swallow them whole, then stand up and walk out.

The Hippodrome stood on the corner of Wharf Street and there my grandmother saw John Merrick, "The Elephant Man", who was a Leicester man and who sadly earned his living by showing his malformed body. As he came onto the stage and revealed his back, women screamed and hid their faces and some fainted and had to be carried out. The date of this is uncertain but it was about 1910 to 1912.

Living with my grandmother, I can remember her house in Woodland Road being one of the first to have electricity installed – I was two years old at the time. It was a terraced house and the switch was on the wall adjoining next door. The neighbours complained of the noise that the switch made when switching on and off.

Tram cars ran along Humberstone Road/Uppingham Road to the Trocadero and the Lido swimming pool. My brother and I used to take a towel rolled up with our swimming costumes inside and go on the tram. We went upstairs and loved to move the seat backs to face the opposite way. When you moved one seat the whole row moved in the same direction.

In 1945, towards the end of the war, dancing in the parks was started off by a Mr Reg Whightman of Fairfax Road. A ring of grass was fenced in and a gramophone with loudspeakers was played. We danced the barn dance, the valeta, the waltz, all the old-fashioned dances. We were charged sixpence and this included a lesson. I loved to dance with the feel of the grass beneath my feet.

There was a celery man who called round with a handcart on Sunday afternoons with fresh, washed celery which smelled delicious. There was also the bread man with his horse and cart – no sliced stuff then.

During the depression my mother and father and myself lived with my grandmother but things became a little better around 1935. Father looked for work on a daily basis and for a time he drove a large Corona soft drinks cart drawn by a shire horse. I was terrified of the horse although it was lovely and had lots of brass and medals on its harness. Remembering the bottles of lemonade and dandelion and burdock, the tops were ceramic and attached to the bottles with metal each side. You popped them off with your thumbs and the top still remained attached to the bottle. There were also special stone ginger bottles with corks in the tops.

Once the war came, rationing was another thing – I remember having to register with a corner shop (aptly named Hubbard's shop) for butter, bacon, sugar, cheese and eggs, but "points" could be spent anywhere for jam, biscuits, tinned meat, tinned milk and so on. Sweets were also on points and when a purchase was made the shopkeeper cut out the number of points for the purchase – believe me, one of the first things a child learned was how many points needed for a bar of chocolate. Many times Mrs Hubbard dived under the counter for some scarce commodity that was not shown above the counter, for "regulars only".

School was very basic in the war years and cookery lessons were very difficult as we had to take our own ingredients and our mothers often would not spare them. The class would watch the teacher make a dish and then take notes. I well remember one day having no ingredients, so I was allowed the privilege of cooking teacher's lunch: bacon, fried bread and egg – I can almost smell it now. I lived on the memory of that smell for ages as bacon was scarce and eggs were one a week and had to be used in cooking.

I lived in a cul-de-sac from the age of five and during the big freeze of 1940/41 our road was so blocked the coal lorry and horse carts could not get down it and we burnt old shoes filled with "slack" (powdered coal). The water pipes were so frozen we lit newspapers to thaw them out and the windows had thick frost patterns on the inside in the mornings.

In 1947–50 the highlight of the week was to walk up and down Melton Road. Lots of boys and girls did so – just as in my grandmother's day they walked up and down the London Road, with a "Bob" side and a "Tanner" side in those days ("Bob" one shilling, "Tanner" one sixpence). In 1947 we would go to the pictures: one shilling and threepence for a good seat, then to the new milk bar in Melton Road for a milk shake and a bus home. In this milk bar towards the end of 1950 they installed a juke box. It was very popular – a great novelty.

On Saturday mornings we would go to Woolworths in Gallowtree Gate and look around – everything was very cheap. At the rear entrance of Woolworths, a small road off Charles Street, horse-drawn railway wagons unloaded and two large shire horses pulled each wagon. I can recall having to walk very close to the horses as there was hardly any room.

Brucciani's was a favourite meeting place for Saturday mornings in the mid 1950s for us girls so that we could have coffee and plan the week ahead – the cinema or perhaps the Palais de Danse.'

SOME OTHER TOWNS AND VILLAGES REMEMBERED

Lamplighters on the streets, the village shop which sold anything and everything, roads quiet and safe enough for children to play in – not so long ago, after all. Here are glimpses of just a few towns and villages, and their inhabitants, in the first half of the 20th century.

MELTON MOWBRAY

'Many of us can remember the days when the streets had gaslights which the lamplighter lit each evening; the shops were independently owned and had smells of ground coffee, smoked bacon, Stilton cheese and spices and also had cash carriers that moved around the shop by the magical pull of a cord; there was maypole dancing; cheap bus fares; new best dresses and black patent leather ankle-strap shoes for the chapel Anniversary; and the necessary little room was a shed at the bottom of the garden with a "two-seater".

But there were many circumstances which were exclusive to Melton. Life before the Second World War depended to a great extent on the popularity of foxhunting and during the winter months the large houses or hunting boxes as they were called were full of wealthy people, including Royalty, who came with their entourage of grooms, maids, valets, butlers etc for the season. Craven Lodge was the home of the Prince of Wales, later Edward VIII and after his abdication, Duke of Windsor, and Warwick Lodge was for many years occupied by his brother, the Duke of Gloucester. They could be seen walking between the two houses in a very informal manner.

The phrase "painting the town red" means today having a good time but it meant exactly what it said in 1837. In an escapade many prominent buildings in the town were daubed with red paint by members of the foxhunting elite. This particular episode is of course beyond the memory of any resident but there were many equally daring and boisterous pranks in the 1920s and 1930s which we can recall.

A typical scene in Hallaton high street at the turn of the century, showing The Old Royal Oak and Mr Pick's butcher's shop.

Many of the hunting boxes were occupied during the wars by troops stationed in the area and a visit by George VI to Newport Lodge to review the troops stationed there in 1944 can be recalled. Meltonians will also always remember the battle of Arnhem, for the paratroopers who took part in that raid were stationed in the area and in the parish church there is a plaque in memory of those who were killed in the battle.

Mention that you hail from Melton Mowbray and the immediate reply is, "Oh yes, where the pork pies come from." This is so but whereas before 1939 there were numerous pork butchers in the town all making their own brand of pie there are now no individual pork butchers specialising in pork products and only one manufacturer of pies, though many more, manufactured outside the town, are still sold in local shops.

Pies are not the only gastronomic delicacy of the area. Stilton and Red Leicester cheeses are made in the town and in 1951 Pedigree Petfoods moved their main factory for the manufacture of pet foods here and established it in buildings which had up to then been occupied by Paton and Baldwins wool mill. Remember the mill hooter which sounded across the town at 8 am and 6 pm?

Many of the town's amenities are administered by a unique charity known as the Town Estate. The street markets on Tuesday and Saturday pay tolls to the Town Estate; the stalls were manned until late in the evening when light was provided by paraffin flares. The cattle market is owned by the Town Estate. Cattle used to be driven to market through the main thoroughfares of the town. The Corn Exchange, a large building owned by the Estate, was, before demolition, used as a butter market and for the colourful and grand occasions of the hunt balls and the annual pageant in aid of the Waifs and Strays Society (now The Children's Society).

Among the many old buildings in the town none compare with the stately parish church where in the 1920s Dr Malcolm Sargent was choirmaster and organist. None, however, were stranger than the three round houses in the middle of the town said to have been built by a father for his three daughters who could never agree on anything. Each house, now gone, faced in a different direction so that no daughter could see a sister.'

'My father was in the fire service in Melton Mowbray, when the call for a fire was the siren or a bell that all firemen had in the house, not a bleeper as they have today. At Melton they didn't have firemen at the station all day; they also had a full time job, but were on call 24 hours a day. During the day they would leave their jobs and go to the station.

At home, I remember, if the bell rang at night while my dad was getting his jacket on I would take his bike out (it was always kept in the kitchen at night) and take it to the top of the passage and put the lights on ready for him to make a quick getaway. I don't think any of the firemen had a car.

There was always a jumble of bikes outside the station as they would just throw them in a pile. It was the job of any fireman who didn't catch the first crew to sort them out.

They would put their uniform and slickers on as they were going to the fire, holding on to a rail on the fire engine. There was no covered-in appliance as of today, and it was very dangerous for them going round the corners.'

BRAUNSTON-IN-RUTLAND

'In the village in the 1920s and 1930s there were at least eight working farms, a post office, two grocery shops, one selling newspapers, two butchers, one baker, a wheelwright/undertaker, a blacksmith and two public houses.

Milk was obtained from one of the farms, collected twice daily. The farm also made Braunston's famous "slip curd cheese". Bread was delivered to the door, carried in a large basket; a large loaf cost, I think, a penny ha'penny. A representative from a general store in Somerby came round on alternate Tuesdays for an order which was delivered the following Thursday.

For hardware and paraffin a large van came from Uppingham on alternate Saturdays. Later, when we had a wireless, a van also from Uppingham came fortnightly to change the accumulator, taking the used one away and replacing it by a recharged one.

Any item not obtainable from these sources meant walking into Oakham, to Furley and Hassan's or George's (for linen and drapery) or Jackson and Boston's for ironmongery. It was a great day when the first Midland Red bus started a regular service, to Melton on Tuesdays and Oakham, I think, on Wednesdays and Saturdays. Two people started taxi businesses running a shuttle service to Oakham on Saturday evenings.

The vicar lived in the village and looked after Brooke in addition. There were three services and Sunday school each Sunday, and a service at the Methodist chapel. Each weekday at twelve noon the bell was rung, originally it is believed to give the time of day to the men working in the fields. The vicar faithfully read the office of matins at this time.

If anyone was seriously ill in the village, the road outside the house was covered with a layer of straw to muffle the noise of the traffic, ie horses' ironshod hooves and iron-rimmed cartwheels.

We had a lady in the village who attended after a death to lay out the body. A funeral meant a procession from the house to the church, the coffin being borne on their shoulders by four men; no mean feat if the deceased was heavy and lived at the end of the village farthest from the church. The vicar met the cortège at the north gate.

In 1935 the village celebrated the Silver Jubilee of George V and Queen Mary; the houses were decorated with flags and bunting. Sports for the children were held in the afternoon, followed by a tea and a concert in the village hall in the evening. May Day was always a special occasion, actually on the first Saturday in May. We had two May Queens with four attendants and the four "seasons". The boys carried the May Bush, and went round with collecting tins. In the morning we toured Braunston, "singing" our carefully rehearsed May Day songs; in the afternoon we went to Brooke, by which time our posies and chaplets were somewhat wilted!

The children's village party was held on New Year's Eve. After tea Santa arrived with a present for each child, games were then played followed by dancing for the grown-ups. How the gallant menfolk enjoyed the Lancers when they whirled round at such a speed the ladies were swept off their feet. The finale was, of course, Auld Lang Syne.

The village school on the Knossington Road consisted of two rooms, one large for the seniors, ie seven to eleven year olds, and the smaller one for the infants. The headmistress, who cycled from Oakham each day, was assisted by someone from the village, a war widow; both had infinite patience and were very dedicated.

I remember one sunny summer day Mr Keeling from the farm opposite rushed over to say that an airship (probably the R100) was passing over – out we all trooped to see the spectacle.'

'DUMMY TOWN'

'Belgrave was once known as "Dummy Town". This name seems to have originated from the fact that Belgrave folk would never inform on one of their neighbours.

The men would often gamble on the "Black Pad", a footpath that ran alongside the river Soar, just off Bath Street. Young boys would be posted as look-outs to warn them if the local policeman was out looking for them, as pitch and toss gambling was illegal.

No one seems ever to have been caught, as when anyone was questioned by the police as to who the culprits were, they were silent or "played dummy". Hence, "Dummy Town".'

NEWTOWN LINFORD

'There were regular motorcycle races round Ulverscroft in the early 1930s, incorporating the watersplash on Polly Bott's Lane. This was a great spectator sport for villagers, especially if any local riders were taking part.

Ulverscroft was a rather upmarket area of large, scattered houses. Some of the children were sent to boarding schools. The village itself was a more homogeneous community. Being, until 1925, an estate village without a Big House, there was little scope for class distinctions. The vicar and the estate agent may have seen themselves as middle class, but the villagers didn't seem to notice and were in no way in awe of them.

There was a tramp known as Old Black Charlie, who used to help farmers. His name was a puzzle, as he was always clean. He slept under hedges and made beautiful bouquets of wild flowers, which he wrapped in paper doilys and presented to people who gave him titbits.

A number of rag and bone men would come through the village with a horse and cart. One always shouted "Ragabone a rabbit *skeen*ick!" and gave about a penny for a rabbit skin, which was considered generous.

As in many villages where there were relatively few surnames because of intermarriage, boys in particular soon gained a nickname, which was then theirs for life. One family of Harrisons, for instance, contained Zaddy, Butcher Ike, Boykin, Wrinkles, Polo, Polly Currants and Fairy. Sometimes a lad would inherit his father's nickname; in fact such names could sometimes be passed down for three or four generations.

1925 brought about the biggest change which had ever happened in the village. Like many landowning families of the time, the owner, Mrs Katherine Venezia Duncombe Grey, put her estate on the market, and this included the entire village of Newtown Linford, with the exception of the cricket pitch (and Bradgate Park, which was sold three years later). The sale lasted for three days and was held at the Bell Hotel in Leicester. Some tenants managed to buy their cottages, while others found themselves with new landlords. As the Bradgate estate agent, Mr Haslegrave, continued to act for some of the new landlords, the tenants continued to pay their rent to him as before. Because of the lack of planning requirements in the 1920s and 1930s, ribbon development was soon taking place along the roads towards Anstey, Groby and Markfield.

Electricity came to the village around 1936. The houses at the bottom of Markfield Lane, which were built just before that time, were wired up for electricity from the start, but the new occupants had to wait a year before they had any power. There were never any gas lamps in the streets, which had to wait for electricity to be illuminated. Water closets were put in just before the Second World War.'

SHEPSHED

'I was born in Queen Street, Shepshed and Queen Street now is very different to how I knew it. The top half is much the same but all the rest is changed. At the top of the street is an Elizabethan manor house but even that has had the top storey removed, and looks nothing like it used to do. When I was young it was an outdoor off-licence, kept by Arthur Jordan. In the yard at the back he also bred bloodhounds for the police, and sometimes we could hear them baying and then it reminded me of *The Hound of the Baskervilles*.

Next door was Kerry's yard and house. Mr Kerry repaired steam rollers and we very often had to get out of the way when we were playing street games. Mr Kerry's son was probably the first man in Shepshed to have a crystal set and when my husband was a boy he used to go into the house after church on Sunday and Mr Kerry showed him how to make a set himself.

There was also a small sweet shop kept by Ann Cook, a very old spinster, and we used to go in for a "ha'porth all round the counter" and she would dip into every box. She had wire netting round the counter so we could not reach over to help ourselves to aniseed balls, rosebuds, humbugs and all the other sweets. A girl in the street used to help her to clean the house, and she sometimes had to go down the cellar to pepper the beetles.

At the bottom of the street was a butcher's shop. First it was kept by Isaac Whiteman and when he retired, by Mr Billy Hunt. During the First World War we had some Belgian refugees in Shepshed, and one day they went in the shop and kept on saying "Sorsay, sorsay". My aunt was in the shop and just after Billy said, "What do they want, Liz?" she realised they wanted sausages.

A street gas lamp was fixed onto the wall of my brother's bedroom, and Jimmy Chapman was the lamplighter. He came to light the lamp and later came back to turn it out. My brothers used to wait for him to come and they made up a little song to sing to him. It went –

"Jimmy Chapman lamplighter
Flea biter, cherry bumper
Last nighter"

which was nothing but gibberish. Jimmy would come to our back door and say, "Mrs Page, your lads are at it again," and she would say, "Right Jimmy, I'll see to them," and that satisfied him till the next time.'

MARKET HARBOROUGH

'Life in Market Harborough in the 1920s was very different from the one we know today. Picture a small market town nestling in the fertile Welland valley for many centuries. People hurried to work on their bikes, women to the two Symington's factories making soups and jellies, corsets and the world-famous liberty bodices, men to a variety of trades making rubber buttons, shoe soles and heels, wooden heels, nuts and bolts.

Farmers and their wives would throng the streets on Tuesdays, bringing their animals to the cattle market and visiting the open market on the Square. There were many family-owned shops, all with their errand boys delivering goods, along with the milkman and his pails of milk, the baker with his large basket of bread, all brought to the door. Everyone was busy, with hardly any leisure time, which was just as well for there was very little in the way of entertainment. Most men would tend their allotments at the weekend, perhaps calling in at one of the old coaching inns on the way home. Their wives would be making and mending whilst the children played whip and top, hopscotch and bowl the hoop. Sunday school at the chapel provided many treats, Christmas parties, concerts and summer outings.

There were many local characters – "Long Liz" who sold the *Leicester Mail*, Christopher Perkins the self-styled disciple, Mr Scarborough with his penny bazaar, and many others, all of whom had disappeared long before the advent of the Second World War. The little shops have given way to supermarkets, the noise of traffic has replaced the clip-clop of the horses, and the peace and quiet of our lovely little town has gone forever.'

'My parents and I moved to Market Harborough in 1925 from Darlington. After living in a town with electric street lighting, trackless trams and modern stores, only a few miles from the sea, Harborough seemed very different.

My father was having a house built on Lubenham Hill, halfway between the town and the village of Lubenham. We had a rented house on the hill while ours was completed. There were gas lamps in the road and just a rough footpath. We had to make sure the gates were closed every Tuesday morning, which was market day, when the cattle and sheep were driven to market and if they saw an open gate they were soon trampling all over your garden. You had to watch where you walked on the path in those days. The grass verges were used for horse riders. The manure was very good for the roses. This road is now the notorious A427, unlike the country road that I remember.

When we first came to Market Harborough I went to the C of E

THE GRAMMAR SCHOOL
MARKET HARBOROUGH

GWEN HUGHES
1985

school. It was very different for me, and one elderly lady had the nasty habit of putting her thumb through two fingers and pinching you on the arm. It was painful and left a bruise. Fortunately I was only there for two years and I passed my eleven plus and went to the Edward VII grammar school. It was much more interesting: tennis and cricket and hockey were the main sports for girls. We had four subjects to do for homework so we did not get much spare time in the evenings. The school was very strict on uniform at all times, and anyone seen in the town without it was reported and either had detention or a severe reprimand.

When I married in 1936 my husband and I lived in Leicester for nearly three years but came back to Market Harborough and lived with my parents during the war years. During the war my husband went to work for the Leicestershire Agricultural Department and apart from farming he had to take Italian prisoners of war to work on the land and transport the land girls from the hostel at Lubenham to their jobs. There was an Italian prisoner of war camp on Farndon Road and towards the end of the war some of them were allowed to take a Sunday evening walk in the light evenings. They had big, round, coloured rings on the backs of their tunics.

In 1943 I went to work for the Ministry of Food and my mother looked after my two children. Everyone had to work, if possible, in those days. They were long hours, especially when I was promoted. During the issue of new ration books we had to work weekends and go round the villages with the new books. Despite the war we were all great friends and all the staff helped each other out.

When the air raid sirens went off at night we used to push the dining-room table into the corner by the fireplace and put a mattress under for the children to sleep on. We could hear the German planes going to Coventry – they seemed to follow the railway line at the back of our house. On a moonlit night we could stand outside and see them in the sky. We felt so sad for the people of Coventry and said a prayer for them.

We had our victory celebrations at the end of the war, first for VE and then VJ Day. These were held in the gardens of "The Hill", the home of the Symington family.'

PEATLING PARVA

'In the early 1930s Peatling Parva was a very small village with about 34 houses, the church and The Dog and Gun pub, a carpenter's shop, a butcher's shop and a very small sweet shop. There was also a small hatchery and a market garden, and the school.

The baker's van called several times a week as also did a hardware van, and groceries were delivered by van. It was an event for the village when a post office and shop opened; the shop sold everything from food to spare parts for your bicycle, and lots more.

For the children the highlight of the year was Christmas, when a party was given for them at the Hall. Tea was served by the maids and then they gathered round a huge Christmas tree and received a present of a toy or book and a bag of sweets. Every child was also given a new red jumper, and the mothers or wives of the estate workers were given a pair of sheets. The Hall employed a lot of people in the way of servants, grooms and gardeners and farm staff. The village school closed when it had only five pupils. They had to go to the next village and the school was pulled down during the Second World War.

The village hall was used for dances etc. When the Bruntingthorpe aerodrome opened in 1943, it brought a lot of RAF lads to the village dances.

May Day was another big day for the children. The May Queen was crowned on the village green and they toured the village on a trailer pulled by Silver, a grey horse, and afterwards had tea in the village hall. All the children were in fancy dress. In the field next to the church was a cricket pitch and two grass courts for tennis, these were looked after by the Hall gardeners.

Peatling Hall was turned into a convalescent home during the war years, for ATS girls and nurses. A café and shop opened to cater for the extra people from the Hall and aerodrome. We also had a doctor in the village and a dentist! The best time to catch him was after the pub closed at night!'

CROPSTON

'I was born in Cropston and over the years it has grown steadily from a community of some 30 or so houses to the large village it is today. Having no school and no village hall, the chapel has always been at the heart of the village. I remember the sewing class on Thursday evenings, when we girls would make pin cushions and lavender bags and would sing as we sewed. The chapel outings were to nearby farms for a picnic tea and games. We played cricket and rounders.

We children attended the church school at Thurcaston, walking over the fields in summer and, in winter, walking by road for three miles. No buses in my day. We took sandwiches for lunch and cocoa was served from a large brown teapot which bubbled on the black coke stove in the middle of the classroom.

Mr Hutton ran the first service bus in the village. It ran between Anstey and Cropston at weekends only and the fare was threepence return. Later he extended his service into Leicester for eightpence return, picking us up at our own front door. No bus stops were needed.

Cropston has only a post office now, but in 1930 we had a bakery, brewery, butcher's and two grocers. I remember my errands to collect fresh bread, still warm from the large oven. The bakery would also cook Yorkshire pudding on Sunday and chicken or turkey for Christmas for any of their customers.

The Bradgate Arms public house served the village by supplying milk. I used to go to the back door with a jug and the milk was measured out by inserting a metal can into a big milk urn and then pouring it into the jug. In the evenings, some wives were to be seen carrying milk jugs to fetch beer for their husbands to drink at home.'

COUNTESTHORPE

'One of my earliest memories of Countesthorpe is of being pushed by my mother in my pushchair to "follow the hounds". If they were in the direction of Peatling Magna we had to pass through the gate in the road to reach the open fields. This gate was manned by "Dolphi" Glass who expected a penny from all who passed through. If the "floods were out" between Countesthorpe and South Wigston we had to use the raised wooden footpath from the bridges to the bottom of the hill.

My parents kept the post office on the Bank and I would be left in the back room to play in a cot – the forerunner of the playpen, I imagine – with tins and jars and picture postcards from the little shop. When I was about two years old my parents gave up the post office, which was moved to Central Street and was kept by Mr Butcher in the house next to Nurse Richardson's. My mother then did outwork for one of the hosiery factories. I remember being cradled on her lap when I needed a rest while she turned the handle of her Griswold stocking machine. At that time there were several hosiery factories in the village: Tom Burley's at the top of Brook Street, Glazebrook's on Wigston Street, Asher's on Leicester Road and Tamplin's at the bottom of Station Road Hill.

We still had a station in Countesthorpe until the advent of Dr Beeching and from there we journeyed on our various outings: to Broughton Astley for the Wakes and for the trips to Skegness, Mablethorpe or Hunstanton, organised by the three Sunday schools. There were three church Anniversary Sundays, or "Sermon Sundays" as we called them. We all had new clothes and from then on these were our "best" and only to be worn on Sundays. Patent leather ankle-strap shoes were the ultimate!

Whit Monday was the day of the Infirmary Fete, so called as the money raised was given to Leicester Royal Infirmary. Charlie Moore's Band started the day by leading the parade of floats, decorated bicycles or ponies, or walkers in fancy dress around the village. This was followed by races for the children and a tea for all held in Charlie Read's field – this was where Gwendoline Drive leaves Station Road up to Linden junior school.

On bonfire night there was a large communal bonfire on the 'reccy' – still the recreation ground today. All the children helped to build

Outside the Navigation Inn at Kilby in the 1900s.

the bonfire and all brought their own fireworks for everyone's enjoyment.

There were two schools in the village: the church school, now the church centre, and the council or "Board" school on the corner of Foston Turn. Those who passed the scholarship at age eleven went on to Lutterworth grammar school. The rest stayed in the village until they left school at 14. The bus to Lutterworth picked up children in Peatling Magna, Bruntingthorpe and Gilmorton. Frank Whittle was just developing his jet engine at Power Jets and when they were testing the engines it was impossible to hear the teachers talking so we had to resort to written work.

Our village shop was owned by the Misses Taylor and Nellie ran the shop while Phyllis and Maggie went out to work. Nellie had a parrot, very vociferous, whose language often left much to be desired, necessitating the use of a cloth to cover the cage when the minister called. Nellie was very scared of thunder and at the first sign retired to a cubby hole under the stairs until the storm had passed.

Some cottages had small gardens to front and/or rear and in our street we had iron railings in front of our pocket-handkerchief sized gardens, but these were removed for the war effort and brick walls built instead.

There were many tradesmen who delivered their products on a regular basis: Henry Ringrose brought our bread in his horse and trap; Cis Randle came weekly from South Wigston with fruit and vegetables and had a sign across the top of his cart which said ، "Wreaths, Crosses and Bouquets"; Mrs Simons walked with the milk in a large churn, dispensing it to each housewife in her own jug. A special treat was when a cow had calved and we had the "beastings", first milk, for a milk pudding. Mrs Simons was the sister of Mr Adnitt who owned the farm on the square, later taken over by the Cosby family who put a pig on the wall to watch the parade go by.

Families generally were very poor, but the slightly better off helped the others by handing on outgrown clothes and I remember some mothers bringing large jugs of hot cocoa to the school railings at playtime and sharing it out among their own children and the less fortunate whose mothers could not afford such a luxury.

Many were the tramps and gipsies who paid regular visits to the village. There was one tribe of gipsies who always camped in a small square field on the road to Peatling Magna, opposite the allotments. One well known tramp was John Thomas Butler, the mushroom king, known to the village children as "Brassy". He was a regular visitor. Each winter he endeavoured to get on the wrong side of the law in the hope of spending the worst of the winter months in Leicester prison. His crimes were minor and deliberate, more often than not just being drunk and disorderly.

It was a wonderful life we lived. We made our own entertainment and I don't believe we knew the word "boredom" existed. I'm so thankful I have those happy memories to reflect on from time to time.'

ARNESBY'S TELEPHONE

'When the first telephone appeared in the village, people were unsure how to use it and would call at The Old Cock for assistance. One such lady wished to speak to her sister. Questioned, she gave her sister's name and the name of the village where she lived. Further questioned as to her sister's "number", she gave the house number. Eventually it was revealed that the sister had no telephone. The would-be caller was under the impression that if *she* had a telephone that was all that was required.'

ROTHLEY

'Rothley, in the early part of the 1900s, had a village crier who would run around the village with a large brass bell, ringing and calling, "Oyez, Oyez, this is to give notice (then the message or news), Oyez, Oyez."

Newspapers came by train and the newsagent cycled to the station to collect them and then delivered them to the houses.

There was no radio or television in those days, and no electric light. We used chiefly paraffin lamps and candles for lighting. People walked about the village at night with storm lamps. Gradually, gas was installed and then we had gaslights with incandescent mantles.

The village policeman, Mr Tom Pratt, was appreciated and feared by everyone. He was a little lame, so carried a stick. If the children did not behave they got a whack with the stick and when they told their parents all that was said was, "You must have deserved it!" He wasn't thought badly of for it. When you required a policeman he always seemed to be there as he patrolled the streets frequently. He lived in a house on the village green, which was very central.

A man with a barrel organ used to come round, with a monkey in a red jacket carrying a collecting box. The monkey would sit on top of the organ. We used to sing and dance round them as the organ played. A one-man band also came, with all his band attachments.

The fire engine was kept in the Court House on the green (later on it had a place of its own), near to where the telephone box now stands. It was a tank on wheels with a rail each side and when in use men would be both sides working the pump.

The Red Lion on the main road is a very old inn; it used to be called Rothley Halfway House as it was halfway between Leicester and Loughborough. The road was called The Turnpike – it had a gate across the road to stop travellers and carriages who paid a toll

34

for keeping the road in repair. It is still known by that name today by some of the older residents. The coaches and brakes would call at the inn and the passengers would have their lunch and continue their journey. On the opposite side of the road was a large tree and the villagers would often sit and watch the coaches coming and going.

Boyers started a bus service about 1911. The buses went to Leicester on Wednesdays and Saturdays, about three a day each way. They were a bit shaky but better than walking. We used to have to walk to Rothley station which was a mile away, or to Belgrave tram terminus five miles away to get a tram in to Leicester. Coming home, we were sometimes lucky as the carrier's cart would pick us up.

If you wanted a day out to Bradgate Park or any other such place, you would have to walk or hire a brougham from the carrier, Mr Fearn. He also owned cabs which were used at funerals, following the four-wheeled bier, all patterned frosted glass and pulled by four bearers.

A man swept the village streets and the village was a credit to him. On Saturday mornings he would distribute disinfectant to the villagers, who brought a bottle to collect it, as there were then only outside lavatories, emptied during the night.

Sometimes a Church Army van came to the village green, where children would gather to watch lantern slides, sing hymns and say prayers. There was also a roller skating rink and coffee house on the main road (now a garage and showroom) where many happy hours were spent by the older generation.'

BITTESWELL'S WAYFARERS

'During the 1920s the life of the village of Bitteswell was enriched by the people who travelled through it. Gipsies were regular visitors, camping in the Woodby Lane outside the village and spending the next few days visiting door-to-door selling clothes pegs, telling fortunes and dealing in anything saleable. Most parishioners seemed to be relieved when they moved their pitch, but I cannot remember that they ever caused any problems.

I can recall walking in the lane and observing their way of life. There were always horses tethered on the grass verge. I expect they may have taken advantage of the pasture in the fields, and probably trapped a rabbit or two after dark. I remember the glow of their fire outside the caravans and seeing a gipsy woman smoking a pipe. There seemed to be several generations of gipsies living together and always dogs of varying breeds. After they had gone we would wander along the lane and see the scraps of rubbish they had left behind, and the heaps of grey ashes where their fires had been.

Tramps were regular visitors to our village. The freelance ones of my earlier childhood would stay overnight in the barns in the Woodby Lane. They would emerge to beg for hot water to put in their cans which might already contain sugar and tea. They always appreciated an added drop of milk and a hunk of bread with dripping or cheese. I rarely heard of them being offensive. I do remember seeing a tramp accompanied by a woman and an old pram with their few belongings piled on it. They didn't stop but passed straight through the village. I was very impressed by this sight as they were quite elderly and I worried about them.

During the 1930s there seemed to be some provision made for these travellers, and tramps could get a night's lodging in the casual wards of the local workhouses. From Hinckley Workhouse a tramp would be given a ticket to get food at a Lutterworth shop (two faggots and half a loaf of bread). He could also spend the night in the Lutterworth casual ward. They were expected to chop wood before they left the next morning, when they would be given another food ticket for Market Harborough.

This pattern of life was still in existence for the tramps during the war and strict tabs were kept on them for security reasons, with identity cards and ration cards.

After the war I believe the practice stopped and tramps were rarely seen.'

CHURCH AND CHAPEL

Going to church or chapel, and Sunday school for the children, was a part of our lives, most households keeping Sunday as a day of rest (though not all women would have agreed!). Much of our entertainment and social life was also bound up with the church, which occupied a central role in the life of town and village.

A DAY OF REST?

'They said in those days it was a day of rest. Well, for the male it was. It was fashionable in the 1920s and 1930s to attend church or chapel. Children were expected to attend Sunday school morning and afternoon. It being a special occasion, only best clothes were worn, then brushed and hung in the cupboard ready for the next occasion. Sunday dinner consisted mainly of roast beef and Yorkshire pudding. They had large families who all sat round a large table covered in a pristine white linen tablecloth, washed, starched and ironed by a long-suffering mother or daughter. There was much discussion over what Mrs So and So wore, plus the latest news and scandal in the village.

The head of the family (father) would give thanks before the meal and one had to have a good excuse to leave the table before he said thanks for what had been received.

Fashions by now had changed from ankle-length costumes and skirts to knee high with sometimes a fringe added for extra sophistication.

You never thought of entering church without a hat – it was unheard of. Hats were wonderful creations and much talked about. Silk stockings had made their debut and because they were expensive items one had to learn to mend ladders with a minute crochet-like hook, sometimes even using a magnifying glass. Then there was make-up, lots of pale powder and cheeks rouged dark red. Lipstick was applied very generously. With all this paint and powder a female could be accused of flightiness or bad reputation.

The hair was cut in a "bob" or shingled, a marcel wave was all the rage. It could be crimped with curling tongs at home, necessitating curling tongs being shoved in the coal fire. Many times there would be a strong smell of frizzed hair or it would fall out, leaving a bald patch and a long wait for fresh hair to grow. No wonder some of us say "the bad old days". It was much harder for females then than it is now.'

PART OF OUR LIVES

'Sunday at Newtown Linford consisted of Sunday school at 10 am, followed by the church service at 11, then Bible class at 2.30 and evening service at 6.30. Sunday school consisted of hymns and stories and then the children were questioned on the story of the day. If children answered incorrectly they were told sharply that they couldn't have been listening. For the adults, there were also Holy Communion services at 7 am and 8 am.

There was a good choir in the 1920s, with about 20 members, ten of whom were children. There were always girls as well as boys. Mr Sills was the organist and choirmaster except for special productions of, for instance, The Messiah or Crucifixion, when Mrs Connie Stopper was the conductor. The church would be full for special occasions, but not otherwise. (There were, after all, four services each Sunday.)

There was a good team of bellringers, and these were all men. The organ had to be pumped, which was rather a noisy operation, and if left to go low it would drone.

The Sunday school Anniversary was always held in May, on a Sunday afternoon. A platform was erected in the Sunday school for the children to sit on, and they would sing songs which they had learnt specially for the occasion. The girls usually had new Sunday best frocks, made by their mothers, and the boys had new suits.

By the 1930s the Anniversary was held in the church and the children took part in morning and evening services. At the Anniversary practices the children were allowed to take turns at pumping the organ, but on the Sunday the task reverted to the usual pumper.

At Harvest Festival time all the farms used to provide sheaves of corn and there were bags of potatoes, masses of eggs and vegetables, a box of coal and sticks by the door and marrows galore – though there were not so many flowers as nowadays. Afterwards the produce was taken to the hospital.

On Christmas Eve, from the late 1920s till wartime, a party of carol singers from the church would meet for cocoa, then set off at midnight to tour the village. They went first of all up the hill to Mr Squirrel's, near the Old John car park, then back into the village, singing at each house, and ending at the vicarage at six o'clock on Christmas morning. Here they always sang Mr Pigot, the vicar's, favourite carol, *Brightest and best*.

There was a well attended Mothers' Union in Newtown Linford and the meetings took place one afternoon a month in the Sunday school, led by the vicar's wife. There would be a hymn, a prayer and then a talk by a speaker. When Mrs Pigot was the leader of the Mothers' Union she would meet all the members at the church gate at eight o'clock communion on Mothering Sunday with a bunch of violets. The Mothers' Union was eventually disbanded by a vicar who was a widower, and who considered it just a gossip shop. Later a Young Wives was formed, which, as the wives got older, became the present Women's Fellowship.

The Girls' Friendly Society was a church-based week-night activity for girls. They had Bible classes in the Sunday school every week. The GFS also used to take part in the Sankey evenings which were held at Mrs Snartt's once a fortnight in the 1920s. Mrs Snartt used to accompany the singing on her harmonium.

The Foresters was a Friendly Society to which nearly all the adults of the village belonged in the days before the Welfare State. They paid their subscriptions and in return could draw sick pay and a lump sum to cover burial costs.'

'When I was small in the 1940s I went to church three times a day each Sunday: Sunday school followed by morning service, 2.30 pm Sunday school and evensong at 6.30 pm. My great-aunt was a Sunday school teacher for many years and in the early days took me to church. She dressed in a black dress with flowers on; everything else was black.

I was in Harby church choir too. We had choir outings and suppers when the rector, a lovely old man, his like never to be seen again, sang *Simon the cellarer*. It was always requested on these occasions and something I will never forget.

Another event was the Sunday school's annual flower service. It was held early in July when we took flowers and gifts, mainly eggs, to church. The flowers were placed on family graves during the "cupping of the church" when the congregation would surround the church holding hands and singing *We love the place O God*. They usually joined up too. The gifts were taken to the local hospital and children's home. Bibles were given to the eldest boy and girl. We always had a new dress for the flower service and sang lovely little hymns, some of which I still hear today.

We had outings to the seaside, also village trips, mainly to Wicksteed Park where there were lots of swings and slides and a water chute which was always the favourite attraction.

We had a village chapel: they had their anniversaries too and a silver service when the collections were supposed to be in silver.

The church had an annual garden fete, held on the rectory lawn. Working parties spent months sewing and embroidering the most beautiful cloths and knitting garments of all sorts and sizes. My future husband provided the music and visiting dancing schools performed. An old piano was wheeled out for the pianist to accompany them. The costumes were always very pretty. The stall-holders wore their best summer outfits with straw hats, some large and with flowers and fruit on them. I remember one with black cherries – artificial, of course. The ladies who provided the superb teas were kept busy with their teapots and all wore pretty coloured aprons.

In winter we had a Christmas fair – another new dress – in the Institute. There was also a Sunday school party when Santa Claus came. We went carol singing all round the village, ending up at someone's house for hot mince pies and a glass of sherry, with perhaps a sip for me. We called at the pubs – I wasn't allowed inside although I did have a quick peep sometimes.

The annual Harby Feast was celebrated in September and the highlight was the Harvest Festival service in the church. The church was decorated and the choir sang an anthem such as *Ripened grain*. Again, all the hats would be on view and best clothes worn.

On the Monday, the WI would hold its competitions, complete with teas and the tea ladies. There was often a lot of falling out over who won the prizes. I remember a major upset over whose eggs were whose. I think they'd been swapped around. Even my granny became involved.

At Rogationtide churchgoers followed the rector and church-wardens round the village blessing the crops, allotments etc and singing as we went.

The bells were rung each Sunday by the villagers, with their shirt sleeves rolled up and red faces. The sound was beautiful, always in tune and no clashing of the bells. The team would ring for weddings and visiting teams would sometimes ring on Saturdays and employ the services of the tea ladies again. When someone died one of the ringers would toll the "passing bell" and would toll the bell at the funeral, too.

Easter was a lovely time. The church was decorated with spring flowers and nearly all the ladies and children had new outfits, including lots of Easter bonnets. My Dad would wear his very best suit, too. One year I had a grey and green check coat with a belt that could be worn half round the coat at the front then disappeared into a slot and round the waist leaving the back of the coat like a swagger. I had grey shoes to match – very smart, I thought.'

'We had a dear old lady at Nanpantan who was the village character. Every Sunday she would come to church with a wad of men's handkerchiefs. If any girl dared to come to church without a hat she would be given a handkerchief, with four knots tied in it, to wear on her head.

This lady was very artistic. During the war she used to cut out animal shapes from cardboard and sent them to people as postcards until one day she was asked to stop doing it as it might be thought she was sending secret messages!'

'In 1921/22 the rector of Glooston had seven chestnut trees planted along the Main Street as he thought it a rare occasion to have seven brides and grooms making their first homes in the village in 18 months. Five of these trees are still here today.'

SERMONS AND TREATS

'My family came to the Anstey district in the early 1930s when Sermons Sundays were very special occasions for the churches and in fact for the whole village. There were then four places of worship in the village – the parish church of St Mary, the Congregational, Primitive Methodist and Wesleyan Methodist chapels. Most villagers claimed to belong to one and those who did not attend church normally would be there three times on Sermons day. All children and most grown-ups too would have an annual complete new outfit of clothes, including underwear, so it was also a fashion parade.

We previously attended a Baptist church but there was not one in Anstey so it was decided to try one of the others and it being the Sermons at the Primitive Methodist ("Prims") that seemed a good start. We did not know that Sermons in Anstey were so popular that you had to arrive about an hour before commencing time. So when we got there the church was already completely full, including chairs in the aisles, and it was impossible for us to get in. We then went up the road to the Congregational church where I am still a member. Needless to say, numbers at the "Congs" were small that evening, some being at the Sermons.

The churches erected special tiered galleries to accommodate scholars for the Sermons, the youngest sitting at the bottom. Great importance was attached to position on the gallery and how high up you were. There was lots of special singing by scholars with an augmented choir and an orchestra. A choral march was always included. Services were quite long so you had to hurry home for a quick meal to get back again and it was a great day for entertaining relatives and friends. In the evening when the church was completely full the service would start early. Collections for the day were abnormally high and there was great rivalry between the Congs and Prims as to which could get the most. The money had to be counted immediately so the figure could be announced at the end of the service.

Sermons day for St Mary's church saw the scholars, teachers and friends assembling on the green to march down Bradgate Road to the church led by a band. As they had to pass the Congs, all the scholars there remained outside until the parade had passed. The Congs caretaker, a very stout man named Bill Pollard, headed the band beating the drum.'

'Most children at Cosby in the 1930s attended Sunday school. There were, and still are, the church and two chapels – Methodist and Baptist. Highlights in the latter were the Sermons, as the Sunday school Anniversary was always called. No matter how poor a family, there were always new clothes for that occasion, and new shoes. The boys had brown crepe-soled sandals and the girls white canvas shoes which were cleaned with whitening from a big ball mixed with water. We used to leave a white trail where the surplus powder fell off when we walked. One year my dream came true – I had a pair of black patent ankle-straps, the ultimate in shoes at that age.

Sunday school treats were to Bradgate Park, where I first saw foxgloves growing in profusion. I was in my seventh heaven when allowed to pick an armful to take home. There were games and sandwiches at Blakes Hay Farm, sitting at long trestle tables, and I remember sheltering from sudden thunderstorms in barns and sheds.

Prizegiving was also a big day at my Baptist Sunday school, when we received a book for good attendance. The Christmas party, too.

Most of the lights would be put out and while we sang a carol, a loud knock would be heard and in came Santa. He gave everyone a bar of chocolate from his sack. When I was very small, I never told anyone but that knock on the door and those lowered lights frightened me – my little heart was thumping. I did enjoy the chocolate though.'

'Annual events at Hinckley in the 1920s were the Sunday school Anniversary, or Sermons, when the chapel services were dominated by the children singing specially learned hymns and showing off their new summer outfits, and then, on the first Sunday in July, "Walking the Town", or "The Treats". All the chapel Sunday schools would parade around the town, each preceded by their banner and a horse-drawn dray on which was depicted a biblical scene. The children following on foot would carry garlands of flowers or paper, push decorated prams, carry baskets or bunches of flowers – anything to look pretty. After the walk we returned to our own chapel where we were given a bun, an orange and an apple, and then off to a field somewhere pre-arranged to run races and scramble for sweets.'

'At Elmesthorpe there was All Saints church, the Baptist chapel and the Congregational chapel. Sunday school days bring back pleasant memories, especially of Mr Abbott, the superintendent, and Mr Law, the local preacher, who used models to make his sermons more interesting for children.

"Mr Davis's Caravan Mission" used to visit and give scripture talks during the summer holidays and we would sing short choruses – very happy times. A Band of Hope was held in the Baptist schoolroom and we would listen to temperance talks and sign the pledge.

Each year we would go by horse and brake for a day's outing to either Bardon Hill or Swithland and several times we even went to Mr Eddie Joyce's farm at Cosby. Whit Sunday was the Anniversary day, when we sat on the platform in our best clothes and sang to the older congregation.'

GETTING ABOUT

At the turn of the century we either got about by horse-drawn transport or we used Shanks's pony – we walked! Then came the trams and the early buses, and a few lucky people had their own car. How things have changed, since the days when the roads were quiet and trains slowed down for the fireman to pick mushrooms by the track.

A GALLOPING PRANCER

'When I was very young I used to visit my grandparents who lived in the tiny village of Debdale. As it was at least two miles from where I lived, my father and I used to go by horse and cart. This he borrowed from the local butcher. The cart was very high with just a back board and a seat without any sides.

The horse was a grey, a real galloping prancer. The journey was sometimes uneventful but on others it was quite different if we happened to meet a heavy snorting steam roller, used for rolling the tarmac when repairing the roads.

This particular horse was frightened of and hated steam rollers. It would rear up in the shafts of the cart with my father hanging on to the reins for dear life. I would hold on to the seat absolutely terrified until we had passed the engine – but to be honest, if we did not meet a roller I was a little bit disappointed as the journey did not seem so adventurous.'

TRAMCARS AND CHARABANCS

'The main public transport in Leicester before the war was by tramcars, some of which had open tops – lovely in the summer time. The seats downstairs were along each side from front to back, but upstairs there were seats for two, facing the front with a gangway down the middle. They were made so that they could be turned round at the terminus to face the way the tram was going, and the trolley also had to be turned around. That was done by the conductor with a long pole which hung along the side of the tram on big hooks. Each tramcar had a driver and a conductor. The driver stood at the front – no seat for him.

Charabancs were popular for outings in the 1920s and 1930s as here at Wigston. Note the '12 m.p.h.' on the bodywork!

When we went on Sunday school treats we often had a charabanc, which was a sort of coach with rows of seats going across it and with a door at each end of the seats. Each seat would hold four or five people and, of course, they crowded more on when it was a children's party.'

TRAINS AND TRAPS

'My first recollection was in 1918 at the age of three taking a journey on a train, when I made the remark that the trees and hedges were running away, to the amusement of the people in the carriage.

The railway was the old Swannington line, one of the first to be built. It ran from West Bridge station, King Richards Road, Leicester to Desford. The track went through the Glenfield tunnel; there were no lights in the train and it was an ordeal travelling for a mile in complete darkness. If one forgot to shut the windows the carriage was filled with smoke from the engine, which caused much coughing and spluttering. My great-grandfather lived with his wife and family in a cottage at the Leicester end of the tunnel. He worked on the railway and one of his duties was to shut the gates to the tunnel when the train had passed through, to keep the farm animals from straying into the tunnel. As a schoolgirl I was the last passenger when the line was closed in 1928.

Roads were surfaced with granite chippings, dusty in summer, icy in winter. The traffic was mostly horse-drawn carts and wagons. We children had a donkey and cart at one time, and the donkey often lost a shoe. It was our job to take him to Mr Chesterton, the blacksmith at Kirby Muxloe, to have a new shoe fitted. Unfortunately there were often gipsies camped along the side of the road. My sister, who drove the donkey, was convinced gipsies made off with donkeys, and children as well, so we turned round and made for home. The donkey had no new shoe that day. I doubt if gipsies were interested in taking on any more animals or children, they had enough to feed of their own. But my sister was taking no chances.

My uncle had a pony and trap and we used to go for rides around the lanes. One of the few vehicles on the road was a steam roller, used for rolling the granite chippings. If my uncle saw one coming he turned the pony into a convenient field gateway where it could admire the view, and so take its mind off the steam roller. Uncle was more nervous than the pony. After the road was clear we set off again at a brisk trot.

The manager from the local colliery was driven from the railway station in a closed cab pulled by a smartly groomed horse. The manager wore a top hat and frock coat, and the driver sat on a box in front. We were very impressed when they drove by.'

VERY FEW HAD CARS

'During the late 1920s and early 1930s buses would go by packed with children waving large white handkerchiefs through the open windows, conveying to us their joy that their long anticipated annual day out to Wicksteed Park in Kettering, via Market Harborough, had at last arrived.

Adults also enjoyed occasional day, or evening bus trips. There was an air of togetherness as they joined in singing songs, mostly from the Great War, such as *Keep the home fires burning* and *There's a long, long trail a-winding*. The return journey's repertoire always included *Show me the way to go home*.

The effluvia of tobacco smoke, petrol fumes, etc, were at times somewhat overpowering, but were all part of the happy atmosphere and were accepted as such. Convenience stops were made where grew the highest and thickest hedgerows!

Leicestershire folk who could, spent a week's holiday on the East Coast. Just £5 covered the return bus fare, full board in digs, and spending money! Hotels were for the wealthier.

On workdays some took the local penny bus ride into town, but most cycled. On Armistice Days, when they dismounted to walk uphill, they fell prey to ardent poppy sellers, but they gave generously and good-naturedly.

Very few of us had cars and if one was given a lift, it was an awesome treat accompanied by a feeling of almost regality.

How lucky those early car owners were! No driving test, no MOT certificate, no traffic jams, simple wooden signposts, hardly any parking restrictions, friendly, saluting AA motor-cyclists, and petrol pump attendants who filled the tank and gave windscreens a wipe. When windscreen wipers were first invented most cars had only one on the driver's side.

The most compelling order to road users was the Halt sign. Traffic roundabouts were built up on the roads and were easily discernible. At the junction of crossroads in town and city a policeman mounted a stand to direct traffic.

The pre-nationalised London, Midland & Scottish (LMS) Railway Company ran special Saturday evening ninepenny trips between Market Harborough and Leicester which were well patronised, as were Thursday five shilling day trips from Market Harborough to London St Pancras. These trips were so popular that the third class compartments soon became full and many travelled all the way standing in the corridor. Only rarely was a blind eye turned towards the hoi polloi who invaded an empty first class compartment!

Trains which ran between Market Harborough and Melton Mowbray on the Northern line via Hallaton, East Norton, Tilton, John O'Gaunt and Great Dalby were non-corridor but every third compartment had a toilet to itself.

As for air travel, mono and bi-planes, autogiros and helicopters were machines which, at the sound of their propellers, we ran out to gaze up and wonder at.'

LOOKING FOR MUSHROOMS

'In the early years of the century there was a carrier service three times a week from Swinford to Rugby, and also from Swinford to Leicester via Lutterworth. After the advent of the railway, parcels were delivered by carrier from Stanford Park station.

A public motorbus service was started in the village by a

Mr Fred Gee, who also had a small garage with a petrol pump. Buses, including an open charabanc, travelled from Swinford to Rugby and to Lutterworth. The Midland Red Omnibus Company provided a service to the village in 1927.

From 1850 onwards, Swinford was well served by the railway, most passengers walking to Lilbourne station across the fields. Others boarded at Stanford Park station. Very old engines were often used on the Rugby to Market Harborough line and the pace was leisurely. On one occasion a fireman was seen walking through a field close to the line whilst the driver was bringing the train gently along to match his speed. An onlooker asked the signalman at Yelvertoft what was happening and received the reply, "Oh, he's looking for mushrooms, they often do that." The train was known as the "Mushroom Special". This line was closed on 4th June 1966 and the Great Central line, which gave Swinford people the opportunity to reach Leicester from Lutterworth, closed on 3rd May 1969.'

DURING THE WAR

'During the First World War the season ticket from Birstall to Leicester cost two shillings and elevenpence. It was a lot to find for my father for each one of us. The trains ran every 20 minutes. When it snowed some of the local men were glad of it for they could pick up good money shovelling snow off the line. They could be at it all night.

The railwaymen's braziers were very handy, not only to warm yourself, but we used to scrump potatoes and onions and bake them in the braziers. Of course they all got burnt, but that didn't really matter.

When Tommy Fielding-Johnston was going on the train from Belgrave and Birstall station it would always be held up for him and you weren't so worried you'd miss it on those particular days. He was a small man with a billycock hat and a walking stick, a person to be respected and feared.

Jimmy Went, headmaster of the Wyggeston, who lived at The Cottage in Birstall, used to patrol the train. All the schoolchildren started to behave themselves very prim and proper when they saw him coming.'

'Seagrave, a small Leicestershire village, in 1945. Transport? The best way for generations was Shanks's pony.

As a ten year old evacuee from Plymouth, who was used to trams

48

and buses, my feet were not really for walking. The village could be very isolated and the weekly trip to Loughborough was an outing, comparable with the big cities of today.

The Trent Traction Bus Company, bright red and very welcome, turned up three times every Saturday. At 1.50 pm, by the local post office, people waited for the bus to manoeuvre this very tight corner at the junction of King Street and Church Street. For sixpence adults and threepence children we could be up and away. Market day in Loughborough, the Empire cinema or just window shopping, a glorious two and a half hour trip before the return journey back to rural Seagrave. Some of the older generation even went out in the evening from 5.30 to 9.30 pm. You could be adult and go to late cinema!

We must not forget Midland Red buses, which went to Leicester at 9.05 am outside The White Horse. Back at 5.15 pm, and again you could go to the cinema for the evening entertainment, and back home by 9.30 pm. Was that really so late?

Of course Sileby station was fully operational, but the two mile walk did take the edge off an outing!

The bicycle was really the necessity of this era. Ride your bike to the Fosse (A46), leave it in Henry Wells's field (it was always safe), catch a Bartons bus (Leicester to the south, Nottingham to the north) and your trusted bike (probably rusty) was awaiting your return.'

'Scalford railway station was well used by the local people. I especially remember mothers going to Melton Mowbray with their babies and toddlers in pushchairs and prams often being allowed to ride in the guard's van to save disturbing the pram occupants, who were usually asleep – we had to stand, of course. It was a smelly journey, as being wartime there were often small animals being transported to the market or sales. Goats, I know, one time were in there and often there would be a hessian bag of horse meat that was for the dogs of the local gentry, Colonel Colman of mustard fame, who lived at the Hall. This would be taken off by the groom, who met the train at our station either on his bike with suitable carrier or with the horse and trap, as it was wartime and there was no petrol to spare. We mothers didn't mind the smell as it was only a ten minute ride for sevenpence.

We returned by the same line if we managed to catch the train, otherwise we walked the four miles, thinking nothing of it, aiming to be home before darkness fell and the blackout. We caught the train on its return journey from Northampton to Nottingham – it always stopped at the small stations – at the Northern station, Melton, which has gone many years ago. There were earlier morning and late evening trains too.

Many munition trains went through our station during the dark hours. We could hear the rumble of them from the village a quarter of a mile away.'

GETTING ABOUT IN THE BIG FREEZE

'Those who remember the winter of '47 will recall that it was a grim time, what with everything still rationed and power cuts. The final straw was the heaviest snow falls that most had ever experienced. My father had managed to keep his Rover 14 going and usually had coupons for a few gallons of petrol. In his spare time he had constructed a sledge and now the weather had come to use it, so we set off from Oadby, where we lived, to Great Glen and then took the back road towards Kings Norton.

Although the snow was deep a snow plough had been through and we travelled along nicely. Unfortunately (and I know the exact spot to this day, I was ten years old at the time) the road sloped and the plough, which must have been towed, had slid off the road. My father, however, did not see this and ended up down the grass verge

The men of Great Easton clearing snow in the Big Freeze of 1947. Some remote areas were cut off for weeks.

where the car became stuck. We had no chains on the wheels and as the car weighed a ton and a half, it could not be pushed out by myself and my mother. After various experiments with sacks under the wheels, my father was forced to abandon the car. We walked back to Burton Overy where we caught a Midland Red bus home.

The car was snowed up for a month and it must have been March before we went to retrieve it. I reckon the snow had been four feet deep round the car. We never went sledging again. My mother would not go in the car in the snow after that!'

'During the 1947 freeze, Great Easton was completely cut off and as most of the men in the village were employed at Stewarts and Lloyds Corby they could not get to work. Each day after the snow had stopped falling, the men cut a way through to get back to work as quickly as possible. Our bread was delivered to us by a bakery in Cottingham, so some of the villagers walked across the fields to collect it, walking on the tops of the hedges at times.'

INDIVIDUAL ATTENTION

'My particular memory is of the kindness I met with in travelling to and from work by train. In the 1950s, this was of course by steam train. In those days there were many lines, now closed, with small village stations en route.

I used the Rugby to Leicester line and the trains used to call at both Leire Halt and Broughton Astley on their way. I lived about halfway between the two stations. When I started work I had to walk across two or three fields to Broughton Astley station, cross the line at the station by means of a wooden crossing laid between the rails (there was no bridge) and on to the platform where I would buy my ticket. The route over the fields was a bridlepath, muddy most of the time, so I used to wear an old pair of boots and change into clean (and what I thought) smart shoes at the station for the rest of the journey.

In those days, although the trains were well used, the numbers catching each train were not many and the railway staff knew nearly everyone. It wasn't long before I was receiving such individual attention as would never be known nowadays.

I was never good at getting up and starting out on time so that normally when I was just leaving the second field I would hear the morning train starting to puff out of Leire Halt. This would be the signal for me to start running and then it was a competition as to who would get to Broughton Astley station first.

If I arrived first, I had to run across the crossing before the train arrived. The signal box was situated at my end of the platform and the signalman would be leaning out of his window, calling to me whether it was safe to cross. If it was, I would be in time to go to the booking office to buy my ticket and while doing so would change my shoes, putting my muddy boots into a bag I had with me. The man on duty would then take my bag into his office to put by his fire (coal of course) where the boots would dry out during the day, ready for me to change into again in the evening.

If the train arrived first I still had time to do all this but on the odd occasion when I was really pushed for time I would jump through the train door, kept ready and open for me by a friend (one always found a friendly group of regular travellers in those days), hastily change my boots, put them in the bag and drop the bag out of the window on to the platform as the train steamed out of the station. The bag would then be taken into the office and put beside the fire as usual.

We used the train for other occasions when we went out as a family. I remember one time standing on a rise in the ground where I could see my mother well in front walking calmly on to buy the tickets while dotted along the path behind at various stages were brother, girlfriends etc all according to their abilities to walk fast or slow, with my father in the rear coming at a fast trot. The train nearly always arrived at the station before my father but the signalman would not let it leave without him.'

HOUSE & HOME

THE WAY WE LIVED THEN

It was a slower pace of life, but times were hard for many and money was short. Three women recall house and home during the inter-war years.

BORN IN 1926

'I was born in December 1926 in a large village in a coal mining area. In the road where I was born houses were mostly semi-detached but so close together they appeared as terraced. Being rather tall houses, they kept the sun off and so the outlook was rather drear. Luckily, opposite our house was an open space used as a garden and an entrance to a field which was used once a year for the local show, with tents, exhibits, teas etc.

Women wore wrap-round overalls and polished the windows or put out the aspidistras, when the rain was gentle, in the very small front gardens. Grandfathers walked their whippets or their grandchildren. One of my favourite outings with my grandfather was a walk to the cemetery. It was the prettiest place in the village, I thought, along the drive with its metal hoops stuck into the grass, by the river and up the steps. We then had to search for the sexton, an acquaintance of my grandfather, and I would be allowed to wander on the well-trimmed grass to pick daisies. My grandfather died when I was three or four. He had been a miner and he had reared eight children so I had plenty of relatives to visit. One of my uncles was a miner, two had window cleaning businesses, one was a policeman in Leicester and another, who had lost a leg in the First World War, lived in Sheffield but visited us on a motorcycle with a sidecar for my cousins. One aunt and her husband kept a public house and my mother had worked in a hosiery factory. This was useful later on as she was able to pick up the fine stitches when I laddered my stockings! My grandmother sold drapery from her home, keeping the stock in oblong wicker baskets. Sometimes her customers ran up bills and would work off the debt by coming in to do the washing.

Children played in the road as there was very little traffic and lawns were not a thing usually enjoyed by the working people. Ground was for digging and planting and for hens. We played with hoops in season, dolls and prams, whips and tops. We chalked the tops which made lovely patterns when spinning. The earth between the granite kerb stones made ideal starting places for the tops. You set it in the soil, carefully wound the whip string round and round the top, then jerked the string and the top would be a dancing thing of beauty. We had snobs or five-stones, going through the routine with right hand and then the left. We played ball up against any large wall until the owners got fed up and moved us on. We sat on the boy next door's shed roof and blew bubbles with clay pipes and I went for walks with a pleated paper parasol which smelt delicious when the sun shone on it. Sometimes on Sundays I would go with my father bellringing, up and up the wedge-shaped stairs to the belfry where eight hot men concentrated on Grandsire Triples or Bob Major, occasionally shouting if someone came in late with their chime. We always dressed up in our best clothes on a Sunday, whether we went for a walk in the woods, visited a farm or a dusty belfry and I always wore a hat. I had a straw or organza hat in summer and a velour brimmed, deep crowned boater for winter. I can remember when very small having some button-up leather leggings and used a button hook to do up my buttons. Another time my great aunt, who was a dressmaker, made me a cream tussore-silk, button-through dress which was much admired. I was the oldest grandchild on my father's side and consequently was made much of, especially as I only saw them occasionally.

The road was busy with tradesmen who came on bicycles, in vans, or by horse and cart. The milkman brought a can and measure to the door and filled your jug. Bakers called daily, butchers came two or three times a week, there were three or four postal deliveries a day and every week, without fail, we had a letter from my paternal grandmother. Errand boys rode bicycles and were always whistling the latest tunes or sometimes Gilbert and Sullivan. The rag and bone man came several times a year and the chimney sweep was a regular on his bicycle or pushing a cart. We would run to where he was working to watch the brush come out of the chimney. This was considered lucky, but only if you kept well clear to avoid being showered with soot. Coal was delivered by the ton and dumped in the road for the recipient to barrow in.

Houses in our road were very similar. Usually the front door opened into the front room, then past a bogie hole under the stairs where my mother kept her rug making materials and into the living room with a linoleum floor and one rug in front of the blackleaded range and then into the kitchen. We had no heating or fireplace in the kitchen but we had a gas ring and a copper with space underneath to heat the water. There was also a small hot water tank in the range which we filled with a ladle – enough for about two bowls of water. The copper fire was lit twice a week, once for washday and once for bathing. We did not ever have scented soap but used a yellow washing soap. However, bathing in front of a roaring fire compensated for the lack of toiletries. One refinement houses in that area had, over today's dwellings, was that rainwater from the roofs ran into a cistern under the blue bricked "causie" and was then pumped to the sink. "Causie" seems to have been a local name, probably from causeway, otherwise known as the backyard.

Behind the kitchen was a large pantry and across the end was a tiled shelf called a "thrall". Here was kept the milk and meat as it was supposed to be the coolest place. At the first hint of thunder, milk would be boiled before it turned sour. The coalhouse was next to the pantry but with an outside door, of course, and next to it was the lavatory. This was set back and once having turned the corner it was very dark for a small girl to visit at night. I was not afraid of the dark but I hated running over the causie bricks after rain when the bricks tilted and sent muddy water up your legs, but even more I hated the noise when you flushed the loo. I made sure I was ready to run with door ajar before I pulled the chain. It was considered etiquette to cut newspapers into squares to be threaded onto a string and hung on a nail but imagine the frustration of trying to read a six inch square of paper!

My uncle kept a farm and visits to his lavatory were quite a social occasion, except for the smell, and that was definitely anti-social. First there was the walk across the yard past the dog and a couple of cats, through a gaggle of hens and into a field to a wooden building. There were two holes in the scrubbed wooden seat and piles of newspapers, including comics. The view was idyllic – there was no need to close the door with only a few sheep in sight, in fact it was not advisable. I could have sat there for hours reading the adventures of Laurel and Hardy, Joe E. Brown and Shane the Wonder Dog Detective had it not been for the smell, which was awful. I washed my hands in the horse trough and flapped them dry. This farm was a three-storeyed house with a huge scullery, dairy, living-room and sitting-room and I forget how many bedrooms. They kept binoculars on the window sill so they could see who was coming across the fields. The table was about the size of some present day kitchens. The sitting-room in winter was the most luxurious room I have ever seen – big upholstered chairs, maroon-coloured chenille curtains and tablecloth and a roaring fire with the soft glow from the oil-filled lamps.

When I was a child many houses had two families living in them. Houses were mostly rented but the front room and one or two bedrooms with use of kitchen would be sub-let. It could not have been very convenient as the way to the kitchen was usually through the dining or living-room but it seemed the accepted thing. We shared a house with my maternal grandparents for the first eight years of my life. It was their house and it took this time for my father to save up for a deposit on his own house. My grandparents also owned the house next door and four small cottages in the next village and I used to go with my grandmother to collect the rents. When she died in 1934 these cottages fetched £100 each at auction.

My favourite breakfast food was Robinson's groats. It had to be mixed carefully or it would go lumpy. It was a fine oatmeal and was taken off the market in the 1960s I believe. It was made by J. Colman, the mustard firm of Norwich. We sometimes had Force and I had a Sunny Jim doll. He was an ugly fellow but mine own, as they say. The advertising blurb went: "High o'er the fence leaps Sunny Jim. Force is the food that raises him." I hated gravy, cabbage and sprouts and wanted HP sauce with everything. We had plenty of fresh vegetables and eggs and we always had a pudding. Milk puddings or boiled suet with fruit in season or jam. We always had a fruit pie on Sunday, usually apple in winter as we bought apples from friends or acquaintances in the autumn for storing. When my uncle's cow had calved my mother made a pastry case and filled it with beastings – the first milk from the cow – and baked it. This tasted like egg custard but the beastings were so thick that no eggs were needed. I had my third of a pint of milk, cost twopence halfpenny a week, when I started school. We rarely had fish – it was not considered fresh enough – but we made up for this when visiting my father's family in Norfolk in August when we had crab, shrimps, whelks, mussels, skate, bloaters and samphire. We had very few tinned foods. Occasionally tinned fruit, never cream, tinned salmon rarely, but tinned tomatoes we enjoyed regularly. I hadn't tasted baked beans or tinned soup until after I was married.

Women worked very hard in the house and most did not go out to work. Washday was a whole day's work, when dinner was usually cold meat and baked potatoes or bubble and squeak followed by rice pudding. Every day the range needed blackleading and the ashes raking out, downstairs rooms needed sweeping and dusting and rugs shaking. We had no electricity at that time and had gas lighting downstairs but candles were used upstairs. Every week all the candlesticks, usually enamelled in our house, were placed on the range so the wax would soften and cleaning them would be easier. They were cleaned with newspaper and rubbed with a cloth. The cutlery needed fairly frequent cleaning as it soon stained.

There was a market to visit on Friday and the weekend shopping to do. We rarely went anywhere by bus but walked miles. There were bus services but these were regarded as luxuries. We went for long walks and knew all the footpaths in the area but the areas beyond that, four or five miles away, were unknown.'

MONEY WAS SHORT

'As one of eight children of a farm labourer, money was very short. My brother had only one grey flannelette shirt for school. In the middle of the week when he had gone to bed Mum used to wash the collar and cuffs of the shirt and dry it overnight around the open fire to get it ready for school next day.

My sister Lily was two years five months old when she was poorly in the morning (she slept in Mum's and Dad's bed) so Mum left her in bed. She sent for the doctor with a message through the farmer's wife. Eventually the doctor was contacted and came to see her. Unfortunately there was nothing he could do so she died that evening after 9 pm (of meningitis, we found out). My father arranged for a coffin to be made locally and Lily was put into it. As was the custom as far as we understood (our parents were Irish) Lily stayed in the bedroom in the open coffin resting on the "box" (a type of ottoman, not padded) from then until the funeral on the Friday afternoon. She died on Tuesday 2nd February. On the day of the funeral Dad and my brother carried her to the church and then up to the cemetery. I had to go into hospital with Liz (seven years) with meningitis, in the ambulance – Mum came with us. Of course the house had to be fumigated out. The bedding was taken into a big van on the road. The villages around collected for us and made £30.

That year I was due to sit my eleven plus but as I had just had meningitis I wasn't allowed to. I heard afterwards that my place had been given to someone else. I was very upset about this. My parents didn't do anything about it as they didn't know if they could. I went to school that September on the school bus to where the grammar school and council school stood side by side. Of course I didn't understand the difference between the two types of education, all I could think about was I didn't have a blazer or satchel. About two years later I got a Saturday/Sunday job and earned enough money to buy my own blazer.

I had an opportunity to go to the technical school at 14 but didn't tell Mum because she had a job to afford the uniform for a younger sister, Winnie, when she passed the eleven plus. She got a £10 grant to help buy her uniform and my brother George helped Mum out. The same brother (the eldest of us) bought bicycles for Chris and me to go to work on (we paid him back later).

We lived in a semi-detached house then with no gas, electricity, flush toilet, or bathroom. Mum cooked over an open fire. We used paraffin lamps and candles to go to bed with. There were not enough blankets so we used our overcoats on the bed to keep warm.'

BEHIND THE SHOP

'The tiny terraced house in which I was born in the old village of Belgrave is now no more. It is part of the car park of the Belgrave Hotel. I most clearly remember the shared yard, which was between the two kitchens of the joined houses, paved with blue bricks and having a small patch of earth near the common lavatory which was edged with house bricks set in cornerwise and in which grew flourishing yellow "creeping Jenny". After rain and more particularly after washing day when the suds were emptied on to the yard and vigorously brushed away, the yard shone clean and bright and wholesome.

In the late 1920s I was taken for a ride in a taxi due, I think, to an emergency at my grandparents' home which was the Salmon Inn in Butt Close Lane (still there today just off Church Gate). There were gaps in the wooden floorboards of this taxi through which I watched the road running at an alarming rate.

Most of my childhood was spent living "behind the shop". That is, we always kept a shop although we moved around a bit. We started with a shop in Checketts Road (before it was widened, of course) opposite the Belgrave Working Men's Club. It was a drapery. At Christmas, my father's boss who was a dentist, my father then being a dental mechanic, always gave us our Christmas dinner. This particular year it was a goose. In addition to being the boss, the dentist was a local character and a practical joker to boot. Our dinner was alive. It was delivered, flapping and hissing into the shop window, among the art silk knickers, cambrian vests, liberty bodices and various hats on tall hat stands! My poor mother had to catch our dinner, cage it and then repair the damage to the window display. I recall she didn't laugh about it much.

We later changed from a drapery to a cooked meats shop and Mother cooked all the meats herself. To this day, I cannot stand the smell of pig's belly cooking! She also made ice-cream (almost a new innovation for a small corner shop) in a wooden tub, turning the cranked handle to stir round the heavy blocks of ice. A hugely arm-tiring job to which I was promoted to take a turn. I have never been keen on ice-cream either.

We moved to Linford Street (the old one, not the one that is now) to take a sweet shop and from the age of twelve I was the one to rise from eating my plum duff to serve a ha'porth of liquorice root or a dab and sucker. When I returned the others had eaten the second helping. I found shop work irritating and complained to my mother that it was debilitating but as I was somewhat sturdy this fell on deaf ears.

During the 1930s and whilst we had the drapery shop my mother ran a "club" for the factory girls. They paid in so much a week and she then gave them credit until they had cleared the debt and were a little in hand when more credit was extended. It was a normal procedure. Nearly everyone bought through "club". Unfortunately, one day the factory closed and Mother lost our liquidity.

"Bankruptcy" was a word never to be mentioned, a disgrace, not to be allowed. Our debts were paid off by money borrowed from my father's boss and the next few years were so dominated by poverty, due to the fact that some of the incoming money went out to pay back the loan, that the "Thirties Depression" really meant that to us.

My father was originally an experimental engineer and eventually was working at the British United Shoe Machinery Co, when there was a lockout. As he was of an independent nature and contrary to boot, he decided that he would not again be subject to the whims and wiles of bodies causing close downs and so asked a friend with whom he took his daily pint at the Belgrave Constituional Club if he could be taught dentistry (his friend being a dentist) and when I was born he was an established dental mechanic. To achieve this, he had worked for two years without earning a penny. Mum had kept them both during this period. And even after achieving this status, the wages were no more than, if as much as, many unskilled jobs. His hours (and also mine when I started to work at the same establishment) were 10 am to 1 pm and 3 pm till 8 pm six days a week. You were definitely "sold to the company store". To augment this income, Dad also installed electricity in gas-served houses, as a sideline.

We had an allotment at the top of Brundle's Hill (a dirt road running parallel to Mowmacre Hill where the old Leicester-Birstall-Loughborough railway line ran at the back). The products from this garden helped considerably in our straitened circumstances and it was many years before I realised that not everybody had their pudding *before* the main course in order that the edge would be taken off the appetite.

As I grew up I joined the Girl Guides, the 19th Leicesters attached to Belgrave St Peter's, and our meetings were held in Justice Street Rooms off Checketts Road. I recall one task set being that, with sixpence, we were to buy a meal for four people, of a well balanced content. We bought two oranges, some pork scratchings, two penn'orth of chips and a large chocolate bar!

We never seemed to go out much, but I cannot recall that anyone else did, either. Summer evenings were spent playing in the street. Winter was by the fire burning in the blackleaded grate, cutting out doilys, melting candles into saucers of water to make flowers or any other occupation my distracted mother could think of to entertain three healthy infants between serving in the shop. And when the shop closed, Mum would play the piano and we were taught all the songs from her favourite music hall turns and light operettas and some of Dad's beery songs as well. We did not have a wireless until I was twelve and then I thought it was boring. My sister and I would much rather bang out a tune on the piano or the accordion and sing anything that came into our heads.

I left school at 14 because that was the thing to do if you were hard up. I went as a dental nurse at seven shillings and sixpence a week, which I did not get unless we had had a few good paying patients, and had been at work just a year when war broke out. My father went back to the BU to work on munitions and I took his job over, being at that time the only female dental mechanic in the county (or the country for all I know).

The war, despite its grimness, afforded lighter moments. No one ever considers, when talking of shortages, that false teeth were in very short supply. I had about 300 dentist customers clamouring for artificial teeth and my allocation from the manufacturers amounted to about three sets each a month. So there were many people trying to tackle wartime rations with very diminished dentitions! It may have been consoling that there was very little meat about.

Under the stairs in all the cramped little houses we have lived in, in the room behind the shop, Dad would install a barrel of beer. My parents would have a glass for their supper every night. When we children reached the age of twelve we could join in if we wished. I would occasionally have one. As I grew up I was uninterested as were my brother and sister. I wonder if this was because as it was never denied, it was never coveted?

Every morning, before leaving for school, Dad would administer a dessert spoonful of pure malt to each of us. It was delicious. He said it was to ward off the cold! He bought it in large stone jars from the Clubs Brewery in Syston Street.

He also brought many of his friends home at night and Mum would don her best grey lace and royally entertain them at the piano. If we children crept downstairs, with our toes turning blue on the cold lino, we were never sent back but allowed to stay.

I had a liberal, loving, laugh-in-the-face-of-fortune upbringing that may have been denied to many, although the softer pleasures and comforts were not to be had.'

THE HOUSES WE LIVED IN

Sometimes overcrowded, usually poorly heated, hard to keep clean and with no mod cons – but we still feel affection for the cottages and houses of our youth.

LIFE IN NEWTON LINFORD

'I was born in Lilac Cottage, now a highly desirable, modernised thatched cottage, but then with just one room upstairs and another room plus kitchen downstairs. When I was eleven, in 1922, the family moved across the road to a larger cottage, two up two down, with stone walls and a thatched roof. This was very warm, due to the thickness of the walls. There was one cold water tap, over the grey slate sink in the kitchen, and a closet down the yard which was emptied once a week by two local men, who came after eleven o'clock at night with a horse and dray. Being local lads, the Night Soil Men used to play tricks on people – hanging a dead hen inside the door, or fixing up a "ghost" on the privy. The sewage they collected was taken to a field, known as the Sewerage Field, off the Groby Lane. Water closets reached the village just before the Second World War. At Blakeshay Farm the privy contained a row of five seats – four for adults and one for a child. In the more remote areas each householder had to make his own arrangements for disposing of sewage.

There was no bathroom, of course. A zinc bath hung on the wall outside. This was brought in on a Friday night and everyone took turns for a bath. Most houses had a washhouse, or the use of a shared one. This held a copper or a gas boiler. Drinking water came from a pump. There were two village pumps by the roadside, and a big well near the allotments, but a good many houses had their own pumps, some of which are still in position. Some people went down to the brook with their buckets. Water was never wasted, and after the family wash the water would be put on the gardens.

Monday was always washday. When children got home from school they were given the task of folding the dry washing and putting it through the mangle. Sheets had to be carefully squared up, corner to corner, and then mangled twice, with the rollers being tightened for the second roll.

The front room was called the parlour, and in Newtown Linford this was often a tea room, where visitors to Bradgate Park called for their teas. Everyone had a sofa. Scratchy horsehair has left itchy memories for the children who had to sit on it when visiting relatives; those with a leather covered sofa considered themselves lucky. There would be a scrub-topped table in the kitchen, and the one in the parlour was probably also scrub-topped, but this was never seen as it was always covered with a chenille cloth with bobbles around it. The mantelpiece was often also covered with a chenille or velvet drape. There was always hot water from the kitchen range.

In Newtown Linford during the inter-war years there seems to have been a general terror of thunderstorms, especially after a house in Polly Bott's Lane was hit by a thunderbolt which went down the chimney. Evelyn's mother threw out the brass fender from the parlour after that occurrence, in case it attracted lightning. All mirrors were covered over and all knives and forks were put in a drawer: no meals were eaten during a thunderstorm.

Most of the cottages had very large gardens, and many of the men also had an allotment. As Newtown Linford was entirely owned by the Bradgate estate, the allotments (like the houses) had to be rented from the estate office. Men, women and children worked on the gardens. The men made sure that their families were kept in vegetables and fruit, while the women looked after the front gardens and took a pride in their flowers – hollyhocks, gypsophila, lilies and roses are specially remembered. Children took it for granted that they would help wherever they could.

Children's clothes were usually made at home. Girls wore pinafores, also made by their mothers. These had a frill at the bottom and a top which had to be starched. New clothes were kept for Sunday best, and I always had to go and show off any new dress to my Auntie Lizzie before I wore it to Sunday school for the first time.

There were dressmakers in the village, who were used for special occasions, such as Miss Warner, who made my Confirmation dress. Later there was Mrs Butler, who came during the Second World War, having been bombed out in London. She and her family lived in the Sunday school until they got a council house.

No woman would think of going out without wearing a hat. Wool or chenille hats were home-made, either knitted or crocheted. Felt or straw hats were bought in Leicester, either from a stall on the market or from a shop such as Grices in High Street.

Shoes usually came from one of the Anstey shoe factories, for nearly everybody had a friend or relative who worked there if they didn't do so themselves, and could get rejects at modest prices.

Several tramps would come round. The best remembered was known as Old Black Charlie, although he was always clean. He used to help farmers, and would sleep under hedges. He made beautiful bouquets of wild flowers in a doily, and he would present these to people who gave him titbits. Rag and bone men would also come round, and would give a penny for a rabbit skin.'

A LONELY FARMHOUSE

'I have many memories of the lonely farmhouse at Peatling Parva where I was born some 70 years ago. Sadly this was demolished at the time of the Second World War to make way for Bruntingthorpe aerodrome. Although I was born in early November, I am told there had been a very heavy fall of snow and as access was either by way of a footpath over several fields or via a mere lane track, my father was obliged to get out the trap, harness the pony and struggle to the nearby village of Walton to fetch the midwife. This farm, called Covert Farm, was occupied by my family for many years.

Later, as a schoolgirl living in Leicester, I spent many holidays with my aunt and uncle at the farm. Aunt Clara was, I suppose, a typical farmer's wife of that time and made excellent use of all that the farm provided. Near to the farmhouse was the farmyard with cowsheds and pigsties, a duck pond and an orchard where Aunt kept her hens, which had free range. I was allowed to collect the eggs, which sometimes had to be looked for when the hens found their own nests in the orchard and rickyard. An evening task was to shut up the hen coops. Any strays would most likely become a victim of prowling foxes.

The farm kitchen of course contained a blackleaded range for cooking and heating some water and a stone sink where one washed oneself in cold water, or alternatively one might have a bowl of water on the bench outside the back door. It was not unusual in spring to find a sickly orphan lamb being warmed by the range or perhaps some newly hatched chicks. Several steps led from the kitchen down to the dairy where butter was produced. After the cows had been milked by hand, the milk was put into a separator to take off the cream. When there was sufficient cream it was put in the churn and then began the laborious job of turning the handle. It took quite a long time to make the butter and there would be several stops in churning to see how it was going.

When the butter was ready my aunt, who was a large lady, would load some of it into the basket on her bicycle, along with eggs, and pedal unsteadily down the lane for her weekly visit to Walton to sell the produce, visit the village shop and catch up on the news. At the shop, sugar was weighed into blue paper bags. Biscuits were sold loose, being weighed from large tins and sometimes broken biscuits could be bought cheaply.

Very little meat came from a butcher as succulent pies were made from wild rabbit meat. At harvest time there would be great excitement when the machine cutting the corn was getting to the last of the crop in the centre of the field and rabbits fled, to be caught by dogs or shot. One of the older hens might be killed for steaming or as a treat there would be cockerel for Sunday dinner. One of the pigs would provide many meals of pork and bacon and on the day of the killing, pigs' fries of liver and offal would be given to friends and relations and sides of fat bacon would hang from the ceiling to mature after being salted. I enjoyed looking for mushrooms in the fields to accompany the fat bacon for breakfast. Aunt liked making wine from cowslips or dandelions and there were apples from the orchard and blackberries from the hedgerows to make tasty pies or very filling suet puddings. Home-produced goose grease was rubbed on the chest as a remedy for colds and a messy process this was. In the summer there was haymaking and trips to the hay field to take the men sandwiches, cake and tea in white enamel cans. If I stayed at the farm in winter we would play dominoes in the evening and Aunt would fill the copper warming pan with hot coals to warm the feather bed.

Fox coverts were close to the farm and during the season there would be visits from the Fernie Hunt. In the early 20th century the royal princes often rode with the hunt and were seen near the farmhouse. At one time my uncle was an earth stopper for the hunt. He would go out the night before a hunt day to stop up fox holes to prevent the foxes going underground.

My father told of his childhood at the farm and his walk over the fields to the little school at Peatling Parva. He and other scholars who made long journeys would often arrive wet and cold and the kind schoolmistress would dry their clothes by the large stove in the middle of the schoolroom.

My grandmother delighted in making pegged rugs. Discarded clothes would be cut into strips, suitable colours selected to make a pattern, then hooked into hessian. These rugs made a warm covering for the floor of the farmhouse living-room. This craft was done in winter evenings by the light of an oil lamp.

It was a very special outing to leave the farm for a day trip to town by pony and trap and later by the local bus. Of course arrangements first had to be made for the livestock. Special days for my uncle were visits to town on quarter days to pay the rent or to go to the cattle market.'

MEMORIES

'There was lino on the floors in most rooms with a carpet square or rugs, ie rag rugs or knitted rugs made with wool cut into three-inch lengths. Kitchens often had red terracotta tiles which had to be scrubbed and polished with Cardinal red polish. Doors and banisters had a dark wood stain and the bottom half of walls might be varnished over a heavy embossed paper. Floors were washed with a thin solution of starch to make them shine without being slippery. The fireplace in the dining/living-room had an oven at the side; some had to be blackleaded but after the Second World War an enamelled type was brought in. Coal fires in bedrooms were lit only at times of illness or when babies were being born. When lighting a coal fire newspaper was put in front to "draw" it up, which often caused chimney fires when the paper caught alight.

Men always washed in the kitchen on returning from work. Brilliantine was used on hair, later Brylcreem. Razors, both cut throat and safety type, were sharpened by using a strop, a long piece of leather hung from a knob. Loose collars, well starched, were worn only on going out and on Sunday. These collars were sent to the laundry, which collected one week and delivered the clean washing the next week; everyone had their own individual mark.'

'The typical village home at Heather could well consist of a small, quaint cottage with no bathroom and a single non-flushing toilet, yards down the garden. Everyone had open coal fires, and certainly no central heating. The door on the kitchen oven was kept open to help warm children on cold mornings.

Feather-filled eiderdowns were a poor substitute for our modern continental quilts; on a winter's night overcoats were used on the bed to give extra warmth. On cold nights the bed would be warmed with the hot oven shelf wrapped in an old cloth. Having a whole bed to oneself was a pleasure few children enjoyed. For many large families sleeping arrangements usually meant several to a bed in the head to toe fashion. If this wasn't a recipe for disturbed sleep one could always rely on someone requiring the chamber pot during the night!

"Donkeying the step" was a term used for the scrubbing of the front doorstep and finishing with a donkey stone, a frequent ritual for many housewives.

Cleaning and polishing shoes was once a daily task undertaken by most families. Children's shoes used to be inspected after assembly at school and had to be clean and polished. If the family did not have any polish available, scuffs would be covered with blacklead grate cleaner, to prevent the children getting into trouble. Shoe repairs were often undertaken in the home, old car tyres sometimes being used to sole and heel family footwear.'

COTTAGE-CUM-FARMHOUSE

'Our home at Harby in the 1940s was a 200 year old cottage-cum-farmhouse with very low beamed ceilings, and a distempered kitchen with cream painted woodwork. The cream paint went throughout the house, with some rooms papered and others "Walpamured", which was an improvement on distemper.

There were some old cheeserooms at the back of the main rooms where Stilton cheese had been made years before. One room had been turned into a pantry with the hastener shelves still standing: they were used for the storage of huge serving dishes, pancheons, bowls etc plus the butter churn with which we made our own butter.

The other cheeseroom was used for storing all sorts of equipment including a Ewbank washer which had a handle that was wound first one way and then the other by hand to clean the clothes. The clothes were put through the wringer and then rinsed and wrung again. We also had an old wringer, painted green with large wooden rollers, which really took out the water. A fire-heated copper in the corner of the kitchen was lit every Monday morning for the weekly wash.

Also in the second cheeseroom were long tiled leads (originally used for the cheese curd) which were used for salting sides of bacon and hams when we killed pigs. After so long in the salt the bacon and ham would be hung to dry before we began to eat them. We made pork pies and brawn too; my grannies' brawn was better though. We made up pigs' fries (a selection of pork liver, kidney etc) and took these round to our friends. We had a large sausage machine and made our own sausages. This was a very busy time: sometimes we would kill two pigs a year.

We had coal fires and a cooking range in the kitchen, graduating to a cream Belling electric cooker in the late 1940s.'

THE EARLY 1950s

'When we moved to our new house in Thurnby in 1952 it was the first house either of us had lived in that we could walk right round, a square Victorian, double-fronted villa – actually built in 1900. The two rooms on either side of the front door, facing north, were the sitting and dining-rooms, both nicely finished and one still with its beautiful marble mantlepiece.

The room behind the sitting-room was the kitchen/living-room. It had an inter-oven grate – an open fire with an oven at the side, a high cupboard for dry goods and an electric cooker.

The staircase went up the middle of the back of the house and the passage at the side led to a back door and the scullery which was also the bathroom. In the corner behind the door was a tall cupboard, and inside, standing on end and hinged on its waste-pipe, was a metal bath. This, when lowered, was filled by buckets from the wash boiler and the cold tap. Incidentally, one had to walk half round the house to drain vegetables after cooking them in the kitchen!

Upstairs there were four bedrooms. One, looking down the garden, had a fitted wash basin, beautifully decorated with chrysanthemums, with a waste-pipe but no taps. There was no inside lavatory but an Elsan in one of three small outhouses just beyond the back door. A little further back was the "coach house" with a stable, hay loft and an older "two by two" – twin lavatories side by side draining to an ash pit and long unused. We think this provided nourishment for the wistaria which now flourishes on this building.

When we moved in, there were considerable restrictions on what we were allowed to spend on modernisations but we were given a grant by the Billesdon RDC for putting in a bath, toilet and wash basin and a hot water tank in a cupboard in the bathroom – the room with the chrysanthemum wash basin.

The scullery became the kitchen with a coke boiler for the hot water system – there was also an immersion heater (electric) in the bathroom tank. The pump was moved outside and the copper and bath-in-a-cupboard were taken out. We also had a toilet-cloakroom in what had been the pantry, with a brick thrall, behind the dining-room. We – and the council – wondered what would happen to our drainage. There was a cesspit partway down the garden and "they" said that main drainage would soon be coming to Thurnby so we could see what happened. I've often wondered about this as we never had the pit emptied – however the drains did come, about 18 months later. A deep trench was dug down the middle of Main Street and Grange Lane and we were connected to this.

I cannot remember how much we were allowed to spend on the "improvements" – can it possibly have been under £100?

An afterthought; all the room doors had a lock and key and downstairs there were bolts so that the doors could be secured from the passage. We had these taken off. We were not so security minded in 1952.'

WATER AND WASHDAY

In the 'good old days' every drop of water had to be carried into the house from well or pump – though that could prove a social experience! The little house at the bottom of the garden had to be cleaned out too. Washday was dreaded in most households, a whole day of steam, flapping wet clothes, cold dinners and hard work.

NO MOD CONS

'At Blaby the lavatories were called closets and they were across the yard or even down the garden path. These were big pans covered by a wooden surround and a lid with a hole in it to sit over. Small squares of newspaper hung from a nail for toilet paper. The men's closet was a drainpipe over a drain behind a wooden fence; four cottages would share the use of this. One such closet in the baker's

Taking a walk down the garden path in the days before mod cons was a necessity. At least this path at Whetstone was straight!

yard had a big hole and a little one so that mother could use it at the same time as her child.

The night soil men used to start out at 9 pm to collect the pans, hence the "nine o'clock horses". A horse would be used to pull the heavy trough on iron wheels, into which the men emptied the sewage.

Bath night meant a large zinc bath in front of the kitchen fire and all the family using the same water. We had a chamber pot under the bed which we would empty into a slop pail and then rinse out with boiling soda water.'

'Our home during the war was a small terraced house in the village of Whetstone. We had no bathroom and no flush toilet, but had to walk down to the bottom of the garden to our "lavatory", which was a round metal bin encased in wood, with a seat scrubbed so often the deep grooves made a pattern on your thighs. There was no light and if you had to go at night you took a torch, but couldn't shine it down the garden path because of the blackout.

Next to this was a coalhouse, with a little coal and a heap of riddled nutty slack. The coal dust which remained after the riddling was put in a heap at the bottom of the garden. The first one to "go" after breakfast (it always seemed to be Dad) would be instructed by Mam to take the remaining dregs of the teapot and empty them on the heap of coal dust. This would bind it together and hopefully help with the coal ration. It worked, too.'

WELLS AND WHEELBARROWS

'There were three town wells in Arnesby, but since mains water arrived in 1953 they have all disappeared. One stood at the top of Baulk Lane (now Robert Hall Road). One was at Bottom End and is now under Mill Hill House. The third, Kerbidge well, was in Town Street as you left Arnesby on the way to Shearsby. This had a little "house" over the actual well and a small drinking trough where tadpoles could be found in the spring.

Some houses had their own wells, others were shared. One such was built into the wall between the Co-op and the next house. This had a "slide" arrangement in the middle with a handle and a spout on either side. All these provided drinking water and soft water for washing was usually caught from the roofs in water butts or tanks.

When we moved to Arnesby in 1947 we had a soft water pump over our sink in the kitchen. I carried water in white enamel buckets from Mrs Kemp's yard for drinking. We first used to get water from Mr Sidwell's pump at his hosiery factory, until we pumped up worms. During the winter, on wet days when I returned from school I had to take my turn and stand down in the beer cellar (at The Shoulder of Mutton) and hand pump the water out. It was a good day when we had an electric pump installed.

Years ago, before there was modern sanitation and dustbins were emptied every week, the old earth closets (which could be either single or multiple "holers") often backed on to the ash-hole. Here tins and bottles as well as ashes were put. Two men with a cart and wheelbarrows would come annually to empty the contents. On one occasion, the weather being very hot, the two men performing this unpleasant task asked the lady of the house whether she could find them a bottle of home-made wine. This being done they consumed the contents while completing the job. When they eventually went home it was with one pushing the other in the wheelbarrow they had been using.

Later "night soil" was collected by George Freer and his "pan cart". The horse was frequently sworn at for its habit of wandering further down the street while the buckets were being fetched. Such toilet arrangements were generally located at the furthest point from the house; although incredibly in one instance the bucket was actually carried into the house through the kitchen. The contents of the cart were tipped in the corner of a field just outside the village. On one occasion some members of the Home Guard, out on an exercise in the dark, accidentally wandered across this area, much to the amusement of their comrades.

At this time there were in fact a few flush toilets in the village. These were connected directly into the storm drains, which went into an open ditch across the fields and into the washbrook. Tomato plants grew in this ditch during the summer months. George was eventually replaced by a Lutterworth RDC tanker and cesspits were installed by some people. Main sewers still had not been installed in 1960.'

'Most houses in the village obtained their water from wells and it is said that one can dig anywhere in Swinford and find water. Many houses in fact had their own wells but some wells served many houses. The parish council was notified in 1947 that a piped water supply would be installed but it was not until 1952/53 that the mains water arrived in the village.

In the early part of the century, sanitary arrangements consisted of bucket lavatories. These were collected by the "pan waggon" in the early hours of the morning before anyone was about, and disposed of on the fields. According to parish records, on 28th September 1905, application was made by the Assistant Overseer for extra remuneration for the collection of a special Sanitary Rate. A sum of ten shillings quarterly was allowed, and this was increased to £1 in 1920. In 1965 a proposed plan for new sewerage was received from the Rural District Council, but for some years after that, as new houses were erected, individual cesspits were built. Since 1970, nearly every house has been connected to the main sewer.'

MEETING AT THE PUMP

'In 1950 I was living in Great Easton with my husband and young daughter. Close to our house was the street pump where all the inhabitants got their water.

Each morning we had to rise early to pump all our water for the whole day. Needless to say, with a young baby we required many buckets of water, and two zinc buckets with lids were kept for drinking water and were stored on the sink draining board.

In the corner of the kitchen a brick-surround copper was built and this was heated with a solid fuel fire for washing our clothes. This had to be filled every night and on the day when most of the weekly wash was done, it had to be filled three or four times. On the days when you needed a hair wash or a bath the same ritual had to take place. In the outhouse we were fortunate to have a water closet (most of the villagers did not) so another full bucket of water was left standing nearby and whoever emptied the bucket had to fill it.

The pump was a meeting place for young and old to share their daily problems and delights. If you were short of time then you had to be short of water too! Villagers expected a daily natter when performing this task and were quick to take offence when you were not prepared to talk.

In the early 1950s there was talk of a mains supply being brought to the village and soon it materialised and there was no longer any need for our pump. It remained solely as a feature until one day a loud bang was heard and we found it had been knocked to the ground by a vehicle. The following week it was removed and the well sealed. Gone forever.'

WASHDAY

'My earliest recollection of life in the home, when I was a child in the 1930s, was Monday, which was washday. It used to take nearly all day washing for five of us children and Mum and Dad. We had a brick-built copper in the corner of the bathroom, which was downstairs, and of course the water had to be heated by a fire under the copper. Water for baths was scooped out of this, also washing was boiled up in it. Then the washing was put into the dolly tub and Mum used dolly pegs to agitate the wash and after this if they weren't to be boiled they were rinsed. The last rinse was in Reckitts Blue which was kept in a piece of cloth and swished around in the water. If any starching was needed this was also used, the starch made by Colman's. The three washing powders which seemed to be very popular were Persil, Rinso and Oxydol, and the washing soap was Fairy and Sunlight.

We used to have a makeshift (as Mum called it) dinner on Mondays, which was left-over meat from Sunday, with potato and vegetables added. She called it hash. We all liked it and it was filling. Suet pudding was my favourite sweet. This was boiled in a cloth and then golden syrup was poured over it. It was lovely. As a treat Mum would make treacle toffee and parkin cake.'

'We lived at Whitehouse Farm on High Street, Castle Donington in the 1920s. My mother always had a woman come in to do the washing. She was paid one shilling a day plus an egg for her tea. The washhouse was separate from the main house. The water had to be carried over in buckets to fill the copper and a fire was lit under it early in the morning. Because the water here is so hard, soft water was sold at a halfpenny a bucket. Wet clothes were put through a wringer with rubber rollers. Dry clothes were put through a mangle with wooden rollers. Household linen was mangled when dry instead of being ironed. Some women took in mangling for a halfpenny a basket. In the washhouse was a dolly tub and pouch and a stone slab for scrubbing extra-soiled garments.

Mr Grimley, the butcher, made soap with his waste fat and caustic soda. It was very hard on the hands. We bought it by the stone (14 lbs) and used it for all household cleaning. We were lucky because my mother bought Knight's Castile toilet soap from a chemist in Ashby to wash ourselves with. She also bought candles there. Candles were sold by the pound in weight: twelve to the pound for household use, eight to the pound for carriage lamps and outdoor lamps. The eights were shorter and thicker.

We had boys to live in on the farm who had been sent "on probation" for minor crimes by the courts. They all had to be cooked and washed for. My mother did all her own cooking but had women in to help with the cleaning and ironing.'

'I remember my mother-in-law saying that the mother of a very poor family used to come and fetch her washing water in buckets to do her own weekly wash because she couldn't afford to heat water or to buy soap.'

'Once a week when Mum did the washing the back boiler was kept going. A big metal bath was brought in to the kitchen and one by one my brothers, sisters, father and mother had a bath. After each of us had finished the water was ladled out of the bath with a white enamel spoon with a long wooden handle and then filled with hot water ready for the next person.'

'At Kirby Muxloe there was one wash for the whole village – a big iron and a mangle. People took it in turns with the coppers. The boys turned the handles of the mangles and sometimes the parents wondered why it took so long. Many a wedding was planned over the mangle!'

TAKING IN LAUNDRY

'When my mother, who came from the north, married my father in the 1930s, it was decided she would help out at my grandmother's laundry at Bitteswell. I well remember as a schoolchild the cold meat lunches on Mondays and Tuesdays and stew on Wednesdays to accommodate the work. My grandmother, who lived in what had been three small cottages, took in laundry from all the big houses in the village. The smallest cottage had become the "ironing house" and there was a staircase which was most mysterious to me, and which I was not allowed to investigate as it was deemed unsafe. There was a washhouse at the top of the straggling garden and so there was ample room for several washing lines.

Early on a Monday morning the brick-built copper was filled with buckets of water from a pump and lit to heat all water. The washing process was begun in three tin baths with rubbing boards, Oxydol and Lux flakes. Soda was used to soak washing beforehand. All dirty water had to be carried to the drain to be emptied. My mother talks of carrying these heavy baths just two days before I was born. The second process involved the use of a small mangle, followed by a huge one, and finally the clothes, weather permitting, were hung out to dry in the large garden.

On Tuesdays procedures began in the ironing house, and I can still remember the warmth here in winter, the smell of the damp clothes, the starch and warm irons. Here three tables were in place and flat irons were placed for heating on a small central solid fuel stove. There was a large pancheon of starch for many items, including pillowcases, vast tablecloths and napkins, and many baby clothes. Clothes-horse airers and a pull-up ceiling airer helped to finish off the process.

If all went well and the weather was kind, by Thursday the laundry was ready to be folded and placed into the well-known wicker baskets, for collection by servants from the houses. If the weather was inclement it would mean vast amounts of washing arrayed around the big stove to dry, and again I remember the not so pleasant smell of damp and drying clothes.

On Saturday fresh loads would arrive at Grandma's to begin the whole process over again.'

WASHDAY BLUES

'As a small child just before the war, washday (always Monday) was to me a series of delights which stay in my mind as vivid memories of special colours, sounds and smells.

The creamy mixture of starch magically becoming clear when added to the waiting bowl of water; the beautiful "blue" for the whites in its own little bag which I wanted to keep for myself when the blue had been used; the copper stick, worn smooth and white by the hot suds – for years after the copper had gone it stayed in its home by the sink and was used every day by my mother to flick the catch of a high window, saving her a climb up to open it; the frothy suds getting higher and higher in the sink during hand-washing and even spreading in minute bubbles over the draining board. The softness of them when my small hands could not resist a little pat; the warm soapy smell pervading the kitchen but not quite masking that other Monday smell – of milk pudding in the oven in readiness for our dinner at one o'clock.

However, it was the mangle that held the greatest fascination for me. I knew to keep away from the massive rollers with their delicious squelch as the water was squeezed out of the sheets, pillowcases and towels, the lovely flat linen sliding through and then guided by my mother into the clothes basket below. Even more fascinating were the dark oily cogs at the side, moving round, fitting into each other so perfectly every time. How shiny they looked in their grease – out went my left thumb for just one feel of that smoothness.

A basin of water, milky with Dettol, turning bright red as soon as my thumb went in it. The doctor arriving. A large padded bandage. A sling. Manoeuvring my pedal cycle round a corner, one-handed. Daily visits to the surgery to have the dressing gently soaked off in warm water and another applied. No memories though of pain or tears. Surely there had been some.

The tiny thumb was too small to stitch. The almost severed top piece had been carefully replaced by the doctor, but not quite straight as was discovered when it had eventually healed. The scar and gap, still clearly visible, and the ugly misshapen nail which grew in place of the delicate pink shell-like one found hours later on the kitchen floor, are a continual reminder of that particular Washday's Blues.'

SHOPPING AND CALLERS TO THE DOOR

How exciting shopping could be when a visit to town or to the market was an event rather than a chore – and each shop had a character all its own. Many of us had goods brought to our doors during the rest of the week, tradesmen providing a service in the days when travel was difficult and expensive.

SHOPPING BY THE CARRIER

'There were two shops in Empingham where everyday things could be bought but the village carrier obligingly made purchases in Stamford on Fridays. We listened for his voice calling "Staamfud", and then ran out to him with a note telling him what we required and the money to pay for it. Late in the afternoon he would arrive back in the village where the boys would meet him and help to deliver all the shopping.'

OFF TO MARKET

'There used to be a carrier from another village go from Peatling Magna to Leicester each week in a high trap; a few used to take advantage of it, but there was no cover from the weather. One person from the village used to walk in pattens and had half a crown to spend when she got there.

It was a big day to look forward to when we went to Leicester, driving of course, and leaving the horse and trap at the Marlborough Head in Marlborough Street.'

'Until cars were introduced a weekly horse-drawn brake took people from Groby into Leicester, putting up at The Fish and Quart public house in Churchgate. The farmers also left their ponies and traps there on their weekly visits to the market. One well known farmer, having imbibed too freely during the day was regularly helped into his trap by the innkeeper and the horse, having been given a slap, trotted home quite happily with his master fast asleep behind him.'

'One of my favourite places was the old Leicester market. Living in Filbert Street as a child, it was easy to get to and two nights a week my mother would take me there. It was a hive of activity, being open until 10 pm and everyone shouting their wares. The butcher shouted, "Here's a joint for Sunday dinner, a slice of steak for husband's supper and six links of sausages for breakfast", and all for half a crown! Then there was the pot stall, where the man would throw all the plates up in the air and catch them, never dropping one. We would always finish up at the hot peas stall and enjoy a plate of peas with plenty of mint sauce. This was in the late 1920s.'

FOOTPADS AND DRIPPING

'On Saturday evenings long ago the women from the villages of Preston and Ridlington used to walk into Uppingham to buy perishable items from the tradespeople. No fridges in those days and bargain-priced meat from the butcher was very welcome to people with large families to feed.

I can only imagine that the women got a lift home in Tiny Thorpe's horse-drawn bus which plied between Uppingham and

Manton station. It was strange that the Ridlington women came to Preston rather than home by the shorter route through Ayston. However, whilst they were walking along the Ridlington road, just beyond Preston windmill (now demolished) past a tall, thick hedge in the twilight, on some occasions they would be accosted by a "footpad" who demanded to look in their baskets and helped himself to their bargains. A husband of the women got fed up with this robbery and, dressing himself up in his wife's long skirt and cloak, he accompanied the women on their walk home. Sure enough the footpad appeared and got the shock of his life for under the cloak the husband had a heavy cudgel and he gave the robber a right good beating and he was never seen or heard of again.

A Saturday morning trip for Preston children would be across the fields to Ayston Hall where the cook would fill their cans and basins with beautiful beef dripping and give them strict instructions not to look in their cans until they were out of sight of the hall windows in case her ladyship was looking out. The children would scamper quickly away and get behind a tree and with great glee enjoy the hidden treats, maybe a slice of plum cake or at Christmas a mince pie! Of course the beef dripping on toast provided the family with several good meals during the week. Full tummies were of more importance than calorie counting or cholesterol problems in those days.'

THOSE WONDERFUL SHOPS

'Shopping trips were made to Leicester occasionally, travelling by train, usually to purchase "Sunday best" clothes from Bridgewater's or Joseph Johnson's and at Christmas there was always a visit to the Opera House to the pantomine.

Of course, there were shopping trips in Hinckley – to Alsopp's the pork butcher's, perhaps, who also made a delicious fruit cake, or to the ordinary butcher's, Frisby's, with sides of beef, pork and mutton hanging from the ceiling, sawdust on the floor and a scrubbed wooden counter and chopping block, steels, choppers, saws and knives hanging round the walls. There were various draper's shops; one selling materials and dressmaking sundries had a whole wall from floor to ceiling of little drawers containing buttons.

The Penny Bazaar opposite was like an Aladdin's cave with shelving from floor to ceiling and on it displayed all kinds of glass, china, etc. How they got things down from the top shelf, I've no idea. A little bow-fronted shop entered up a flight of steps sold sheets of scraps and almost next door was "The Maypole" which

The Co-op store in Bell Street, Wigston in the early 1900s.

sold butter, patted up before your eyes on a marble slab, along with other groceries. Simpkin & James, another high-class grocer, always had biscuit boxes with glass lids round the front of the counter which were purchased "loose". Sugar was weighed up too, granulated and caster in blue bags, and soft brown in purply-pink. Dried fruit was all weighed up on the premises and the bags were made by the men behind the counter.

In "Aucotts", a little Queen Anne double bow-fronted shop – down a step this time – I was always fascinated by two very elegant glass jars on the counter, one containing chocolate marshmallow biscuits with a walnut on top, the other, apricotines, two sponge drops sandwiched with apricot jam! The bakers delivered bread and buns daily by horse and van, but had a shop too where "fancy cakes" were available, usually on Fridays. Our baker, Squires, also made Grantham gingerbreads and brandy snaps but only at Fair time.

Milk and greengroceries were also delivered by float and a covered dray. The dairy float had a canopy fitted in the summer when they sold ice-cream; penny and twopenny cornets and wafers and halfpenny boats. The second ice-cream man made his living in the winter making and selling muffins. The shoe repair shop was interesting as the man always had his mouth full of sprigs [tacks]. Why didn't he swallow them when he talked?'

'I have wonderful memories of Charnwood Street, Leicester or "Charny" as it was affectionately known. The whole length of "Charny", which was quite considerable, was filled with all types of shops. All your needs could be met there somewhere. There was Bagnell's the draper's for all the ladies' requirements, Forster's the men's outfitters, Dalton's the hardware shop, Chaplin's for all musical needs, Joblin's the sweet shop, Paddy's Swag Shop, a tripe shop on one corner of St Saviours Road, Hynard Hughes for all kinds of drink on another, and Kirby's for meat on another. One of Wilkinson's first shops was opened in "Charny" and opposite to it was Issitt's the pawnbroker's with the familiar three brass balls on show. And of course the main grocer shop was Walker's, with the sides of bacon hanging in the shop and the butter patted up into the weight you wanted. For the local residents it was a must to visit "Charny" on a Saturday and pedestrians had pride of place.'

'The shops at Blaby included two drapers, a chemist, a barber, two butchers and several grocery shops which also served as sweet shops. These would sell paraffin, firelighters and soaps and also had a bacon slicing machine. One shop sold poultry food which had to be weighed out from open sacks, and another sold locust beans to chew. From the butcher you could buy sixpence worth of shin of beef and that plus vegetables from the garden or allotment would feed a family of five. Co-op dividend days were a great help to people and often enabled them to have a little luxury.

One of the draper's shops in Cross Street had holes in the window frame where the shutter bolts fitted and if you blew into them all the tissue paper went flying off the counter. Good fun for the kids but not for poor Mrs Henney!'

CALLERS TO THE DOOR

'When I was very young my friend and our next door neighbours at Harby all bought their milk daily from an elderly man with a pony and trap who came from the next village. He carried churns of milk in the trap. The neighbours would bring out their jugs to have the milk measured into them, the measure being dipped into the churn. He had to be watched so that he gave full measure and that the milk was not watered. A hardware man called each Saturday, with his big yellow van which smelled of paraffin and Vim. We called him the Saturday man. The van was packed full of everything under the sun. He always came at lunchtime when we were listening to

Tommy Handley in *Itma* on the wireless. The Saturday man was a Christadelphian and was often trying to put over his views, which sometimes caused a lot of friction. A baker from the next village called two or three times a week but sometimes my mother made her own bread. Another baker would buy his bread from this baker and bring it on the bus in a very large square basket. He would leave it on the customer's doorsteps! He also had a great big carbuncle on his neck. I didn't fancy his bread!

A butcher had premises in the village – he killed our pigs. We bought meat from him. When he died, butchers from neighbouring villages traded in the village. The occasional knife grinder and gipsy called, also the rag and bone man.'

'A man called round the houses in Market Harborough to sharpen knives, scissors etc. He had some sort of bicycle which he sat at and pedalled and which drove the grinding wheel round. He also spat on them as he worked!'

'There were eight farms round the centre of Cosby in the 1930s, all long gone now. Two herds of cows went by our door every morning and evening on the way to and from the fields near our houses. Two of the farms delivered milk. They had a large can which they brought to the door from the horse and trap. There were two measures inside for one pint and half a pint, poured into the jug which you took to the door. Mostly, however, we would be sent to the nearest farm with a jug to fetch a pint of milk when it was needed. The farmer's wife always served us at her kitchen door. That kitchen had a smell all its own – sort of apples, vegetables, cooking, soap and milk and cheese all mixed up. There were sides of bacon and huge joints of meat hanging from the ceiling in muslin covers.'

'Until the early 1920s in Leicester we looked forward to the Saturday afternoon ringing bell and cry of the muffin man, then without warning, it stopped, never to be heard again. However, for a long time to come, we still had the organ man come round – an added bonus when accompanied by his little monkey.

Daily, crusty bread was delivered while still warm, transported by horse-drawn vehicle. The milkman pushed his two-wheeled contraption with churns and measuring jugs. There was excitement when a load of coal was delivered, with the two lovely shire horses sometimes gaily bedecked with coloured ribbons, manes beautifully plaited. I must admit, I was always glad it wasn't one of my chores to go out on completion of the delivery with bucket and shovel to collect that which the horses invariably left behind!

The one thing I remember getting from a corner shop, was treacle. For this, we took our own jam jar and this was filled beneath the tap of the barrel of treacle – and how delicious it was, especially on suet duff.'

STREET CRIES

'A hot cross bun man would come round Rothley with a big wicker basket on four wheels, calling, "Hot cross buns, one a penny, two a penny, hot cross buns." They were really lovely and hot. The only trouble was there weren't many currants in them and we used to say "He stood on Mountsorrel hills and threw them in."

There was also the man who came round with a big basket on his arm, covered with a white cloth, selling lovely pikelets. There was Old Tom the fishmonger who rang his bell and called out, "Fish alive-o, herrings and mackerel alive-o." He also sold oranges, four a penny. Then the greengrocer would call, "Apples penny a pound, plums the same." He would also ring his bell.

I mustn't forget the ice-cream man who used to call, "Ice-cream okay." He had a pretty yellow cart and with his nice white apron, he would sell cornets at a halfpenny each and ice-cream sandwiches at a penny each.

And there was the hot tripe and cowheel man – that was a real treat on a Friday night.'

FOOD IN SEASON

In the days before refrigeration we ate our food in season, part of the joy of each new month. We were far more self sufficient too, gleaning being carried out well within living memory, and pig killing day part of many childhood memories. The village bakehouse was still important in the days when ovens were by no means universal in the home, and Sunday saw a steady procession of meat and Yorkshire puddings on their way to be cooked!

EVERYTHING IN SEASON

'The years were defined by the food that was in season. I don't remember much about New Year's Eve – except the church bells ringing, but soon it was Seville orange time and marmalade making. Lovely orangey smell! Next Shrove Tuesday and pancakes, with lemon juice and caster sugar. Hot cross buns on Good Friday – the boys selling them and shouting, "One penny, hot cross buns." Easter brought Easter eggs (not before!). Strawberries next – my sister's birthday was in June and my parents always managed to get strawberries for her birthday tea. Living in Belgrave, July brought Belgrave Wakes when it was usual to have the first garden peas and gooseberry tart on the first Sunday in July. When lemons were cheap we had lemon curd. Soft fruits, summer beans, apples and pears followed in their maturing time. Brussels sprouts (especially after a frost) and Bonfire Night brought toffee apples and gingerbread men.

Then December and all its preparations for Christmas. The first box of small mandarin oranges – some in silver paper – usually meant Christmas was near. All the goodies for mincemeat, puddings and the cake were prepared and the lovely fruity smell of it all. On the day – turkey and trimmings and afterwards mince pies and nuts, raisins and muscatels and almonds, and lemon and orange slices and Turkish delight. What a feast and all in their seasons to look forward to.'

TO THE BAKEHOUSE

'The bakehouse at South Luffenham was attached to The Boot and Shoe public house. On Saturdays the women would take along pies and cakes to be cooked for the weekend and on Sundays the joint and Yorkshire puddings were taken to be cooked for twopence. The Yorkshire pudding was cooked in a large tin and the children used to fall out over who was having the piece of pudding the meat had dripped on.'

'At Knossington we would take the prepared joint on a tray in its roasting tin with a jug containing the Yorkshire pudding batter, covered with a clean tea towel, to the village baker. For a few pence he would put it in his bread oven to cook and at the right time he would add the batter to cook round the meat, ready to be collected for one o'clock dinner. The smells up the street were mouth-watering!'

'Mother, born in 1895, remembered taking Christmas cakes to the local baker in Castle Donington to be baked in the large oven. Price: a penny for a small one, twopence for a larger one. Little fingers sampling the fare may have reduced the weight when they arrived!

Dakins, the butcher, made savoury ducks each week. To obtain these delicacies folk took their own basins to carry the gravy home.'

GLEANING

'Many years ago at Empingham the gleaning bell was rung after the harvest cornfields were cleared of their sheaves and it was then that the farmers allowed the village women to pick up the spilled corn. It was a very merry annual festivity. The gleaners paid threepence each to the bell ringer and all through the gleaning season the bell would ring at 8 am. The women would meet at the church, about 40 of them as a rule, all laden with their lunch and with large linen sheets. The oldest woman was mistress of ceremonies and she walked out of the village in whichever direction gleaning had been arranged, leading the rest, waving a flag.

The women stayed in the fields until 5 pm. They then gathered up their sheets, heaped with heads of corn, by the corners and made them into big squares which they balanced on their heads. It was a sight to see 40 women marching home, thus laden, to cook their husbands' evening meals.

One of the farmers lent the women a large old barn to do their threshing which they did with a flail. A miller in the village ground their corn for one shilling per bag. One woman, Mrs Pugmore, always gleaned enough corn to keep her family of nine in bread all the year round and to feed a pig throughout the winter. Women also walked back from the cow common of Shacklewell carrying buckets of milk, using wooden yokes.'

'School holidays at Cossington were arranged to fit in with the harvest so that every child should be free to spend all his time in the fields.
They gleaned the corn, which was carefully garnered and afterwards threshed and ground into flour at the mill. This was made into bread by the mothers and baked at the public bakehouse on Fridays. There was formerly a barn called Sunhill on Mr Astill's farm where the gleaners used to gather for their midday meal.'

PIG KILLING DAY

'I remember pig killing days at Little Dalby – I can still hear the screams. Delicious sausages, pork pies, scratchings and pig's fry.

Bacon and sides of ham hung in the kitchen to cure, fat rendered down for lard. With boiled fat bacon for breakfast we ate potted beef in the winter and crisp shredded lettuce with sugar and vinegar in the summer.

We picked watercress from the brook on our way home from school. Butter was made in a wooden churn and Colwick cheese from sour milk. At harvest time we had frumenty made with creed [hulled] wheat and raisins for supper.'

'Pigs were kept by nearly every cottager in the old days and when one was killed it was the custom to send the neighbours a plate of fry. The following ditty was quite common then at Cossington.

"Blessed is the man that kills his pig
And sends his neighbour a fry,
After that a quart of ale
And then a good pork pie.

Cursed is the man that kills his pig
And sends his neighbour none.
May he have neither grains nor swill
To feed another on."'

RABBITS AND PIGS

'We five children were woken up each morning on our farm at Bitteswell around six o'clock by the clanking of metal milking buckets in the cattle yard outside the windows, and the yellow light from hurricane lamps swinging backwards and forwards as the men carried them across the yard to the milking sheds. The milk was emptied into the cooler in another shed and then into churns, which were then stood in a large tank half full of water to keep the milk cool. In the farmhouse all was rush – breakfast of bacon and eggs and sausage (sometimes mushrooms from the fields when in season) for eight people. All was cooked on a three-burner paraffin stove as electricity had not arrived at the farm. To have a morning cup of tea, the fire in the Triplex range had to be lit. If the sticks which had been left to dry in the oven overnight were still damp, the fire would not go, so there would be no tea and no heat in the house.

After breakfast the puddings for the midday meal would be made and put on to boil or steam. My father would often take his gun and shoot a couple of rabbits for rabbit pie. We used to kill three pigs a year for the household. All the meat had to be dealt with in a couple of days and this involved making faggots, pork pies, pig's fry, etc – no fridges in those days. Father went to Lutterworth to a local fish shop and brought back large blocks of ice wrapped in sacking to put in what looked rather like a large refrigerator with shelves. We put the ice on the bottom shelf. The pig's head, together with trotters and any other pieces of meat, were all boiled in a very large cast-iron oval pan with a handle over the top. All the pans we used were of black cast-iron – the bacon never stuck to the frying pan in those days!

When I got married in 1948 I could not believe how easy life was, just switch on the kettle, electric cooker, and joy of joys, the electric iron. Bliss, absolute bliss!'

'In the early 1920s my great grandfather and grandfather were farmers in the village of Stoney Stanton. Father and his young friend would go into the fields and with old netting and stones would secure a trap around a hay rick – well known for harbouring rabbits. Then, putting a ferret under the net, they would patiently wait for one or two unsuspecting rabbits to fall prey. After wringing the poor animals' necks the two lads would then wait for village quarrymen walking to work. One or two would give the boys a shilling – hoping for a rabbit stew as next day's meal. And all this before school-time at nine o'clock.

In the 1940s my father would walk a fat pig from our farmyard to the village butcher in the morning for a killing. My brother, sister and I would watch a while, hearing its squeaking objection as it staggered its way up the road. By late afternoon my father would return a second time with some meat, offal and the pig's bladder. This he would blow up and tie with string so that we children had a "football" to play with. During the rest of the week I would help my busy mother to prepare faggots – how I loved putting the lacy caul-fat over the uncooked faggots and watching her pop them into the oven. Mincing the pork ready for pie-making took a little longer.

It was in the 1920s when quite a few village folk kept a pig and some poultry at the top of the garden. As well as other days my father remembers going along with *his* father in horse and cart to collect the manure. Particularly on a Good Friday, the householder was required to tip the loose pig and poultry muck into the gutter during early morning. This was carted some half mile away to the men's allotments. There the men would follow to dig in the manure.

And all of this had to be done before the church bells rang for Good Friday morning service. The rector at the time, the Reverend Mr Disney, would send his sexton to see that no man was left on the allotments since he hoped to spot him in church.'

FROM THE CRADLE TO THE GRAVE

We were far more likely to be born, to suffer our illnesses and to die in our own homes in the past. Often to call the doctor was a last resort, families relying instead on home cures passed down through the generations – the doctor had to be paid for! Diseases such as scarlet fever were common scourges for children, and medical treatment of children left a great deal to be desired.

BORN AT HOME

'All South Luffenham babies were delivered at home. A Mrs Cole would move into the family home for the duration of the confinement to look after the family, do the washing and housework etc until the mother was considered fit enough to take over the household tasks again. Women were always churched after childbirth (a service to thank God for a safe delivery); they were considered "unclean" until then. Unfortunately, stillbirths were commonplace.'

'I remember the shushing when I approached groups of women in a huddle, obviously talking of a new pregnancy. Little girls were to be ignored! The children of a family would be taken in by their neighbours when a new baby was due so that the man of the family could stay in work. Having babies was a mystery to us all, but when we woke in the morning to find a neighbour's small child in bed with us, we knew!'

'There are fond memories in Appleby Magna of the midwife who was shared between a few local villages. One lady recalls being left in the early stages of labour while the midwife went off to a more urgent call and being told not to make too much noise so as "not to upset the rector". Later in the day she produced a healthy ten pound baby.'

'The year was 1957 and as I had one perfectly normal birth, I opted to have my second baby at home.

In due course the midwife arrived and took one look at my then red hair and asked to see the contents of my rag bag, from which she selected suitable cotton material. I was then asked to carefully boil the cottons in my old gas boiler. She told me that she would need these cloths during childbirth as due to my red hair, I was very likely to "lose a lot". This did not inspire me with confidence.

December 25th, 1957 (two days before "D" day) duly arrived, together with the tinned chicken which I had bought in view of the circumstances. This promptly fell to pieces and did not even inspire our cat, who promptly smelled it and walked away. We therefore had a chickenless Christmas.

December 27th ("D") Day) came and went, as did every day until 11th January 1958 when I finally went into labour and produced a lovely baby girl on 12th January. And I never needed one of the cloths!

Then followed a lovely week in and out of bed, a roaring fire in the bedroom, friends to call at will, and a husband to do all the work.'

HOME CURES

'A basin of hot milk with bread in it at bedtime for a cold. Camphorated oil in ears for earache. Goose grease rubbed on chests for coughs. Mustard mixed in lard for chilblains.'

'Brimstone and black treacle were used for coughs and Carr's Fever Powders for colds. Father's old socks placed around the neck were good for easing a sore throat. Dock leaves would be placed on stings, especially from nettles. For lumbago, people used to place brown paper over the pain and proceed to iron the sufferer!

Constipation could easily be cured by mixing castor oil in warm milk; liquorice powder and senna pods also helped to keep the bowels open. Chilblains could be eased by dipping the feet in the full chamber pot. For bruises or gathered breasts (caused by breast feeding) a poultice made from white lily petals and olive oil could be used and this was stored in a glass jar.'

'Mother made cough mixture with sticks of blackjack etc and rubbed our chests with goose grease. Iodine was used for cuts and sweet nitre for toothache. Cod liver oil and malt in winter for colds. Parrishes' Food (an iron mixture) was taken if you were thought to be anaemic. Chilblains were a common complaint – running out in the snow in bare feet was among the many remedies, and one of the most painful.'

'A home-made remedy from Edwardian times – slice Spanish onions in a dish, sprinkle with demerara sugar, then add another layer of onions and another of sugar and so on. This was laid in the hearth and the juice taken for coughs.'

'In our family, every Friday night senna pods were put in water in a big earthenware pot, which was left all night in the oven beside the fire. The next day everyone had a cup of the liquid.

Blackberry vinegar in boiling water was almost worth having a sore throat for.

My friend's family believed in taking brimstone and treacle in spring and at the fall of the leaf to keep spots away. She liked the linseed and liquorice which was produced if she had a bad cold. She also had to have Scott's Emulsion, which was cod liver oil.

Another friend had a little block of camphorated oil sewn into her liberty bodice.'

DOCTOR, NURSE AND CLUB

'The doctor at Great Easton lived in the village but had his surgery in a neighbouring village. If you needed a prescription, he would make it up and leave it on a shelf outside his back door for you to collect. Can you imagine this happening today?'

'The doctor used to visit Harby twice a week and those requiring a visit had to write their names on a slate in the porch of The Nag's Head and the doctor would call, unless, as occasionally happened, the list was washed off by the rain.'

'Miss Mary Cragg came to Higham on the Hill in 1948 as the first District Nurse/Midwife when the NHS was formed. She covered Higham, Stoke Golding, Wykin, Dadlington, Upoton, Atterton, Fenny Drayton and Lindley, which was a disused airfield turned into a squatters' camp. The salary was £235 per annum.

Market Bosworth Benefit Nursing Association

For providing Nurses for the Sick in Country Parishes.
1909.

Rules for Persons Requiring a Nurse. Price One Penny.

1.—Applications must be made to the Committee Lady, to be transmitted by her to the Secretary. No Nurse can attend a case without an order from the Secretary, or in case of urgency from the Committee Lady.

2.—Subscriptions and fees must be paid to the Committee Lady. Subscriptions are due quarterly; if in arrears the patient will be charged non-subscribers' fees. Board, lodging, washing, and decent sleeping accommodation must be provided for the Nurse by the patient or their families. The following is the scale of charges :—

Class		Yearly.	FEES FOR NURSES PER WEEK. Subscribers.	Non-Subscribers.
1.	Labourers	2s.	2s.	
2	Artizans and Servants	3s.	3s	} 10s.
3.	Small Farmers, School Teachers,	5s.	5s.	
	Upper Servants and Tradespeople	5s		
4.	Large Farmers, Gentry and others	10s.	10s.	£1

A charge of 15/- weekly is made to non-subscribers living outside the area of the Nursing Association

3.—A double charge will be made for mental and infectious cases, also for cases lasting over six weeks, or when the patient has already had six weeks nursing in the current year; cases of small-pox are not nursed. The Committee regret that they cannot *guarantee* to supply Nurses for infectious cases, as this is only possible if one of their own is available.

4.—Non-subscribers can only have a Nurse when one is disengaged, and on condition that she leaves if the Secretary requires her. No person will be allowed to join when ill A woman wishing to join not less than two months before expecting her confinement, may book a Nurse by paying one year's back Subscription, provided she has lived *less* than a year in the District.

5.—The services of a Nurse (when not otherwise employed) may be had within two miles of home for occasional nursing on the following terms:—

Class.	Visits per hour.	One Day (12 hours) with Board.
1 and 2	2d.	6d.
3 „ 4	3d.	1s.

Non-subscribers double fees in all cases, excepting where more than two days together of occasional nursing is required. Where more than two days' nursing is required, the days must be charged at the same rate as per week. *See Rule 2.*

6.—Notice of not less than two months must be given by Subscribers when engaging a Nurse for a confinement. In Classes 3 and 4 the fee is charged from date of engagement, but in Classes 1 and 2 a margin (not exceeding a fortnight) is allowed before payment begins. Nurses do not attend cases without a doctor. Classes 1 and 2 can book for a fortnight's nursing; Classes 3 and 4 for three weeks. If necessary to keep the Nurse an extra week in confinement cases, double fees will be charged.

7.—When night nursing is required, the Nurse shall have six hours' rest during the day, and be off duty one night in three. She should be allowed some daily out-door exercise.

8.—The Secretary must receive two clear days' notice before a Nurse is sent home.

9.—When attending a cottager's wife the Nurse will be expected to do all that is required for the care of the patient's family, excepting the family washing. Where servants are kept, no washing or work un-connected with the patient or sick-room.

10.—No Nurse may receive a gratuity, and must not expect either beer or spirits.

11.—In cases of emergency, such as burns or accidents, when a Nurse is required at once, she may be sent for without applying to the Committee Lady.

12.—The patient's friends must pay or provide for the conveyance of a Nurse to and from a case within the radius of the branch of the Association.

Committee Lady _____

Nursing Associations, such as this one based at Market Bosworth, provided an essential service for many families, for an annual subscription.

Before the NHS, Mrs Povey-Harper was president of a Nursing Association Committee raising money to pay the nurse's salary by holding fetes, whist drives etc and collecting contributions.

A driver was able to take Miss Cragg to some calls, but other times she went by bicycle, not having a driving licence herself. Called to a patient on Lindley camp one foggy day, using a short cut, she was completely lost until she heard a man's voice and went in that direction and found the road, which was a great relief as the patient was very sick.

She was often called to confinements at the camp. On occasions babies were delivered on mattresses on the floor and when no cot was available a drawer was used. Jam jars were used to drink from and once a chamber pot was offered to the nurse to wash her hands in. Luckily it was clean. To sterilise instruments a large saucepan was used, boiling them on a small stove. Dressings were packed in a large tin and baked in the oven.

She remembered a gipsy living in Blacksmiths Yard, Witherley, in a cottage of one room up and another down, who walked miles selling pegs to buy things for her confinement. Her first child was sleeping in the same room where the second was to be delivered, and was told to stay under the bedclothes until after the delivery. When attending her on the second day, the nurse found the door locked and all the curtains drawn, which was very frightening. On making enquiries however, she was told that the woman had put both babies in the pram to go shopping at Atherstone market. She was back in bed in the evening with no ill effects.'

'Sproxton had a "Sick and Dividing Club" – people paid in a shilling a fortnight and received money when they were ill. There was also a coal club. Money was paid in and a load of coal delivered when it was paid for.'

SUPERSTITIONS

'Going under a ladder, looking at a new moon through glass, or putting shoes on the table were all unlucky. Don't wash clothes on New Year's Day – or you'll wash somebody away. Don't wash a blanket in May for the same reason. Never cast a clout till May is out.

If there's two deaths there's sure to be a third; everything comes in threes. They used to ring the bell if anybody died: it was so many pulls for a man, and quicker for a woman. They used to say, "There's

been two this week, there'll be a third!" One magpie's a death –
you've got to see two.

There used to be a Leicestershire saying: "Hold your collar and
do not swallow." If you saw an ambulance, you'd say this, and do
it until you saw a four-legged animal. If you saw a pin in the street
you'd say,

"See a pin and pick it up,
All the day you'll have good luck.
See a pin and let it lie,
The next day you will die."

And if you saw a cigarette, a Woodbine packet, you used to put your
foot on it,

"Woody Woody Woodbine you'll bring me good luck.
Today or tomorrow I'll pick something up."

If you saw a white horse, you could spit –

"White horse, white horse, bring me good luck.
If I spit three times, will that be enough?"

With bus tickets I used to keep adding up the numbers, to get a
single number: .

"One for sorrow,
Two for joy,
Three for a letter,
Four for a boy,
Five for silver
Six for gold
Seven for a secret never to be told."

Then:

"One for dark,
Two for fair,
Three for a boy/girl with ginger hair.
Four for curly,
Five for straight,
Six for a boy/girl and a date." (1950)

Don't step on a paving stone. Don't let a lamp-post come between you and your best friend. Anything sharp, such as knives or brooches, will cut the friendship. Purses shouldn't be empty when given. I wouldn't give gloves; they spoil a friendship. You can't give red and white flowers in the hospital. They are the blood and the bandages. Yes, if you were in a hospital years ago, they wouldn't allow the red and the white flowers together. Or bring may blossom in the house. Or snowdrops. A bird hitting the window signified a death. Peacock feathers are unlucky.'

SCARLET FEVER

'One of my sisters had scarlet fever and another had scarlatina, a milder form of the virus. They were kept at home in the bedroom as the isolation hospital was full. When the fever passed the room had to be "stoved", as they called it then. This meant that the windows and door had to be sealed and some sulphurous smelling candles put inside. The remaining three of us couldn't go to school or mix with other children for about six weeks. The smell of Dettol still reminds me of the fever as Mum had to wash her hands each time she left the room.'

TONSIL TERRORS

'As a very small child, in the 1920s, I was weak and thin and always suffering from colds and sore throats. This meant frequent visits to the doctor, of whom I was terrified. It seemed to me that everyone else in the waiting room was frightened too as all the people tried to be last to go in to see the doctor.

After one of these visits Mother said, "You're going to have your tonsils and adenoids out, then you won't have any more sore throats." That sounded good – no more visits to that horrible man in a white coat.

Presently, Mother and I set off to walk to the hospital pushing baby sister's pram. The pram was empty which I thought was strange as baby had been left with a friend. We arrived at a very grim looking building in Knighton Street and went inside. From a large room came the sound of awful screams and crying. Round this room in a semi-circle sat mothers with their children on their knees, and we joined the group. At the far end of the room was a row of sinister-looking screens behind which the children were taken in turns, screaming as they were pulled from their mothers. They were carried out to Mother with blood running from their mouths and a bowl to catch the blood. Eventually it was my turn to go behind the screens – I can't remember screaming like the others, perhaps I was too petrified. Back in the room I sat on Mother's knee for a while – then home with me in baby's pram!

My next encounter with the doctor was the time that my sister and I had a bad attack of measles. Mother and Father had brought our bed downstairs in order to keep an eye on us. The doctor arrived and after a quick look at us he turned and shouted to my mother, "Light the fire, woman, and get some warmth in the room, these children are very ill." Had the doctor not heard that it was the year of the General Strike? We had no coal and therefore no hot water – no hot food and no fire in the grate.

Fifteen years later I was nursing at the LRI and assisting in the theatre during operations on children's tonsils, and I wondered at the giant strides that had been made in medicine during those intervening years.'

THE LAST JOURNEY

'It was thought in Cossington that if a person lay dead in the parish over Sunday, there would be two more deaths before the next Sunday.'

'The church bell tolled in Sapcote when anyone died, once for a woman, twice for a man, and this was still the custom in the 1950s. The open coffin was kept in the sitting-room on trestles and the lid put on just before leaving for the cemetery. Blinds in the street would all be down.'

'When someone died at Harby, a little old lady from the village, with a bun of hair on each side of her head, would come and lay the dead person out. This lady would also officiate at the funeral tea, always dressed in deepest black. The funeral director in the village was also the wheelwright and carpenter.'

HE GETS US ALL IN THE END

'Married in 1945, I came to Sheepy Magna to live in 1946 and in 1949 began working for a family in the village and continued to do so until 1988. The son was a wheelwright, carpenter and undertaker and from here I gained my knowledge of the undertaking business and funerals.

The bell was tolled first to announce the death and then again at the funeral service. The hearse with decorated glass sides was pulled by two black horses, and the bearers wore black suits, black bowler hats and black gloves. The undertaker always wore a top hat and he walked in front of the hearse on short journeys with the mourners following on foot or in horse-drawn carriages. The church bell was always muffled for the funeral of a VIP. A very haunting sound.

Coffins were made of oak, elm or chestnut. The wood was sawn on the premises and the coffin boards planed, sanded and polished by hand. Hot pitch was used to make watertight the joints then the coffin was lined with satin and lace in pure white. This lining of the coffin was a work of art. A white pillow trimmed with lace and filled with sawdust was placed in. The brass fittings, name plate handles etc completed the coffin.

Forty years ago 90% were buried and 10% cremated, a situation that has almost reversed with 80% cremated and 20% buried these days.

In the event of a death the undertaker would be notified and the deceased would be laid out in their own home, and in lots of cases the task of laying out would be done by the undertaker. The coffin would be made immediately and the deceased placed in it and the next day loved ones could pay their last respects, the coffin having been left open. If a person died in hospital the coffin would be taken there and the deceased brought back to their own home until the day of the funeral. The coffin lid would only be fastened down immediately prior to the funeral. From the undertaker being notified it would normally be three days before the funeral, but frankly, behind the scenes it was hectic. The coffin had to be made quickly, the funeral service to be arranged to suit relatives and the vicar, the grave had to be dug and continual comfort and helpful advice on registration and form filling given to the bereaved. If there was a post mortem then this could delay the funeral for two days.

It was then customary to draw the curtains until after the funeral service and neighbours and houses on the funeral processional route would do likewise. All mourners wore black and the traffic would stop as the funeral procession made its way to the church. People would stop and stand quietly, men would remove their hats until the cortége passed, even if they had not known the deceased. Women continued to wear mourning and men black armbands months after the funeral, all in respect for the dead.

I lost my husband after 40 years of a good and happy marriage and was devastated. Luckily I had the support of my family and friends.

They say that the undertaker gets us all in the end. Well, the undertaker got me and I've lived to tell the tale. I married him five years ago.'

CHILDHOOD &
SCHOOLDAYS

WHEN WE WERE YOUNG

So many childhood memories – of family musical evenings, of staying with grandparents, of the fears, delights and freedom of growing up.

GROWING UP IN LOUGHBOROUGH

'One of my first clear memories is of being in bed at Shelthorpe Isolation Hospital in Loughborough suffering from scarlet fever and seeing my parents appear at an open window at the foot of my bed and toss a packet of iced ABC biscuits to me. The year was 1931, I was aged three and the youngest but one of six children who never got a whole packet of anything to myself as my father was frequently out of work due to the depression. This treat, and the good food (especially the rice puddings), cancelled out any bad impressions of being ill and in hospital.

We lived in a terraced house with two gas-lit rooms downstairs and two bedrooms lit by candles upstairs and we had an outside toilet near a small paved area with a piece of garden following on, flanked by the open backs of the rest of the terrace. Epidemics were common and our family usually had a victim or two, including smallpox, but they recovered. My second eldest sister caught pneumonia, leaving her with weak lungs which in her teenage years developed into tuberculosis. This was a common disease and whole families were known to die from it. My sister was sent to Markfield Sanatorium at 18 and despite new treatments being found was sent home incurable and sadly died at 21 years of age.

We left this small house for a larger one when I was ten. We had few bought toys and made our own from various boxes. Shoe boxes were made into doll's beds and peep-shows, matchboxes made doll's furniture with shoe buttons for knobs, cotton reels were used for French knitting, and our favourite – clothes-peg dolls. Our highlight was getting a toy at Christmas (a Shirley Temple annual once) with chocolate money, fruit and nuts in our stockings.

We never went to the seaside as a family and I was thrilled to be taken by my eldest sister to Skegness for a day trip when I was nine years old. I was overwhelmed by the vastness of the sea, greatly disappointed by its colour and awed by the length of time it took to reach there as the furthest I had previously travelled was to Swithland Woods on the Sunday school outing. The latter was called the "treat" and believe me it was one, as kind neighbours and older friends of my sisters gave us coppers to spend at a shop near the woods, while the superintendent of the school used to scatter toffees and sweets in all directions for us to pick up. We played in the woods, ran races, and simply going on that little bus ride singing all the way there and back filled us with a pleasure I can easily recall. Nor will I forget being made May Queen down Allsopps Lane – my "coach" being an old pram bedecked with May blossom.

We paddled and fished in the brooks around that area, picked iodine on the Big Meadow to sell to Mr Larrad the chemist and made houses out of the bales of hay at haymaking time. Making houses seemed to dominate our play and when old houses were demolished near us we spent hours creating our own with the outline of rooms done with house bricks. Our walks sometimes lasted the most part of a summer's day and our refreshments were very meagre, usually consisting of bread and jam and a bottle of water with fizzy lemon tablets to flavour it, if we were lucky.

My religious background was varied as I went to the Band of Hope (Baptist) and the Sunbeams (Salvation Army) as well as regularly attending Sparrow Hill Methodist chapel. I loved the feeling I got from them all of joy and belonging to a greater family.

Another bright spot in our lives was the annual fun fair and to avoid any child not having a ride on the amusements free tickets were donated by the Mayor and councillors to all schoolchildren over a certain age. This caring attitude was again shown at Christmas when a "Robin's Breakfast" was held in the town hall for underfed children.

There were at least four carnival bands in Loughborough and many contests were held on Brown's Lane ground for bands from the surrounding area and provided great entertainment. An annual ox-roasting was also held there and it certainly made the nostrils twitch and the saliva of the hungry youngsters run.

I can remember magic lantern shows, especially one on the night of George V and Queen Mary's Jubilee, and the excitement, revelry and dancing that filled the streets. At the age of twelve I was a member of the Odeon Mickey Mouse Club committee, formed to help on Saturday morning matinées with competitions and keeping the queue orderly! A perk for being on this committee was a free visit to the cinema on one night of the week with a seat in the balcony –

Three little terrors enjoying the freedom of childhood in the 1920s.

what a contrast to the magic lantern show watched from a wooden bench.

Industry in Loughborough was very varied and Taylor's bell foundry was only one street away from my home. I often stood at the open doors watching the workmen in its dark, dusty interior working on the bells. My grandfather, who died before my birth, had worked there. There are some old shovel-like tools still hanging up there from those days, on which the men placed their bacon etc to cook in the furnace when they arrived at 6 am to start work. Another factory near to us was the Zenobia perfume factory. I used to take silver paper there which we had collected at our school for a charity supported by the factory owner, Captain Emerson Huston, and I always looked forward to seeing their products on display and the lovely smells. Their perfumed scent cards were very popular to put among hankies, underwear etc and my favourite was a bean blossom one given to me by a friend.

There were two people who frightened me in my childhood, one being a one-armed man who ran a rag and bone business and paid sixpence for a rabbit skin. I scuttled into his dingy, smelly premises at great speed, holding my breath, to receive that princely sum from his good hand. The other was a turbaned Indian door-to-door salesman who came selling silk ties and scarves from his suitcase and who, older children told us, could put a curse on you or perhaps kidnap you and put you in his suitcase.'

MUSICAL EVENINGS

'As a small child in the mid 1920s, I spent a lot of time playing in my grandparents' shop in Humberstone Lane, Leicester. They sold gramophones, the type that had big fancy horns. It was my job to dust and polish these. There were also rows of early cylindrical records on shelves which I was not allowed to touch. My mother did some of the repairs, like putting in new gramophone springs, cleaning and oiling, and she also served in the shop. I spent many happy hours playing the HMV records we used to sell, my favourites being *Mighty like a rose* and *In a monastery garden*. It was noticeable how many records we sold on a rainy day!

After the shop closed at night, the family gathered together and had musical evenings; Grandad played the violin, my aunt played the piano and Grandma and everyone else would sing. After school I was made to take violin lessons – on a Stradivarius. I got on fine until my parents moved house and then it was too far for me to travel each day and so that was the end of that.'

GLOW WORMS AND NICKNAMES

'Looking back on early childhood, the 1920s in South and North Kilworth evokes memories of glow worms on the long walk home, a field of mainly quaking grass, and wild strawberries galore – big, juicy and flavoursome, which grew in the bank at the top of the field behind our cottage. Yeasty herb beer, made from Mason's Extract I believe, but just "pop" to the children, was always taken on our picnics "down to the mill". Everyone went "down to the mill" to picnic and paddle in the pool that the cattle walked through on the way to milking and wasn't it always hot summery weather?

Home-made mushroom ketchup, eaten on real bread spread with home-cured lard: holes dug into that and the ketchup sprinkled on . . . nectar!

Why are there no more nicknames? Everyone in a village, mostly men and boys, had a nickname. There was Taffy Palmer, Budge Maddison, Yakky Carter, Proccles Bennett, Governor Ball – to mention just a few. My sister Alice and my brother were both called "Pop", I suppose because our name was Allsopp, or was it because we always took our "pop" on picnics?

103

I remember at the tea table one day when my niece Barbara had invited a playmate in to tea. Barbara was misbehaving and my sister Olive said to her, "Look at John sitting there like a Christian", to receive the reply, "He's no Christian – he's Chapel."'

THE BARRACKS CHILDREN

'I was born in Glen Parva Barracks at South Wigston. My father was in charge of the catering for the sergeants' mess and we lived in the barracks. I had a very happy childhood as there were always parties and other social events like cricket matches, tennis matches and dances taking place. The Christmas party was an extra special occasion as the Army really went out of its way to entertain the children of the soldiers who lived in the barracks. One of the sergeants dressed up as Santa Claus and he even came down the chimney! The presents were wonderful and every child received one.

On Sunday afternoons when the barracks seemed to be a place of solitude and quiet, as soon as the barracks clock struck three o'clock, it was as if the Pied Piper had materialised and children appeared from nowhere. The reason for this activity was, of course, the Walls Ice-Cream Man who came pedalling into the barracks on his tricycle. I have never tasted such ice-cream since that time. There were all kinds of flavours and my favourite was lime. It was so delicious and ice cold!

In those days, just before the Second World War, when parcels were delivered to the NAAFI they did not come by motor vehicle but by a horse-drawn van. The horse was a great favourite with the children as the railway man used to bring lumps of sugar so that we could feed it. He seemed to us to be a huge horse and when he opened his mouth, his teeth were enormous!

Another great event was the cricket match. A marquee was erected on the barrack square and my mother and her staff prepared all the sandwiches. These were, of course, salmon sandwiches and after the teas had been eaten, we children used to crawl under the guy ropes of the tent and my mother gave us the basin in which she had mixed the salmon so we could eat what was left in it. Happy days!'

A POLICE CHILD IN LEICESTER

'We lived in Magazine Square, Leicester, sadly no longer standing. My father was a police officer and I had two brothers. My elder brother and I attended King Richard Road School and Hazel Street. We had a truckle bed each, a blanket and a symbol that we could recognise. Mine was a blue bird. Each day at school as infants we had to have a rest on our beds.

My "best friend", Doreen, lived at the house at the castle as her father was the keeper. She had a swing on top of a hillock and it overlooked the castle gardens which we walked through to go to school. In the spring the daffodils on the hill were beautiful. Mr Cashmore took us to see the dungeons where "bad people went" and I can remember the huge key used to unlock the doors. When the assizes were due, beautifully embroidered banners were brought to our house and Mum would hang them over the back of the settle. We children were forbidden to go into the front room. Next day they were taken and hung from the trumpets which heralded the arrival of the judge in all his finery. My father was the mounted policeman who accompanied the procession. I was very proud of my dad when he was on traffic duty in the city centre. To think he could make the cars do as he wanted!

We had a dog, "Chips", who bit the rag and bone man so he had to go, I know not where. The rag and bone man would give us a balloon on a stick if we gave him rags. I also remember taking empty jam jars to a man in a shed and we got a halfpenny each. A treat was to follow the lamplighter as he lit the lamps in the winter.

On summer evenings we would go by tram to Victoria Park, all dressed up in our Sunday best. Another treat was to be taken to Western Park to play cricket and ball games. My grandpa lived in Regent Road and I would take my younger brother to visit him and my aunt and uncle who lived in Noel Street. We knew no fear of crossing roads.

For a short time my mum worked at the very smart county shop, Adderley's. As I say, for a short time as police wives were not allowed to work prior to the outbreak of the 1939 war. On her half day she would bring us an iced cream bun each.

I suppose my nine years in Leicester cannot have been all happy but if there were sad times I don't remember them. Living in the square we had no fear of cars and could play whip and top, hopscotch and knock ginger, and we had some lovely bonfire nights. The sad time was when Dad was posted to Hinckley and I had to leave my friends and school and start all over again.'

COUNTESTHORPE MEMORIES

'My family moved from Fleckney to Countesthorpe in 1917, when I was two years of age. My father was to earn £5 a week as manager of a hosiery factory, instead of £4, which was the rate in Fleckney.

My friend was nine months older than me, so I went with her to the Board school on the corner of Foston Road when I was four and a half. The first morning my brother, who was seven years older than me, took me on his sledge. We ran up the bank in Green Lane, in the snow, and couldn't go on for laughing. When we reached the school I had to stand in the porch until the children had finished singing the first hymn at assembly.

Our teacher was Miss Williams, a tiny woman who lived at the Vineries on Station Road. Huge greenhouses flanked the wall on the west side, but I never knew them to be used to grow vines. Miss Williams, and most pupils, wore white pinafores patterned with sprigs of flowers. She was a strict disciplinarian, but my first memory of her is when she stood with arms outstretched as we sang *In our dear Lord's garden*, showing how Jesus would protect us from evil.

At first my friend and I sat together and I copied her work. We were separated, so she ran across to show me what she had put down. This was also stopped, which puzzled us at first.

Our chief occupation on the mile long walk to school was walking through all the puddles, or stamping on ice in winter, hearing the sharp report as it broke. We jumped across the ditch which ran along by the spinney in Leicester Road and the boys fished out gobbets of frogspawn in spring which were put in jam jars on the window ledges at school so that we could watch them develop into tadpoles.

To keep them warm, children wore big scarves, crossed on their chests and fastened at the back. Some also had big white handkerchiefs pinned to their clothes.

Children from the Cottage Homes came to our school. The boys worked on the farm there and the girls did domestic work. Their hands were rough and they smelled of carbolic soap. I only identified with them when one girl fell over outside our house and my parents brought her in to rest.

When my father was walking to work one day he met the farmer from Linden Farm. His mother, wife and little girl had died in the terrible flu epidemic of 1918. There were many poor people in the village. Small houses were built round courtyards, with a communal lavatory serving six families, and a pump from which water ran down a central gulley into the drain. People who had no water supply fetched it from the pump in Main Street, outside the cycle shop, carrying brimming buckets balanced on wooden yokes across their shoulders. The blacksmith's forge was a great attraction, with its raging fire and the acrid smell of burning hooves. Once a year everyone who weighed or measured commodities had to take their scales to the Square to be checked. Huge weighing machines from the farms were brought on carts.

Children from Leicester churches came by train for their Sunday school treats. These were held in a farmer's field from which the cows had been excluded the previous day. I refused to scramble for unwrapped boiled sweets which were thrown into the grass as our treat. Poor children were allowed to attend all the outings.

On 29th May, which we called Royal Oak Day to commemorate Charles II hiding in an oak tree, my brother picked bunches of oak leaves for us to wear so that the village boys would not sting us with nettles.

The fields and ponds were our playgrounds, and we made houses under the gnarled old roots of hawthorn hedges. There were wayside seats where gates spanned the roads into the village.

There were many distractions to hinder our progress to and from school: we sampled the "bread and cheese" of the hawthorn leaf buds, the tooth-clogging taste of haws, and the sharp bite of sorrel leaves. A real bonus was gathering beech nuts when they fell in the autumn. We cut our initials on privet leaves with thumb nails, put heads of wall barley down our socks and later looked to see how far they had travelled. We foretold our future by reciting, "Tinker, Tailor, Soldier, Sailor," as we ran our fingers along tufts of rye grass. The earliest sweets I remember were locust beans, horrible dry tiger nuts and tiny cubes of liquorice root. In summer we dissolved boiled sweets in water in medicine bottles, and in winter the boys made hand warmers by setting cotton rags alight in tins, which they pierced in several places and swung round holding string handles. Every year, like Chaucer's pilgrims, we children knew by instinct when the cowslips and early purple orchids would be in flower in a field at the end of Bambury Lane, and set out to gather just a few.

In 1921, when I was six, great excitement filled the school. The Duke of York (later George VI) was to dedicate the war memorial in the Square. We small children stood in the front row until a contingent of the Loyal Antediluvian Order of Buffaloes, who had been celebrating in the pub, lined up in front of us. Unable to see

107

anything, I lost interest in the proceedings. Afterwards someone said, "Their breath were 'eavenly."'

STAYING WITH GRANDMA

'I was born at Kilby Grange in 1924. Farmers in those days rarely, if ever, took holidays and so from a very early age I was taken in the pony and trap to stay with my maternal grandma and auntie at the Manor House at Arnesby. Grandma was a widow and Auntie was still single at that time. They both wore their hair in a bun.

As they kept the post office, our day was punctuated by the sound of the old fashioned shop bell. I liked being with adults and would hover near Auntie and listen to the conversation as people came in. The main event of the day was the arrival of the postman, who cycled up from Wigston twice daily, calling at Kilby on the evening run. Just before he was due, Auntie would unlock the postbox and take out the letters and stamp them. If anything had to be registered, she sealed it by holding a match under a stick of red sealing wax. I was fascinated to see the melted wax dripping like blood. When I was old enough to reach the counter standing on a stool, I was allowed to stamp the letters.

I was an industrious little girl so Grandma always found me something to do. I learnt cross stitch with lovely coloured wools on a square of canvas, and Auntie let me have oddments from her leather work and the puncher so that I could punch holes and thread them up into a little purse. With great effort and concentration I managed to knit on four needles with white silk thread, with which socks were made at that time. Grandma sat on a Queen Anne-style black horsehair chair which pricked my legs. She always seemed to be at hand to thread my needle, untangle my wool or pick up dropped stitches. The big orchard produced fruits of every kind and Grandma spent hours peeling and preparing it for Auntie to make into delicious preserves. I loved to watch her peel an apple in one long thin strip.

About teatime we would take a bowl of maize and feed the hens of all sizes and colours and then collect the eggs from the nooks and crannies in the old outhouses. It was a novelty to me, coming from a farm, to go up the lane to Mrs Freer's to fetch the milk. I took a pretty Victorian jug for the next day's supply, and brought back the one which stood on the cold hall floor, already filled, as were lots of other people's jugs.

It was usually summertime when I stayed at Arnesby, but if I went in the winter I slept with Grandma, in her big feather bed, which Auntie warmed all over with the warming pan and then put in a stone hot water bottle with a cover. When Grandma came up she always brought the post office till and put it under the mattress. On Sundays I had to put on my best clothes to go to chapel. Life at the Manor House was so serene and I loved it. I never go by Arnesby Turn without thinking of Grandma and being grateful for her patience in teaching me so much.'

CLOTHES AND DOLLS

'We lived in Hose in the 1950s. We had three sets of clothes as girls: Sunday clothes, school clothes and play clothes, and the Sunday clothes always came off as soon as we were back home from chapel. We used to have a new dress for the Sunday school Anniversary and white canvas sandals which had to be whitened and put outside to dry. We had one pair of winter shoes, plus wellington boots. In winter we wore liberty bodices and winceyette petticoats with drawstring necks, and thick navy blue school knickers. We changed our clothes once a week, on Sunday, and Saturday night was bath night in a tin bath in front of the fire, with everyone following on into the same water. Afterwards for a weekly treat we had a bag of Smith's crisps with salt in a blue paper.

Indoors we played Snakes and Ladders, and we played a lot with our dolls' houses and our dolls. I remember the first soft dolls and dolls with "pot" heads made out of a sort of clay which went bubbly when it got wet. Some had stick-on hair which became very matted and couldn't be combed or washed. Vinyl dolls with knotted hair were a great improvement.

Outside we played paperchase and we used to go off up the fields fishing for a whole day. When we were older we used to cycle to Gunthorpe and swim in the Trent, which can't have been very safe or hygienic.'

TREATS AND HOLIDAYS

Outings and holidays were rare treats for children in the first half of the century and are still vividly remembered – summer holidays were much more likely to be spent with relatives or just playing in the fields. More common were the excitements brought by seasonal celebrations such as Easter or May Day, and visits to the theatre or cinema.

OFF TO THE EMPIRE EXHIBITION

'I don't remember the exact day, but in the summer or autumn of 1924 a party of schoolchildren over the age of eight (I just qualified), accompanied by helpers, made their way to Lutterworth railway station. We all had name labels attached to us with pink ribbon and a safety pin. We were going to the British Empire Exhibition at Wembley.

We arrived in London in due course and this wonderful exhibition was such an eye-opener to most of us. I remember being impressed by the turnstile which admitted one at a time (I thought I would surely be trapped in it).

That hurdle surmounted, I was overawed by the sight of elephants and camels walking about freely and the different nationalities mingling with the crowds. The whole atmosphere was like a dream and I was quite unaware of the rest of my party. The thing I remember best was in the Canadian Pavilion, a huge model of the Prince of Wales (later Edward VIII) in butter! There were also tableaux of rushing rivers with logs floating down, a wolf standing on the edge of a precipice and apples from Ontario being packed.

We saw natives panning for gold on the Gold Coast of Africa, the rubber plantations of Malaya, the apple orchards of Australia and much, much more.

We were taken on the footplate of the *Flying Scotsman*, and in the afternoon saw an epic reproduction of the battle of Zeebrugge. This last was so real to me that I thought it was actually happening, whereas it must only have been a film.

The whole experience was wonderful and that day I thought I had seen all the rest of the world. Thanks were due to a gentleman in the village whose idea it was and who paid all our expenses.'

THE LEICESTER MABLETHORPE HOME OUTING

'I remember waiting in the hope that I would be one of the chosen ones. My brother, older by 14 months, had been the year before and had come home full of his fortnight there. The very fact that we were poor, and had never seen the sea, was the reason we were chosen.

Not like nowadays with lots of clothes and big suitcases, my few pieces were soon put into a small, much battered attaché case and, with great excitement, I was off to the seaside for a whole fortnight. A train journey, never taken before, and there we were.

The Home, situated on the beach among the sand dunes, was reached and we were given our beds in a large dormitory and had all the rules read out to us.

I was a little disappointed when I knew that part of each day we had to do our school work. However, that part over, and a good dinner eaten, out onto the beach we went. The sight of all that water, the waves trickling over our feet and oh, those lovely shells! Searching among the rocks: what would we find? Trying to puzzle out where the sea went when the tide was out was fun too.

Good plain meals three times a day, when at home we never knew whether or not there would be a meal. Blankets on the beds, not old coats, and, joy of joys, a bathroom with warm running water.

The kindness of the staff, making friends, giggling in bed, for once in my life not a care in the world. Looking back now, about 63 years later, I am still grateful for that wonderful holiday, provided by donations and given to the children who had never seen the sea.'

SUMMER HOLIDAYS

'Every summer when I was a little girl, my uncle cycled over to Kilby from Cosby to fetch me for a holiday. I would ride on the crossbar of his bicycle with my bag of spare clothes strapped to the back carrier. Halfway he would stop for me to get off and walk for a few minutes to relieve the discomfort!

My aunt and grown-up cousins made a big fuss of me and gave me a shoebox and a doll for which they helped me to sew covers and clothes from scraps of pretty materials. I loved being there and at the end of my stay my uncle returned me to Kilby on his bicycle. Those were my holidays when I was young.'

111

Children in Queen Street, Oadby in the 1930s off to the fancy dress parade.

'We had no seaside at Elmesthorpe but lots of time during the summer holidays was spent paddling and fishing on the ford where the river Sence crossed the lane. When the flour mill was working, however, it was not safe there. We used to have picnics in a field called "the peace", where the boys would settle their quarrels and the schoolchildren would gather to watch the fights. When it was haymaking time we were allowed to follow the load from the field to the farm and then have a ride on the dray back. At harvest time the threshing machine would come to Hall Farm and the boys would gather with sticks to kill the mice as they ran from the straw. The curfew bell was rung at eight o'clock during the summer when all the children should be in bed – or so they were told!'

SCHOOL OUTING

'We did not have much money and our parents were unable to provide much in the line of trips and outings but of course it was a real treat when we did leave Witherley. Our school outing was always to Sutton Coldfield Park. Our mothers came to the school gates to wave us off in our open-topped charabanc, and we had a picnic lunch and later games and races. Another outing I remember was due to my being a member of the church choir. Considering how small the village was, we boasted 15 members in the all male choir. The outing was considered to be a great distance as we visited New

Brighton followed by a journey through Liverpool centre to see the cathedral, at that time under construction.'

SEASONAL TREATS

'At Easter time we children used to go round to the Fielding-Johnstons' to sing Easter songs. We were given a hot cross bun and a new penny if we sang up so we all "halleluyah'd" like nobody's business. And it was, "Please could I have one to take back to my little sister (or brother) who had to stay at home?" There wasn't always this little sister, of course.'

'School at South Kilworth was regarded as a necessity; only if ill did children stay away. There was an occasional truant, however, especially when the hunt met in the village, the outcome a possible caning by the headmistress. On the occasion of the meet, the children went out from school with the teachers, standing in line to watch the horses and hounds until they moved off, then went back to school for the rest of the day. A special thrill was to see the Prince of Wales when he was riding.

May Day was a grand occasion for the village, when a vote was held for the May Queen. She was crowned by the previous queen and all paraded round the village on a wagonette loaned by a farmer and driven by the wagoner. A tea followed in the afternoon with games on the recreation ground. There was always Maypole dancing.

Each year, in August, all children were invited to Stanford Hall by Lord and Lady Braye. Each of us was dressed in our best clothes. The chauffeur from the Hall collected us in a Model-T Ford lorry and an excellent tea with games was provided.

Bonfire Night was an exciting time. A huge bonfire was built in the rectory yard and the fireworks were followed by cream buns and mugs of cocoa in the house.

Scouts, Guides and Brownies were the main clubs. Captain Coates was Scoutmaster and the rector's daughter Miss Craise was our Brown Owl. It was a serious business passing the "Tenderfoot" to gain a badge. Tasks included darning a sock, making a cake and other household jobs.

The follow-up to Brownies at eleven years of age was the Guides under the captaincy of Miss Thomas. We were taught "The Promise" and for enrolment a Miss Spencer, the County Commissioner, came from Leicester. These enrolments were taken very seriously. Weekly meetings were held in The Observatory each Monday at 6 pm when around 30 girls attended. A black stove gave a lovely warmth, being fuelled with wood. Round blocks of wood, stacked when not in use, were used as seats. The ashes were cleared, the stove blackleaded, the mats shaken and floors swept on Saturday mornings by the Guides on a rota system. This worked well as all children had the support and interest from their parents. In the summer we had lots of games, songs and a camp fire when we went over Thomas's Farm. On the fire we cooked "cheese dreams" on forked sticks, and fried eggs in greased greaseproof paper. How delicious these tasted. This was instead of going away to camp as no one could afford to do this.'

CO-OP DAY

'When I was a little girl of five or six, my mother would take me to the Co-op Day at the De Montfort Hall. There would be stalls and competitions and a fancy dress – with prizes for everyone. One year I was dressed as Winter, another a stork and another a mermaid. My crowning glory as a child was always my long, shining hair and though I never won first prize the *Leicester Mercury* photographer always picked me out for a photograph in the newspaper. This made my mum very proud, except the year that she dressed me in a skin-coloured swimsuit with a hobby-horse to go as Lady Godiva, but I refused to go on stage for the judging as I thought everyone would think I had no clothes on!'

BANK HOLIDAYS AND CINEMA

'Bank holidays were special in Castle Donington, when whole families traversed Park Lane to Kings Mills for the day. Then, the mill race thundering under the bridge emitted a damp, green, foamy aroma heralding the delights of the picnic to come. The adults would take a stroll along the river bank whilst the children in bathing costumes and waders played in the shallow pools at the side of the weir. One very hot year we walked across the dry weir to the other bank, so low was the river. Towards dusk the adults would reminisce about their youth, forgetting that the little ones listen and remember. Tales of crossing the river by ferry: the ferry keeper, responding to a call from either bank, pulled herself and the passengers across by hauling on a chain stretched between the banks. What stories they told of courting in the moonlight on Daleacre by the ruined monastery, reputed to have been destroyed by Cromwell whose troops, in turn, are said to have been buried in the "barrows" up on Daleacre Hill. All fascinating stuff to the youngsters of yesteryear who, believing every word, would act out the stories in play over the next few days.

Until the late 1950s Castle Donington had its very own cinema. Because my grandpa was caretaker during the war my cousin and I were allowed to "help" him during school holidays. This, an adventure in itself, often boosted our pocket money for when we "found" any loose change it was finders keepers. The County Cinema at that time had the cleanest balcony ever because we always found more silver than copper upstairs.

The fivepenny matinée on Saturday saw us bursting from the doors at the end slapping our sides to urge our horses on if the film had been a "cowboy" or, following a historical romance, sword fencing all the way home to tea of new bread and home-made jam. Such simple pleasures.'

EXCITING TIMES

'Our entertainment for the most part was self-made although we did listen to the wireless – especially in the long, winter evenings, but we still played card games and draughts, ludo, tiddly-winks and snakes and ladders from the compendium of games given to us one Christmas. We played all the usual street games. The little ones in our road liked "The farmer's in his den", "Here sits poor Sally" and "Big ship sails through the alley alley O". We bigger ones preferred the chasing games like "hot rice", "cockarusty" and "So many men come to work" – a more boisterous version of What's my line. Perhaps they got the idea for that from the old street game. Always for Pancake Day we had a whip and top or shuttlecock and battledore.

Every January we went to the pantomime at the Opera House in Leicester. We would get there very early to queue up and would eat our lunch of sandwiches as we waited. I can still remember the little murmur of excitement and the shuffle forward when the men came to light the little gas lamps on the stairs and passages, because we knew that soon afterwards the doors would be opened. If we were near the front of the queue we could get seats in the amphitheatre – a single row just below the gallery with real seats. The gallery or the gods as it was called, had seats that were more like padded steps with no divisions or arms. We loved those pantos with the hubbub of excited children and the smell of oranges.

When I was just a little older my auntie took me to see my first play at the Theatre Royal, *Paddy the Next Best Thing*. She also took me there to see my first musical, *Rose Marie*.

It was so sad in later years to see these wonderful old theatres close down along with the Palace where, in our teens, we went to see the well known stars of variety. Sometimes, on Sundays, we would go to see the big hands at the De Montfort Hall; Oscar Rabin, Harry Gould and many others.

In the village there was always a carnival on Whit Monday when most of us children would be in fancy dress. It was a big day and our relatives from Leicester would come over to my aunt who lived here. She always made salmon and cucumber sandwiches and jelly with bananas sliced into it. The proceeds from the carnival were for the Leicester Royal Infirmary. When they had enough money, a bed would be purchased. There would be a little dedication ceremony and a plaque placed above the bed, saying that it had been given by the people of Cosby. Several beds and cots were provided in this way before the National Health Service was formed.

Sometimes a cinema show would be given. They were silent films but well attended and enjoyed. Sometimes they were semi-educational dramas like Joan of Arc but often it was comedy with Charlie Chaplin.'

GAMES AND CHORES

Games followed the seasons, and we all knew when it was time to stop playing one and start another! They required little money or equipment, but lots of enthusiasm and energy and in those days the streets were our playground, with little to fear from traffic. Pocket money usually had to be earned, but what fun we got from our Saturday penny.

SPENDING MONEY

'Most children at Rothley between the wars had a penny a week spending money and would buy sweets in halfpenny-worths – there would be quite a lot in a three-cornered bag. Pear drops, aniseed balls, liquorice laces and pipes, small bars of chocolate, dabs and suckers, cigarettes made of sugar, sugar mice – what a choice!'

'We had one penny on Saturday and that had to last the whole week. I used to go to the sweet shop and spend half of it on Saturday and save the other half to spend during the week. My grandmother lived with us until 1925 and when the old age pension came in she used to meet my brother and me from school and take us with her to the post office where she collected five shillings, from which she gave us each one halfpenny. We thought it was grand.

On Saturday morning I had to help with the housework. My task was to clean the cutlery. In those days we had steel blades to the knives. I also had to clean the Venetian blinds in the front room, a very tiresome job.'

'Chores could be helping with the washing-up, running errands for parents or neighbours, or keeping the kitchen and outside closet scrubbed. This was just your duty – and often there was no pay involved!'

'There were five small general shops in Cosby in the 1930s and all sold absolutely everything. When we had our Saturday morning penny, the dilemma was whether to buy sweets or to wait and get an ice-cream cornet. The ice-cream man always blew a loud, shrill whistle when his van pulled up. One shopkeeper made his own ice-cream. It was quite yellow in colour and had lumps of ice in it. That was the favourite shop for sweets because you could have a halfpenny look in the box – or if you were rich, a penny look! We could get the same sweets in the other shops but it was not quite so exciting as spending five minutes looking at all the bits and pieces before making a choice.'

'ICE-A-COKE-A-COLA-COLA'

'As a child in Leicester we didn't have too much money. We lived with my grandfather in a terraced house until I was seven. I always went to the corner shop to collect my grandfather's tobacco. I never grumbled as this was the highlight of my week. There was always a farthing change which I was allowed to keep – and what a farthing would buy in the 1930s! I used to ponder for ages over how to spend this magnificent sum. I could buy four gobstoppers, liquorice laces or eight toffees. Sometimes I would buy an ice-cream cone. The Okey-Cokey Man, as we called him, used to pedal round the streets on a three-wheeled bicycle with a kind of trunk on the front which kept the ice-cream cool. He would shout, "Ice-a-coke-a-cola-cola", which used to bring all the children from their houses.'

TOYS AND GAMES

'Most of our toys we made. We got a box like a Woodbine box and made it into a pram by folding the lid to become a hood – placing inside a wooden doll from Mrs Reilly's shop in Sanvey Gate and pulling it along with string.

We also bought a farthing's worth of ravel cotton from Mrs Reilly's to make clothes for the doll.

The rag and bone man exchanged windmills (made from sticks of wood and with sails made from folded wallpaper) for old rags. We made hoops from wire taken from apple barrels or wood bundles and used buttons or matches etc as prizes for our contests.

We ran around singing,

"Who'll play me marbles? I'll play them.
Who'll play me buttons? I'll play them!"

We used either buttons or stones for the game of "fives" and to play marbles we scraped a hole in the cobblestone and aimed to pot our shots from a distance into the hole.

A children's sports day at Leicester in 1924. Locally organised, and informal, events such as this were great fun.

Another game was "diabolo" – made from two wooden sticks joined together by string on which you attempted to catch a wooden reel. I can remember this going through a window once and others have heard of children being able to throw a diabolo over a building which was caught on a diabolo the other side.

We played "faggies" where you had to flick a cigarette card against a wall – if your card covered another one when it landed it was yours to keep. We played card games, ludo and snakes and ladders in winter. We used nuts as prizes for the winner.

Washing lines were taken down to be used as skipping ropes by all the children in the street – no one was left out. As many as 20 children joined in and the line stretched out across the whole street. We sang,

"All in together
All in together
All in together
This fine day"

and, "Salt, mustard, vinegar, pepper", when the rope was turned faster on "pepper". If you fell or caught your toe you were out and took a turn at turning the rope.

We played hopscotch and "tin turkey". For this game someone kicked an old tin and everyone else hid. If you could return to the tin you were still in the game but if caught you became the "turkey".

Another favourite was "ghost tapping". A pin was stuck into the wooden frame of a window. Then a button and a piece of string was attached out of sight and pulled so the button could tap on the window, hopefully alarming those inside.

We went down to the canalside facing The Pastures and took turns on the see-saws, or bumpers. The boys had whips and tops and the girls played shuttlecock and battledore. If we fell out we chanted,

"Sticks and stones may break my bones,
but calling never hurt me.
When I'm dead and in my grave,
you'll wish you never called me."

or,

"Tit, tat, tale,
Your tongue wants splitting."

Often we went and played on the rocks at Abbey Park. If possible we took margarine sandwiches and a bottle of water. You could buy lemonade crystals to turn it into lemonade.

When we were older we went to the dances on the park. They cost twopence. This included a supper of spring onions and cheese. The band played the valeta, the military two-step, the gavotte and the waltz.

More rarely we travelled further afield. We took the train to Aylestone Gardens – "Japanese Gardens" – where there were monkeys in cages and a buttercup field. For refreshment we bought a glass of lemonade.

We pretended that Birstall was the seaside and called it "Birstall Sands". We sat at the water's edge and imagined lighthouses and boats while our parents crossed a narrow plank to the pub – The Plough. We used to say, "We are going to Birstall to see the lighthouse!"'

SUMMER EVENINGS

'In Newton Burgoland schoolyard at playtime, we played lots of singing games including .Oranges and lemons, Here we come gathering nuts in May, In. and out the windows, When I was a teacher, Looby loo, and' Oats and beans and barley.

In the spring and summer evenings at home we played whip and top, various games with marbles, snobs or five-stones, battledore and shuttlecock (sometimes the shuttlecock would be home-made with about half a dozen wing feathers from a hen). We ran miles with our hoops. Our gymnastic skills were acquired on the tubular-like rails by our local brook where we caught minnows with a net. We took them home in a jam jar with a piece of string around the neck forming a handle. We played various skipping games with a long rope which stretched from one side of the village lane to the other. When an occasional cyclist or horse-drawn vehicle came along, we pulled the rope to one side. We chanted rhymes as we skipped. One favourite was:

"All in together,
this fine weather,
I saw Esau, sitting on a see-saw,
Shoot, bang, fire."

On the word "fire", everyone ran out. It was quite tricky getting the timing right to run in and out as there would probably be six or seven skipping at a time. "Running under and over the moon" required considerable skill with the timing. Hide and seek was played in the lanes where there were a lot of bushes and big hedges.

The boys flew home-made kites when the wind blew, kicked pigs' bladders for footballs, and learned to swim in the canal about two miles away.'

EVERYTHING IN SEASON

'When we were children in Market Harborough, there seemed to be a season for our outdoor games. When marble time came round I was given some clay marbles, but they were never as exciting as the pretty glass ones. I remember making my own marble bag. Sometimes it was nearly full and lots of times it was empty, but it was great fun.

Then we had whip and top time. There was one called a carrot top but I liked the one they called a window breaker. We chalked on the

Schoolchildren of all ages looked forward to May Day, here at Witherley in the 1920s.

top of these and when they were spinning they looked very pretty. Indoor games consisted of ludo, snakes and ladders and lotto, and we played snap with cards.'

'We had a season for everything. The autumn brought great fun at Witherley, with conkers for the boys and hopscotch for the girls. As nights got darker (and we had no street lamps) we played "sound yer holler" which involved the leader going off and making a cry for the others to follow and chase. By various devious methods, if the leader got back to the base he or she had won. However, if they were caught, the captor then became the leader. November brought bonfire night; huge bonfires were built, the "top" bonfire by the riverside and the "bottom" bonfire outside the parish rooms. These had to be guarded carefully as there was great rivalry between the two!'

STREET KIDS

'I attended the Taylor Street junior school in Leicester, which had a flat roof for part of the playground. I learnt to walk on stilts up there, and I remember going into the dark cellar with the class so that the teacher could illustrate the solar system with a special lighting system showing up all the planets.

In 1947 there was a terrible, hard, long winter and we had to walk to another school because our heating system had broken down. The pavements were treacherous: it was freezing cold and, although I had a good winter outfit and boots, there were children who were poorly clad for the conditions.

Behind St Mark's church in Belgrave Gate there was a coal depot and I would push an old pram to collect coal for Mam and Dad. I'd put the pram under a chute and a measured amount of coal would drop in. This was after the war had ended and everything was on ration. I'd do errands for Mam and my two grandmas but always armed with the little ration books.

The kids in the street (Grafton Street) used to play some good games together. A favourite – hide and seek – was great fun: there were so many entries and yards to hide in. Skipping and whip and top were my favourites but these were girls' games and the boys would always try to spoil the fun. I used to decorate my "carrot" top with coloured chalk, stick it in the earth between the paving stones and the kerb, lay the whip string loosely round the top and, with a jerk, spin the top into the road. I could keep the top spinning for ages by whipping it carefully.

I also liked to play "faggies". This was a flicking game with flattened cigarette packets (Craven A, red packets with a black cat; Players, with the bearded sailor, Park Drive, are just a few I can remember). Some packets were leaned against the wall and, standing back, one would flick other packets at them and the ones you knocked down you kept. This was also played with cigarette cards – sets of picture cards on a theme (sports, famous people, animals etc) and I could soon collect a set as I was quite good at this game, although it was not classed as a "girls' game"!

There were plenty of bat and ball games we used to play too. My favourite was French cricket when one person used to bat to "protect" his legs and feet and the rest of us had to try to hit these parts to get the person "out". There was always an argument on whose turn was next. We sometimes played cricket and football in the narrow street but people from the houses would soon clear us off, and could we run if a ball hit a door or, worse still, broke a window!

Of course, there wasn't too much traffic about then so we kids could play in the road. The main traffic was bicycles as the men went to and from the factories at the bottom of the street.'

'RELEASEO'

'As a child, growing up in Belgrave in the late 1940s and early 1950s, one of the favourite outdoor games for summer evenings was "releaseo", or "unlock" as it was sometimes called.

The children living in our street would divide into two teams, usually of six or more each side, and then decide which team would run off and disperse first. The object of the game was to chase the opposing team through the neighbouring streets, and if they were caught, to return them to a designated area that had previously been decided upon and was called "the den". This was an area marked on the pavement in chalk outside one of our houses in the street.

When a member of your own team was captured and placed in the den the object was to try and find a way to sneak back and by "ticking" them on the shoulder release or unlock them – hence the name. Of course, when trying to do this it was paramount not to be captured yourself, so the moment had to be carefully chosen when the den was not being guarded.

As the street in which I lived, Justice Street, was connected to the next two streets, Evans Street and Mellor Street (all demolished in the early 1970s) by a "jitty" or long entry between the houses about three quarters of the way down the street, it formed a perfect area, being completely free of traffic and providing many hiding places. One could be running along the bottom of the street, and upon sighting the opposing team coming down the top of the street, a quick exit could be made through the long entry into the next street and thus we escaped capture.

Many summer evenings would be passed playing this game, and only reluctantly would we be called in to bed at around nine o'clock, when mothers would magically appear on doorsteps of the terraced houses, shouting in loud voices for their offspring to come in, the threat always being "or the nine o'clock horses will get you!" This was a reference to the days when the lavatory closet would be emptied of ashes by a man on a horse and cart who only came around after dusk, and no respectable person would want to be around when that was taking place. This phrase was still being used although water closets had long been invented!'

THE BEST YEARS OF OUR LIVES?

Schooldays – were they really some of the best years of our lives? Certainly for some of us, receiving a good general education in small village schools, but there are tales too of strict discipline and of long and wet walks to school. Schools changed very little until after the Second World War, and many grandparents must have relived their own schooldays through their children's children.

SCHOOLDAYS BEFORE THE FIRST WORLD WAR

'The girls wore black dresses with white pinafores on top. My grandma goffered all the pleats on the pinny. We also had to wear vests, stays and a flannelette petticoat. We wore our hair in plaits and used a clean rag for a hankie.

My mother and I really liked the Scotch plaid dresses with a lace collar and she sometimes managed to get one cheaply from the pawn shop on "marking off" day. We had slides for our hair.

Both boys and girls had to clean their shoes and scrub their nails before school each morning. The boys had to wear short black trousers. I felt sorry for their scratched knees when they fell. They also wore a brown, navy or green patched jersey. They used to wipe the "candles" from their noses on the sleeves. They wore grey socks and black boots. When they were 16 they often inherited a pair of their dad's cast off trousers.

I went to Elbow Lane Junior School in Leicester. There was another school nearby and we used to shout to them, "All saints and no sinners, wears frocks no pinnies." They used to chant back, "Elbow Lane Greasy Guts!"

I remember some of the teachers' names: Miss Middleton who became Mrs Potts, Miss March, Miss Roberts and Miss Hardy the headmistress. She wore a black dress. All the teachers were strict, but Miss Hardy also used "The Red Cane". It was kept at the side of her desk and hurt you more than the black cane. We spat on our hands or rubbed them with soap so we would not feel the pain. One teacher was considered a real bully and all the boys picked up their inkwells and chased her down Cumberland Street!

We learnt the three Rs and also had a little history or geography for

125

A group of Leicester teachers from before the First World war, taking a break on a schools outing.

a change. We were given a six by three inch piece of calico to make a hem or oversew or make a French seam or smock. We stroked each stitch to make them go the right way; if they didn't we were caned.

At break time we used to hide a carrot under our desks and scrape pieces off with a tin lid, for a snack.

Every year there was a school outing to Rothley, but only if you had been good! We travelled on a steam train from Central station and a farmer lent us his field for the afternoon. He also provided the picnic and brought round lemonade on a cart. It was lovely. On our return we used to stick our heads out of the train window and sing,

"We've just come back from Rothley,
We've just come back from Rothley,
We've just come back from Rothley,
And we want to go again!"

to the tune "For he's a jolly good fellow".

On Shrove Tuesday we had a half day. My mother used to make pancakes for everyone. We liked orange or lemon juice squeezed on them. We had another song for that day,

"Pancake day, pancake day
If you don't give us a holiday, we will all run away.
Where shall we run? Down the lane,
Here comes teacher with a big fat cane!"

'Until 1907 there was a small school for the children at Groby, but the Leicester County Education Committee built a larger school which children attended until they were 13. The boys then worked at the quarry and the girls at various factories round about. The first school was built by the owner of the estate, the Earl of Stamford, and the tale goes that when his wife, who lived at Bradgate House, was intending to drive through the village to Leicester, word was sent to the teacher to line all the pupils up outside the school to curtsey to her as she drove past.'

VERY STRICT

'I was at the village school at Newtown Linford between 1916 and 1925. The head teacher was Miss Garner and the infants were taken by Mrs Naylor, who was very strict and always had a cane in her hand. First thing every morning there was the register ("Present, Miss"), a hymn and a prayer, then half an hour's scripture. The other subjects were mostly the three Rs, plus history, geography, nature study and needlework. Boys did carpentry. Children wrote on slates, progressing to pencil and paper when they were older. There were all sorts of monitors, who did such jobs as filling the ink wells and fetching material from the stockroom for the teachers. Children never got up from their desks once they had sat down, unless they put up their hand for permission to "leave the room".

Parents, as well as teachers, tended to be strict, and children learned to do as they were told, or they would be kept in or forbidden treats. One teacher had a thimble on her middle finger and would rap it hard on the head of any child with whom she was displeased.'

'The first thing I remember is being taken aged two and a half with my brother to join the Hemington schoolchildren – the leader brandishing a large Union Jack – to march to Lockington church to a thanksgiving service for the 1918 Armistice. We were all under the command of the formidable but much loved and respected headmistress, Miss Hall.

All the children walked to school in those days, some from the

127

outlying farms as much as four or five miles each way. For a five year old this was too much, and there were no school dinners. Some brought bread and cheese, but for those who came empty handed my mother arranged hot soup.

Discipline at school was strict. Any visitor entering the classroom was greeted by everyone standing up and staying, "Good morning, Mrs . . . or Mr . . ." We were a happy and cheerful lot and were taught right from wrong. I have an idea that a light cane lay on Miss Hall's desk!'

CLOTHES AND SCHOLARSHIPS

'When I was five I went to Melbourne Road School in Oadby, quite a little walk from our home. Once we were not able to attend school for several days due to heavy snow; I think that was in 1917. During the Great War, or at least part of it, I only went to school half-days as Medway Street School was taken over by some . Department, and so Medway Street and Melbourne Road schools had to share. One week Medway Street went in the morning and we went in the afternoon and the next week it was reversed.

I suppose some of my friends might have envied me because I may have had more shoes and clothes than they had, but so far as shoes were concerned I did not feel at all to be envied as my father, working in a shoe factory, used to bring me shoes and would say they were a really good pair of samples, and the fact that they were brown and I wanted white was just too bad! For clothes I really was fortunate, because my mother was a good needlewoman and marvellous at getting a dress out of the smallest piece of material. I also had a cousin who was two or three years older than me, and lots of her dresses and coats came to me when she grew out of them, and my mother altered them to fit me. When she went to boarding school I fared even better because she had often outgrown dresses bought for her on the previous holiday.

In 1920 I was allowed to sit the Secondary School Examination although I should not have taken it until I was eleven, but I was scared stiff of tests and exams so the headmaster let me sit it to give me confidence for the following year. To everyone's surprise I got a free scholarship to the Wyggeston Grammar School at my first attempt, mainly I think because that school preferred to have younger girls, so I was fortunate – more fortunate than we knew then, because by the next year the rules had been changed and free places were only given to girls whose fathers earned less than £1 per head in the family, which meant less than £4 in our case. I do not think I could have gone as a paying pupil as the fees were, I think, £12 per term at that time, and my brother was being paid for at the Alderman Newton School for boys.

School uniforms were expensive for those days as we had to go to Shipleys – a rather dear shop. We had navy tunics, cream Viyella blouses, blue and white striped ties, black velour hats in the winter and real panamas in the summer. I was glad the hats had just been changed from straw boaters which didn't look very comfy! We were never allowed out without gloves on and any girl caught without them was given extra homework, and once three girls were punished after being seen eating buns in the street after a games session.'

STANDING IN LINE

'We had a diphtheria epidemic at our school, which was Hinckley Road, now Dovelands, and I must have been a carrier as three boys who sat next to me had it and two died. My mother put a pocket in my vest and there was always a square of camphor in it. Maybe that killed germs – it nearly killed me.

We went to live in Glenfield Road when I was twelve. I had to walk to school, which was Narborough Road School, so I had a very long walk and was often late. Our teacher, Miss Waite, went my way home and if we were not walking straight we were told to straighten our shoulders and walk sedately. On reaching school we had to stand in lines whilst the headmaster, Mr Hull, walked down the lines seeing if we had clean shoes, clean hands and a clean handkerchief. Then we had to walk in twos into the hall for assembly, which was prayers and morning hymns, then into classes for lessons. At the end of the day we again assembled in the hall for evening prayers and hymns, then we were dismissed and again went out in two's to cloakrooms.

We went from Narborough Road School to the playing fields for hockey and netball. We all walked in lines of two, quite a way to walk.

We made our own navy blue knickers in hard-wearing serge in sewing class; all hand-made, they were terrible to wear, all itchy and scratchy. Most girls made dresses but my mother would not let me so I had to sew a nightie for Miss Farmer. It was a delicate pink satin and I had to do very small stitches and I got commended for my work. One day a week we did cookery and one afternoon housewifery, which included laundry and housework.'

129

THE VICAR WAS A FAMILIAR FACE

'The village of Witherley has changed greatly in the last 60 years. However, the original village school, built a little over a century ago, still stands today in the shadow of the beautiful 12th century church of St Peter. The memories my sisters and I have of school go back to the 1920s and 1930s. The infants and juniors combined in one building separated by a folding screen with wood at the bottom and glass at the top, making two completely separate rooms when closed. In the larger room the juniors were kept warm by means of an open fire made safe by a large fire-guard.

Being a Church of England school the vicar was a familiar face. We had Religious Instruction on Fridays and the Reverend Mr Wood thought nothing of throwing a piece of chalk at you if he suspected you were not paying attention. I do remember one brave soul picking it up and throwing it back but that's another tale! We regularly enacted the parables, for instance the Good Samaritan or the Prodigal Son.

Of course, all this was before the days of school uniforms in village schools – we wore much the same as any other day, hand-knitted jerseys, caps, boots, and of course the boys wore short trousers as all schoolboys did in those days. You went into long trousers when you became "a man" and left school at the grand age of 14!'

CHANGES COMING

'I attended Newtown Linford School, where I started in 1926 at the age of six years. My mother kept me at home for an extra year as there was no transport. We lived on a fairly remote farm between Anstey and Newtown Linford which was across three large fields. We had no road and the track could be very muddy, especially in winter. When we reached the main road at an area called the "Wide Piece" the distance was about one and a half miles, making a total distance of just over two miles. My mother thought this distance too great for a five year old, but the following year the Midland Red buses started to run to Newtown and I could ride there to school. We only had two teachers, Miss Bailey, the head, and Miss Cordon who was unqualified. She was a local lady and taught the children up to standard one.

Children who came from a distance such as from Ulverscroft Priory, Polly Botts Lane, Blake Hayes and Ulverscroft Lane and myself and my brother, all had our own packed lunches at school.

We took our own cocoa, tea or whatever hot drink, which was made for us by Mrs Harrison, who lived in an old thatched roof cottage by the side of the Bradgate Hotel. Two of us were delegated to fetch the drink when we were considered old enough. The headmistress watched over us with an eagle eye whilst we ate and drank – no talking allowed and we were not allowed to leave anything! After lunch (dinner in those days) we were allowed outside and if we had a penny to spend we would trek off to Zaddy Harrison's shop in the "Old Post Office Row" and decide how to spend our wealth: perhaps a box of Marston's Snow Mints for a penny or four aniseed balls, or perhaps one large gobstopper or two small ones for a penny, sherbet dabs or liquorice, maybe a lucky bag, what delights! For threepence a lovely bouncy ball, among other things. The owner of the shop was a coalman and chimney sweep – not much hygiene there, and there was even less at school with no running water. The only water was from a pump in the playground which we couldn't use as it had been condemned as unfit. Dead mice were found in the well. The lavatories were situated at the bottom of the playground and were the pan type with newspaper as toilet paper, but as everyone had the same facilities at home no one knew any different.

It was not until about 1930 when returning to school after the August holidays, we found we had a drinking fountain installed and a tap plus a wash hand basin! The old one had been taken away; gone was the privilege of using Miss Everard's (new head teacher) small bowl of hot water provided by the caretaker every lunch time for her to wash in. We girls lined up and waited while she washed and then she would say, "You may use it now." There were about five of us!

All the children were lined up to be shown how to use the fountain for a drink. None of us had come across such a wonderful invention as this. However, we were not allowed to use it indiscriminately, certain restrictions were imposed and permission had to be obtained.

Another wonderful change had been made. The old lavvies had undergone a facelift. They had been replaced with gleaming white flush toilets called WCs! These too were a great fascination and again we were not allowed to play near them or "go" too often. Along with these modernisations we found the old pump had gone.

Our wonderful days at school were marred by the death of a little girl from consumption. She was about six years old, a pretty, curly haired child with a delicate waxy complexion. Most of the children at school went to see her as she lay in her coffin, though my mother flatly refused to allow me to see her. On the day of her funeral the children were all kept in school until it was over and as you can guess we were all disappointed.

Most children wore pass-on clothing and footwear. Most children wore hobnail boots though some were lucky enough to have shoes: wellingtons were deemed to give you bad eyesight! We always changed into our normal boots on reaching school but believe me, the wellies were a godsend and kept our feet nice and dry.

From the age of eleven years the girls spent a full day at cookery school in Anstey. The bus fare was paid for us but we had to take ingredients for the items we made. Household management, cleaning and laundry were also taught here by Miss Gardener, from Leicester. We all really enjoyed this day away from normal school.

I left school in 1934 aged 14 years. After this I started to work for my family, receiving little pay as it was expected of farmers' children to work at home.'

OPEN FIRES AND PICKLED BITS

'The infants school at Cosby had large open fires with a coal scuttle beside and very large tongs with which the teacher picked up the coal to make up the fire throughout the day. At seven years old when I went to the "big school" as the junior school was always called, I saw radiators for the first time. The infants school had three classrooms and the junior, four. Both had separate playgrounds for boys and girls. At that time the schools took children from four to 14 years of age. After my first year at junior school there were great changes and children left the village at eleven years old to go to the newly opened girls' and boys' schools at South Wigston. Also around that time a number of families came from depressed areas in the north and Wales. They moved into a little settlement of specially built houses with large gardens.

Children who passed the scholarship with a high grade went to Lutterworth Grammar School. The exams were quite a highlight. The screens were put back between two classrooms making one large room so that we sat well apart. The examination papers were then completed. It was very quiet as only the scholarship sitters were allowed in that day.

Other highlights included Empire Day when our parents were invited to come and we would entertain them, mostly with patriotic hymns, songs and poems. We would wear a daisy on that day. We would wear or carry an oak leaf on Oak Apple Day. If we did not, the boys would sting our legs with nettles.

Another wonderful infants school memory was a visit to London Zoo. We went by bus to Narborough station then by train to London. As Cosby had no station, it was a rare treat to travel by train – almost as exciting as going to London Zoo. I was packed up with egg sandwiches and given money to spend. At St Pancras on the way home, I bought three penny bars of chocolate from the slot machines as presents for my Mum, Dad and brother. On the long journey home, however, temptation overcame me and I took home one bar of chocolate between the three of them. It was Nestle's chocolate in a red wrapper.

A man once came to talk to us about the evils of drink. "Beer is best left alone" was the theme running through his talk. He had all these little jars with different things pickled in alcohol, presumably to tell us what awful things it would do to our insides. At one point, he asked all those whose fathers drank beer to put up their hands. I was not going to let him know that my dad did this evil thing so I kept my hands firmly clasped. Unfortunately, my brother, who was sitting near the front, shot up his hand immediately. That little deception on my part certainly did not come off! We all had to write an essay. I was awarded a certificate for mine so I guess he must have made quite an impression on me – pickled bits and pieces and all.'

NO MIXING THE SEXES

'Looking back on my school days I am amazed at the difference between then and now. I lived in Syston where I was born and went to Humphrey Perkins Grammar School at Barrow on Soar. I went there in 1931 when there were approximately 120 pupils, both boys and girls. The school did accept state scholarships but also fee paying pupils of which I was one. The fees were £10 yearly paid in three termly amounts of £3 6s 8d. If any child left school for work before 16 years of age a penalty of £10 was payable.

We travelled by train from Syston to Barrow on Soar and had reserved carriages for boys and girls. There was no mixing of sexes either on the·train or in the school playground and only in the top class were boys and girls allowed to sit next to each other – before that boys sat on one side of the classroom and the girls sat on the other. School prefects were empowered to make sure that rules were carried out. The cane was still in use but only for boys. Pupils were not allowed outside the school premises between arriving and leaving unless they lived in Barrow on Soar.

Each generation in education is different. My mother was a teacher from roughly 1909 to 1920 and had attended Alderman Newton Girls' School. At that time their training was done in practice and exams – no college training. She taught at St Margaret's and Slater Street School in Leicester. I can remember her telling me that when children swore they were made to wash out their mouths with soap and water. If they were naughty they were sent into a corner. We had a teacher who made you stand on a chair.'

LEAVING IN A HORSE AND TRAP

'Medbourne was very prone to flooding – in fact right up until about 1984, when the new flood control was built. After a storm the brook would rise very quickly and houses in the village would get water up to the door, and sometimes even into the house.

The brook runs along one side of the school playground and after heavy rain the floodwater could completely encircle the school. Fortunately, the school and playground are on slightly higher ground, but the children and teachers could be marooned. Many children walked quite a distance to school from outlying farms and hamlets. These children would take their lunch with them and would be allowed a drink of water from the pump outside the headmaster's house.

One mother, whose children walked a long way to school, asked if there could be a rack to dry the damp clothes by the fire. At first it was considered to be unnecessary, but eventually drying facilities were provided.

If the floodwaters became too deep, two farmers, Mr Lygo and Mr Sharp, would collect the children in their horses and traps. The children would be driven home with the little ones sheltering under a big black umbrella.'

THE WORLD OF WORK

ON THE LAND

Farming has always been the backbone of our county and every village had its farms and smallholdings, employing many more men in those days. Before the days of the tractor and combine, the horses did the heavy work and whole communities would be involved in harvesting and threshing days.

HIRING HIMSELF OUT

'I was born in Empingham in 1899 in a farmhouse known as Glebe Farm because it belonged to the church.·

When my father was 17 he went to Bourne Fair and hired himself out to another farmer as a farmhand to learn the tricks of the trade. He lived in with the family and received £5 a year as wages – paid to him at the end of the year. This money, all of it, he gave to his mother.

Eventually my grandfather took over Glebe Farm from his father and the whole family moved to Empingham. Later on my grandfather moved to Nook Farm and my father married and became manager of Glebe Farm. For this he received the princely sum of 14 shillings a week, a pint of milk a day, one lb of butter a week, half a pig at Christmas, and there were chickens and eggs in the yard and plenty of rabbits in the fields.'

'My gran and granpa kept the village shop at Peatling Magna. My grandpa also worked for the Hall family at Manor Farm, something like a foreman, earning 13 shillings a week to bring up six children. He went to the farm every morning at harvest time to take the small barrels to be filled with beer for each man from the boss's cask. He had the orchard near the shop to keep a cow, and they also grazed the roadside. When the harvest was finished, the gleaners moved in. My mother said they had enough flour ground at Gilmorton Mill to last them through the winter to make their own bread.'

Haymaking at Aylestone Lane in the 1940s. The horse was still the main source of power on the farms.

MOVING DAY

'On 25th March 1919, as a six year old with my parents, we moved from Station Farm, Bardon Hill, Coalville, to Park Farm, Swinford, Lutterworth.

The cows were handmilked at 2 am ready for the journey but Bardon station did not have any loading facilities so the cattle and sheep were driven through a blinding snowstorm to Coalville station. There was so much snow on the ground the cattle had to be driven in front of the sheep to enable the sheep to get through. The Coalville stationmaster was peeved because they all arrived a little after 5 am! The sheep and cattle were eventually unloaded at Stanford station.

Throughout that winter, the horses had been fed a generous ration of corn to get them fit for their long haul on 25th March. Leicester was roughly halfway. I remember discussions taking place as to where would be the best place to stop to feed the horses, taking them out of the shafts to let nature take its course without the load. Great care would have to be taken with the shaft props when taking the four year olds out and buckling them in again. Bonny, the grey mare, was considered too old to make the journey and had to be taken away by Dan Sitdown, the local horse slaughterer. Blossom and Dolly, the heavy horses, set off, followed by my father with the chestnut Welsh cob and a float-load of sundries, including a recently killed and salted bacon pig, an oil lamp, candles and matches.

Laddie, the Scotch collie, followed the float quite happily until, in Leicester, he took a dislike to the trams and turned tail. My father had to go back a mile or two to find him and then put him on top of the load.

The furniture van was a steam-driven one and the driver declined to go any further than Leicester on the first day. The menfolk, therefore, upon arrival at Park Farm made a good fire and bedded down on straw.

My mother, her younger sister and myself came by train to Lutterworth station. An uncle who lived at South Kilworth met us there with a black pony and governess car. We spent the night at The Old Timbered House, in South Kilworth. I remember my three year old cousin asking if "Bonny had come to Swinford?" When told Bonny had gone she enquired if "Jesus had fetched her" and I replied "No, Dan Sitdown did." The next morning my father and Dolly came to fetch us to Park Farm, our new home.

With cars, tractors and cattle trucks, moving a farm nowadays must be much simpler!'

HARD DAYS

'In the late 1920s and early 1930s things were very bad for farmers. With the depression, general strike etc, I well remember coming home from school one day to find my father in a very upset state. In fact he was crying – very unusual. My mother warned me to leave him be and not ask any questions. However, it transpired that he had taken sheep to Leicester cattle market and they were sold for the magnificent sum of sixpence and ninepence each. This meant bankruptcy for most farmers and nearly for us too. I don't know how my father avoided it. Some of his friends committed suicide and others went across the Herring Pond to seek a new life in Canada and America, leaving behind unpaid debts. Some came back but others stayed. Around this time wool was almost unsaleable. The price of wool in the fleece at the wool sale at Granby Halls, Leicester, held in June each year, was fourpence per pound. I remember my father kept a year's wool over and sent it the following year, as he hoped the price would be higher. However, he was penalised and received even less for it.

Milk was at an all time low when Wathes, who owned the Oaks Dairies, closed in Leicester and we had nowhere to send our milk. In common with all neighbouring farmers we felt that the end had come, especially when an agent came with the wonderful offer of fourpence a gallon! Cows still had to be relieved of their milk for their sake and this milk was fed to pigs or poured down the drain. No buyer could be found in Leicester. After a time a buyer from Uttoxeter was found but they couldn't collect so a certain Mr Brentnall from Newtown agreed to transport the milk from the farms round about. Everyone called it a syndicate. The milk was sold to this dairy for several years until things changed and the Milk Marketing Board was formed and things began to look up a bit.

During the 1930s best house coal was around £1 per ton and every May we bought around ten to twelve tons (a coal truck full) to last the following winter, from Meadows and Ottey of Ibstock. By buying a truck load we got it a bit cheaper.

Cattle food could be bought cheaper than growing it and I well remember best barley and wheat flour for pigs and poultry on sale at £5 per ton from wheat imported from the USA. Most of our land went to grass.

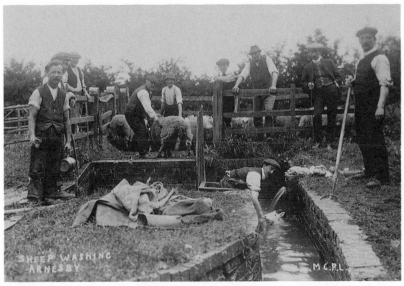

Sheep washing at Arnesby. This arduous task often proved a magnet for local children.

Twice a year farmers in the district and as far away as Copt Oak and Ulverscroft brought their sheep to Newtown to be dipped. This was the law, and we children had a wonderful time helping with the penning of the sheep. Well, perhaps the boys more than the girls, and we were given pennies for our help.

Another attraction was the Newtown Sale. This was a sale of agricultural equipment and cattle, sheep and horses, plus any surplus household items such as tables, crockery etc and anything saleable. This took place on site in Groby Lane at the rear of the vicarage, twice each spring and once in the autumn. It was conducted by a John Shakespear, auctioneer, who owned a site which was really part of a farm site. The barn and farm buildings were there and were used to store hurdles etc which were used on sale days. The farmhouse was bought for the vicarage.

Back home Mother would be rearing chickens, ducks and geese, all incubated under hens: some to replace our poultry flock, some to sell to local folk, mostly for Christmas when we had many days of killing, plucking, dressing and delivering to customers. They were sold for about three shillings and sixpence to five shillings a bird. Not much profit there. Some of our pigs, sheep and cattle were sold to George Lowe, butcher, of Anstey for perhaps around eightpence per lb, at best tenpence per lb. Pigs were five shillings a score lbs (20 lbs) if you were lucky.'

BEFORE THE COMBINE

'Sid Jones farmed Lindley Lodge Farm at Higham on the Hill. He kept the Topton herd of British Friesians, and attracted media attention when he bought and operated one of the first combine harvesters in the Midlands in the late 1920s. Until those days the corn was cut by a binder drawn by three massive Shire horses; a "road" had to be mowed round the field to accommodate them and this was done by scythe. My maternal grandfather taught me how to do this. A hazel or ash wand was tied to the top hand grip, into a position above the point of the blade. Hedge to the left, a full swing of the scythe and hey presto! – the mowed corn was laid neatly, heads to the hedge, butts just clear of the left foot, in a row ready to be gathered into sheaves bound by a few stalks of corn twisted into a "bond" and thrust under itself to secure it.'

A SELF-CONTAINED VILLAGE

'Most villages were self-contained as regards industry and Knossington was no exception – farming or hunting being the predominant employers. Horses were the transport, either ridden or in traps, governess carts, drays, floats or heavy carts, all doing their particular job.

Village life started early in the morning. From five o'clock onwards candles would be lit to "get up", then the fires kindled and tea made, followed by breakfast for some or out to work for 6 or 7 am and back to breakfast later, after the cows were milked and the milk ready for collection in 17-gallon churns at the roadside.

After breakfast the other animals were fed and looked over. Depending on the season other activities were fitted in. Spring-lambing and sowing, summer haymaking – up at 4 am to mow the fields before breakfast and it too hot for the horses to pull the heavy mower; later they would pull the swathe turners, tedders and sweeps as the various stages of haymaking progressed. The farmworkers were often joined by casual workers (others in the village hoping to earn a bit) in the evenings or weekends as haytime is labour-intensive. Likewise the harvest which followed, from the reaping, stooking, carrying and stacking of the corn, to thatching the stacks to keep the corn dry and later on the arrival of the threshing machine and crew to finish the cycle before it all started again with ploughing the fields once more.

After the harvest, the food all gathered and stored for the winter both on the farm and in the garden, the preparation for next year begins – sheep and cattle sales, preparing sheep for next year's lambs, fattening poultry which have been hatched and reared for the Christmas market. Not forgetting cheese makers – also a long process. It was Stilton in this area.

The local bus service was well used, especially to market in Melton. At one time you were allowed to take small animals along for sale and return with your purchases, safely in the confines of a sack.'

FARMS AND SMALL HOLDINGS

'Some men at Newtown Linford men were tenant farmers of the Bradgate estate, and boys often had their first job after leaving school helping on a farm. Surprisingly, it was not common for Newtown men to be employed directly on the estate. The agent lived in Newtown, but the workers, such as dry stone wallers, tended to come from Markfield. Newtown men were often called upon, though, at holiday times and on busy Sundays to help on Bradgate Park in a voluntary capacity, with fire watching and crowd control.

There were ten farms and smallholdings in the village at the time of the sale of the Bradgate estate in 1925, and everybody, even the children, helped at harvest time, if it was only by taking the workers' tea out to the fields. The farmers allowed the women to glean around the edges of the fields after harvest, just as in the story of Ruth. This kept the cottagers' chickens in free grain for several months and was also valuable to the farmer, for it prevented remnants of last year's crop seeding into next year's rotation.

Until the coming of the combine harvester in the 1950s, one of the local steam threshers would be booked after the harvest by each farm in turn. Twice a year, in spring and autumn, there was a sheep fair off Groby Lane, and people drove their sheep and lambs in from nearby villages like Groby and Cropston, and even as far afield as Nanpantan. There was a big wooden ring in the field which you could look over to see the judging, and the winning sheep fetched more money when they were sold. Afterwards the stock had to be walked home with their new owners. There were also cattle sales at different times. The main farming occupations were sheep and cattle, including dairying, and wheat, barley and oats. Potatoes were not grown in bulk, but a farmer would usually keep part of a field for his own potato patch.

A particularly local seasonal occupation was the stooking of fern (bracken) on Bradgate Park. Each farmer had his own piece to cut, and in return he would receive a piece of venison from the park. The cutting of the fern reduced the fire risk on the park, and when it was carted into the village it was used to line potato clamps and as cattle bedding. Farmers would have fern stacks at the side of their haystacks, and manure heaps containing fern heated up particularly well.'

COAL, QUARRIES AND FACTORIES

Collieries, quarries, factories producing hosiery and garments, boots and shoes, biscuits and bicycles – we all knew someone whose work took them each day to one of these tasks.

THE MEN AND THE GIRLS

'During the years after the First World War, most of the men of Newtown Linford worked in one of the nearby quarries, mostly either Groby Granite or the Victoria Stone Works at Groby, though a few went further afield to the Cliff Hill quarry at Markfield. Some men worked in the mines and cycled each day to such places as Snibston, Ellistown, Ibstock and Desford. Evelyn's father worked at Ibstock colliery and said that once the men were underground they had to walk as far as to Bardon chapel. All the men either cycled or walked to work, and if they worked close enough, their children would sometimes take their dinner out to them at work – perhaps a wicker basket containing two basins, one for the dinner and the other for the pudding, plus a white can full of tea.

When the girls left school, at 14, they usually went to work in Anstey, which was an industrial centre, with boot and shoe and boxmaking factories. Florrie hated the idea of going to work in a factory, but nothing else presented itself and her friend Ada got her a job at Palmers Shoes. It turned out to be not as bad as she expected, for the girls were allowed to sing while they worked, and Florrie, a noted local singer, was soon leading the singing of rounds. She was paid 13 shillings and fivepence a week when she started in 1925. Gwen also went to work at Palmers, but Evelyn, who lived on the old A50, travelled all the way into Leicester to go into the hosiery industry.'

'Groby in the early 1900s was a very small village, the inhabitants mostly being very poor. Most of the men worked for the Groby Granite Company, which also had workers from Glenfield. The Victoria Stone Company employed a few men and there was also work available on the few farms.

Some married women got work at home with the Anstey or Ratby hosiery factories, as frame knitters.'

'There was a thriving hosiery industry in the village, Cock Hill as it used to be known. The women worked by day in the factories or as outworkers, as linkers and overlockers.'

STONE AND SOCKS

'In the early part of the century, a number of people at Elmesthorpe had knitting machines in their homes for the making of socks. These were superseded by the establishment of factories for the manufacture of hosiery and knitwear, Hinckley being very prominent in the furthering of this industry. The neighbouring villages of Barwell and Earl Shilton were very well known in the boot and shoe trade.

Stone quarrying was carried out extensively in many villages, a few being Mountsorrel, Enderby, Huncote, Stoney Stanton and Sapcote. The granite quarried there was used for the construction of roads. Farmwork was another source of employment.

During the depression in the 1930s, areas in different parts of the country were purchased and used to build estates consisting of smallholdings, one of which was at Elmesthorpe. The land there was acquired in 1936 by the Land Settlement Association for the provision of holdings, the tenants coming from the north of England where unemployment was particularly bad. Produce was sent to a main packing station on the estate and from there it was sold to the wholesalers, the profits being passed on to the tenants.'

AN ARMY MARCHING UP THE ROAD

'In the early years of the century I remember the Rothley men going to the quarries at Mountsorrel to work. They wore hobnailed boots and at six o'clock in the morning it sounded like an army marching up the road. They wore jackets with trousers of corduroy which were tied just below the knee with a piece of string. They carried their snack in a red handkerchief and also carried a can of tea. At midday their dinners would be packed at home and their wives or children hurried to the quarries with the food. Once a month the men had a bit of extra pay; this was called "the month up". Some got drunk on it, others put it on one side for extras which were hard to come by.

There were five factories then in Rothley – boot, shoe and hosiery – and they would sound hooters for the working hours. You always knew the time! There was also a building and contracting firm.

When the children left school at the age of 13 most of them got employment locally owing to transport difficulties. Some of the girls went into service at the big houses.'

THE QUARRY AT ENDERBY

'My father, who was born in 1885, was one of four brothers who worked practically all their lives at the quarry at Enderby. It was owned at one time by Mr Rawson, who had two daughters. Two engines were used to pull wagon-loads of stone to various points in the quarry, and each engine was named after one of the daughters, one being "Jessie" and the other one "Trot".

The stone was conveyed by horse and wagon to various sites, and the eldest of the brothers was one of the men who used to deliver it. I know it was taken for building to Narborough Mental Hospital (later known as Carlton Hayes) but my eldest sister, who is now 87, tells me that it was also taken to the site for building Leicester Prison.

This sister also tells how she and lots of other employees' children used to have to take the men's breakfasts to the quarry as the men had to start work so early in the morning; this was before they went off to school. If it was an egg for breakfast, the tea would be brewed in the billy-can and the egg would be placed in the hot tea. I guess it was deemed that the egg would be cooked by the time the child reached its destination. My sister was only four years old when this became part of her daily programme.

My father and a younger brother had the job of blasting, which entailed ramming the explosive (the shot, it was called) into a small hole and then laying the fuse. One day when they were in the safety shed (my father was actually further inside than my uncle) a piece of granite flew through the doorway and struck my father's head. It cut his forehead severely and cracked his skull, but it did not cut his cap. He was away from work for a long time, and was awarded £200 compensation, and a lighter job in the wheelwright's shop. Some years later when the company changed hands the new company was not obliged to find him a job, and so he was made redundant.

In 1931 I won a scholarship (later the eleven-plus) and was awarded a free place at the Newarke Secondary School for Girls in Leicester. The manager of the quarry, a Mr Grace, was so pleased on hearing this that he sent for my father and gave him £5 towards buying my school uniform. It was very much appreciated.

My uncle carried on with the job of blasting for some years until he also met with an accident. He and another man were ramming in the shot when it suddenly exploded, killing the other man, and my uncle took the blast full in the face. There were some dangerous aspects of quarrying and I guess it was a great relief for the workmen and their wives when later more stringent safety rules were applied and men were issued with safety helmets.'

COLEORTON COLLIERY

'The Coleorton colliery, known as "Bug and Wink", was opened in 1915. The miners reached the colliery by walking the numerous paths which criss-cross the village and its environs.

Most wore caps, and corduroy trousers tied beneath the knee. They usually carried a purple-blue enamel water bottle and a snap-bag. This white calico bag (about ten inches square) was usually looped to the upper arm. Down the mine the bags were strung high so that mice didn't eat their snack!

Some miners cycled to work – I remember well the cycle shed at the pit head. However five miners, not wanting their cycles damaged or pumps stolen, housed their cycles in our shed. For this privilege I was paid twopence a week and I had to buy PO savings stamps.

Often the miners worked only two or three days a week and "played" the other days. Sometimes they worked half or three-quarter days – if there was trouble with the winding gear or the water pumps. A hooter sounded round about noon, indicating whether the pit would work the following day.

Miners were paid for 19 cwts in every 20 cwts hewed. The extra hundredweight provided the miners' monthly "free" coal.

Coal was delivered to households by horse and cart, but the bulk was shipped from a railway siding coming up to the colliery yard. The monthly loads of coal were tipped on the roadside and many miners' wives, donning hessian aprons and gloves, carted the coal to the shed where it was usually packed neatly. Sometimes a lump of coal had to be broken down to a size suitable for handling. Several houses in the village were colliery houses. They provided homes for the manager, under-manager, engineer, blacksmith, carpenter etc. There was also a colliery farm. Most of these properties were neglected when the mines were nationalised so they fell into disrepair and eventually vanished.

Pit ponies used to pull tubs in the mine and were looked after by the caring ostlers and had regular visits by the vet. Most miners took tit-bits to their beloved ponies which were brought to the surface, heavily blinkered, annually.

All stone waste was heaped in the pit bank. In all weathers men worked at the top of the bank emptying the tubs. After a day shift, many women and children scavenged the bank for lumps of coal and wood from the pit props! During the 1926 strike this was an important, though illegal, source of fuel, but I do remember a group digging coal from an outcrop in one of the woods, though this was soon stopped.

There were no pit-head baths – so miners' wives lit coppers to heat water and filled the baths ready for the miners' daily wash. The mine closed in the early 1960s when a more modern mine was opened at New Lount.'

SAPCOTE LIVES

'In Sapcote, until the 1940s, there were still one or two cottages with long low windows showing framework knitters had lived there, but before 1900 hosiery factories were established. Workers went either to Stoney Stanton or Hinckley, if they possessed a bicycle to do the four-mile journey, and the hours of work were 6.30 am until 6 pm on weekdays; 6.30 am to 12.15 pm on Saturdays. Girls started to work aged 14 and (if memories are correct) were paid four shillings a week. Women doing outwork still had a knitting machine (Griswold's to knit circular socks) in their homes after the First World War. By the 1950s outwork was mainly mending.

In Hinckley, the factory hooters denoting starting time (8 am by the mid 1920s) ruled the life of the town. Doors would be opened to admit workers and after ten minutes firmly closed. They were usually given another chance to get in half an hour later. Large factories had clocking-in machines which recorded the time of starting. Hosiery was the main work for women and even those at home could do outwork. In the 1890s my mother as a child had to "turn" a dozen socks before she was allowed out to play. This I think consisted of turning socks rightside out after the linking of the toe seam. Linking was highly skilled and trying on the eyes as each stitch on the sock had to be placed on the needles. Most operations were paid piecework – priced per dozen – so dexterity was important.

The knitters just watched over perhaps twelve machines to make sure all was well and to tie in new yarn when a bobbin was used up. If anything went wrong, a mechanic would be called to repair the machine. Work was moved around the factory floor and to outside operations of dyeing and finishing in giant wicker skeps, providing jobs in another industry, basket making, the firm I know of being in Leicester. Counter work - the pairing up, folding and packing of finished hose was well paid and a male preserve before the Second World War. When nylon yarn came in, the men were provided with hand cream to keep hands soft and prevent snagging.

There was much variety in stockings from pure silk down through rayon, wool and lisle; fully-fashioned or the cheaper circular knits which were sold in Woolworths in the early 1930s for sixpence a stocking. I still have some bright-coloured fishnet stockings from then, though I don't think they ever caught on.

On Friday afternoon, pay day, each girl in the work room contributed a few pence and there would be a tea party with cakes and a tin of salmon. At Christmas, a fund would be started in October to purchase food and drinks and on Christmas Eve the festivities went on all afternoon. The only time I experienced this was in 1940 and I found it horrifying to drink whisky, followed by port, then perhaps gin – no wonder everyone went rolling home.

Holidays comprised Christmas Day, Boxing Day, Good Friday, Easter Monday, Whit Monday and the annual week beginning the Saturday before August Monday when there was a mass exodus to the seaside. During this week, the factories would be painted, machines overhauled and giant factory chimneys swept.

Both men and women from Sapcote worked in the boot and shoe trade either at Earl Shilton, where there was a factory making slippers, or at Barwell, where boots and shoes were made. Outworkers in the village stitched the leather uppers but had to buy their own machines before they could get this work.

There was a factory in Stoney Stanton (making toe puffs the inner stiffening in boots) which burned down and many dashed from Sapcote to watch the spectacle!

Cheesemaking certainly was taking place in Sapcote around the turn of the century. One resident, aged 93, recalls her mother taking washing back to a farm and coming home with a quarter of a fresh Leicester cheese. The farm I worked on in the 1940s had the remains of a cheese press and a cheese storage room. These were both outlying farms where perhaps the sale of liquid milk was difficult, unlike in the centre of the village where folk would take their jug to the back door to buy daily pints.

Simple curd cheese was made from sour milk for home consumption and small cheesemaking was still being taught to prospective farmer's wives at Farm Institutes in the late 1940s.

Many girls from surrounding villages worked in service in Hinckley, usually in houses of professional people. In some areas there was little other work available for girls. They were, literally, maids of all work, washing, cleaning, waiting at table and child minding. A few of the bigger houses had cooks or housekeepers too and an odd job man, or gardener, for outside work.

Some of the larger farms had inside staff and in these cases the house was split with two staircases and only connecting doors between servants' quarters and the main house. Servants would occupy the kitchen and, if lucky, have another communal room as well as their bedroom. Wages were low but, of course, they had board, lodging and often uniform provided.

Quarrying around Sapcote was for granite. Men started work early and children were sent with hot breakfasts for their dads before going to school, involving a walk of two or three miles.

Blasting took place on weekdays at noon, warning being given by a horn, and men were posted on roads to stop any traffic passing. This regulated the dinner hour which was noon to 1 pm, roughly an hour earlier than in the factories. When work restarted the stone would be loaded on to carts, extra large lumps being broken by the "knockers-up" swinging large, extremely heavy hammers. It was hauled to the surface by horses and thence to the sett makers' sheds where men would chip away making the square-surfaced setts familiar to us all in the cobbled yards and streets, or to the crushers. These were machines where the stone was broken into three-quarter inch or quarter inch chips for road-making, or the fine crusher which made dust for the cement works alongside the quarry, making slabs and sewer pipes, and the tarmac plant. Stone would also be carted to the siding at Shilton pit to be trained away to different parts of the country.

Some horses were owned by the company, but some carters had their own animals and small paddocks in which they grazed. It is said that often on pay day and a visit to the local the horses would bring the carters home! After the demise of horses, the stone was loaded by mechanical diggers, winched out to the surface and on to small trains for movement round the units. The company had its own siding at Elmesthorpe station where the stone was put on to the national railway system.

All operations needed were on site: sharpening sheds for the drills of the shot-firers; the blacksmiths for shoeing horses, repairing and making tools; and carpenters for general repairs and maintenance. There were also two weighbridges – one in the quarry bottom and one on the surface, with the offices, which besides weighing stone off the premises was also available for the public and was much used by farmers selling loads of hay or straw.

The quarry was constantly filling with water so a sump was dug in the bottom and a pump installed to keep it dry. The water was conveyed to storage tanks where it was chlorinated and provided Stoney Stanton and Sapcote with a piped water supply long before mains water reached the area in the 1950s.'

THE BISCUIT FACTORY

'When I left school I was 14 years old. The problem was how to get a position of some kind. If you wanted to go into an office you had to have an introduction or know someone, or wait for dead men's shoes. I lived in Ashby-de-la-Zouch. It was pretty easy to get in at the soap works because at that time (1928) any girl who thought anything of herself would not deign to lower herself for there; you see, even then, class distinction. The next thing was into service and you had to be more or less recommended. Well, until I was 15 years old I worked at a little lady's, I was called a "companion help". I was help definitely, but not companion. I was paid two shillings a week and if I wanted a drink during the morning I had to nip home, but I was naughty. Upstairs the little lady had a bottle of whisky. I was very careful. I used to take one teaspoonful of her whisky, I thought I was entitled to a morning drink and it never dawned on me that I was stealing.

In the meantime I was trying to find something else to do. Then I heard they were going to build a new factory, the firm was coming from London, a biscuit factory. All agog, everyone was trying to get on the list and we kept trekking up to the offices. Big day comes, I had a message from the forelady, who happened to be my auntie's friend from girlish years, "Tell Nancy to report for work." I did; we all had to be kitted out in overalls and caps. I might add that unless you were one of the chosen ones they were all too big.

We were told to report to different groups. I was definitely not one of the chosen ones. I found myself in the bakehouse, eight girls to the machine which rolled and cut the biscuits. We started at 7.45 in the morning and finished at 5.45 with one hour for dinner. I had to run all the way home, a mile and a half, and back. We used to get threepence halfpenny an hour and overtime was fourpence farthing. Plus we had to work Saturday morning cleaning the machine and scrubbing the floor. We had to scrape the floor first with a long-handled hoe and when that was swept up then the buckets and scrapers came into force. Each girl had about 20 square yards to scrub and scrape and it was a rush to get finished by twelve o'clock.

My wage was ten shillings and ninepence a week. Mum had ten shillings, I had ninepence for myself. Ninepence? Sixpence to join a club at a shop to buy my clothes and threepence to spend willy nilly. We all got together at the factory and decided we wanted more money so we went on strike. Messages were going back and forth through the offices. Success! They gave us the sum of one shilling.'

HOSIERY AND GARMENTS

'Leaving school at 14 and going out to work was a culture shock to me. We were not given any idea in those days of what working life was about – no careers officer to direct us or even to ask about what we intended to do in the future. I remember thinking that the best thing about it was being paid at the end of the week and it would relieve me somehow of all the polishing and cleaning I was expected to do at home. I still remember the smell of Mansion polish that we used to polish the furniture Mother was so proud of and the Lysol disinfectant she washed the floors with.

Uncle George worked in the washhouse at Chilpruf Ltd in East Park Road. He put in a good word for me to join the workforce of round about 1,000 people. It was a well known firm of underwear makers. We worked in pure wool and made garments from beginning to the end product. Mother took me as far as the prison-like gates of the huge, red-brick building which looked to me to be a very forbidding place. I felt nervous and small. As I entered the gates clanged shut behind me – there was no turning back now as I waited to see the manageress, a poker-faced, stern woman dressed in a green striped skirt and a black velvet jacket. Her haughty manner didn't relieve my anxiety. At one time she told me sternly always to address her as "Miss".

I was asked what I liked doing. I quickly replied that I liked sewing, making my own clothes and mending the family socks, writing letters and most of all I liked reading any books and magazines I could get my hands on. I was also happy painting and drawing which Mother frowned on. She said I spent too much of my imagination on things which, after all, didn't earn me a living. I was assigned to the design and pattern cutting department where I was introduced to Miss Alice Preston, who bore the same name but was not related to "old sour puss". I liked this kind, gentle lady with a bad limp, hare lip and scraped up hair. She took me under her wing, read me chapters from the Bible and went to the prayer meeting on Tuesday mornings.

The day started sharp at 8 am. The hooter would sound as we all trooped through the factory gate with the spikes on top. I don't know if they were designed to keep us in or to keep undesirables out. Woe betide anyone who was half a minute late for the gateman closed them for 15 minutes. If it happened three times in one week you had to report to the management and it often resulted in dismissal. How I managed to get there on time was always a mystery to me. I found the journey irksome, sometimes walking from Evington where I lived to save a few pennies. My father met me when the darkness came. I used to feel tired and lonely walking back from the day's work and scared of the long, deserted roads.

I was paid nine shillings and ninepence a week and after giving up my pay packet I was allowed enough to cover my bus fare. Mother was eternally grateful for the money I brought home, it being a very scarce commodity. There never seemed enough to feed eight children and two adults but she didn't ever get into debt. I served my apprenticeship and finally I was asked to go and see "MP" as she was known. What, I thought, had I done now but she only asked me if I cared for the job. As I was interested in design I should go to evening classes at the polytechnic and take a course in dress design. No question of who was to pay and no day release in those days. I did take the course there and became an efficient pattern cutter. One had to wait to go up the ladder to such heights as a designer and I didn't feel I could leave to join another firm so I accepted the offer to go to the cutting room instead and if a vacancy came up I would fill it in design. In no time I became an experienced cutter earning approximately £4 a week. It was very heavy, hard work and required a lot of stamina and dedication. I was paid by the amount of work I did. The quicker I worked the more pay. On Friday at 4 pm precisely I was handed a pay packet. We worked a 48 hour week and some parts of the year when the shops were stocking up we worked 60 hours. Not a lot of time for leisure and enjoyment.

Perhaps I can describe work in the other departments. The machine room was huge, consisting of rows and rows of machines for different operations. Each girl sat on a wooden stool with a large hamper on one side for the finished work. When all the machines were turned on the noise was terrific and one had to raise one's voice to be heard.

Women working at J D Broughton's hosiery factory at Wigston in the 1920s.

The garments we made were costly, made up of pure wool fabric, unglamorous styles. I used to imagine a lot of old officers parading up and down the barracks in their long johns and vests and combinations with sleeves and a convenient flap at the back. How the young of today would have laughed.

Each completed garment was inspected twice before it was packed to be sent to a shop. I worked for the firm until the war came along. Then afterwards I started back again and eventually became a pattern cutter and grader until the firm was taken over. It was really a hard life and heavy work to get a reasonable wage in the 1930s and 1940s.'

'Leicester has always been known as an industrial city, but mainly as a producer of good class hosiery garments, both outwear and underwear.

I worked for many years for one of the most well-known factories – Corah, founded by Nathaniel Corah in 1815 after the battle of Waterloo.

I worked in the trimshop which was responsible for the "setting" of all fabrics. If a fabric was not set it would not hold its shape when made into garments. Steam was pushed through the fabric and then it was cooled by cold air forced through by compressed air on a machine called a Stentor.

A Stentor was a very large, long machine which required two operators. One man fed the material into the machine and the other ensured the fabric was either rolled or layered at the other end, depending on the next stage for the material. Each type of fabric had to be treated differently, so the two men kept in touch by intercom. Underwear fabric of vests, pants etc would have to be dry cleaned to get rid of any oil in the material otherwise it would not hold the dye when put in the dye vat machines. This type of fabric was set in an autoclave, a smaller, round machine using a similar system to the Stentor.

The trimshop was a very hot, humid room in which to work because all the machines used steam as part of their processes. Windows couldn't be opened, to prevent dust and dirt getting into the fabric, and the air conditioning system was always breaking down.

There were other machines in the trimshop besides the Stentor and the autoclave and I was able to operate all of them. If there was a breakdown in any of the machines I could usually fix them too. We were supposed to let the maintenance men do this but we, the operators, couldn't afford to stand around as we didn't get paid while the machines stood idle.

After the fabrics had gone through their various stages in the trimshop, the material was passed on to the cutting and making-up departments. Most of Corah's garments were made for Marks and Spencer, Corah being their main supplier.'

'Working in the hosiery began for me in 1944–45 at R. Rowley at Fleckney. The village had three factories at that time. Hours of work were 8 am to 12.30, 1.30 to 6 pm and Saturday morning 8 am to 12.30. For this the wage was 30 shillings which was quite good for doing odd jobs while learning to mend small ladders in lisle stockings. On leaving, about one year later, the wage was £3.

On piece work we were paid by so much per dozen and the fastest workers earned more money, double the wages of the textile industry. Most factories had quite good conditions, some had clean canteens but some small ones didn't have any facilities at all.

These were the boom years for the industry. I knew of young girls earning more than their fathers. I also found a great sense of comradeship and lots of fun. Obviously quarrels took place but usually were soon forgotten. I finished my working life in

Countesthorpe and still have many friends who meet from time to time although houses are now being built where the factory stood.'

'I left school at 14 years of age and started to work in a hosiery factory, Hall & Earls. I was a runabout for ten shillings a week, and five shillings bonus. I had to "cut off": a girl worked the machine (we made directoire knickers: "passion killers") and put the elastic in knees and waist, my job was to cut the elastic to the right size at waist and knee, and in between, fold the knickers to make it easy for the girl to pick them up. If she earned a good wage (about 30 shillings) I got sixpence for my help.

After twelve months, I was put on an overlocking machine, doing back seam and gusset for seven-eighths of a penny a dozen. Some were a penny and some, one and an eighth of a penny (per dozen). We were on our own time so had to work hard.

We were not allowed to talk, and the forelady would come round and watch. If you went to the loo, you were timed.

Later on when I was 17 I changed my job to cutting, which I really enjoyed. I worked for Wolsey on Abbey Park Road, and we made very exclusive dresses. We worked on the Bedaux system: instead of being paid in money, you had minutes. For example, 30 minutes for two dozen garments. At the end of the day, all minutes were totalled, and your wages then worked out in money. I worked there until I married in 1937. When the war began, I went back to Hall & Earls, cutting out vests and pants and directoire knickers for soldiers, ATS, WAAFS and WRNS.'

FROM THE FIRST BICYCLE

'When I was only a twinkle in my father's eye my grandfather, William Spiers, built the first bicycle to be made in Leicester. Not content with making cycles he joined in partnership with a Tommy Grieves to form Spiers and Grieves, manufacturers and repairers of hosiery machines with a works down the yard of Messrs Rowley and Co Ltd, next to St George's church in Queen Street. There was a sudden crisis when a fire brought down the whole works together with the steeple of St George's church, which lay for several years in the church grounds facing Rutland Street.

This event brought about the severing of the partnership – Grieves formed his own company of T. Grieves Ltd, making hosiery machinery, and later moved to Coalville.

My grandfather formed William Spiers Ltd to manufacture hosiery machines and purchased the factory from a firm named Wathes in Walnut Street, the rear of which faced the Filbert Street football ground. He manufactured several such machines but the best was his Autoswift which produced a complete gent's sock with a draw thread to each sock and with only the top and toe to be spliced.

He also produced the first superimposed circular cylinder machine called the Spenser Reel which made pullovers, followed by the Regent and later a 26 inch Leda for making stockinette.

During all of this period of William Spiers Ltd, they had started two iron foundries, one in Graham Street, off Humberstone Road, and one in Clarendon Street near the Walnut Street works, called the Eclipse foundry.

For a time we traded under the name of Porter Spiers (Leicester) Ltd and finally sold out to the Ratby Engineering Company Ltd of Peckleton.'

BOOTS AND SHOES

'My father's business – shoe manufacturing – was in Baggrave Street, North Evington and I joined him in 1915. It was a small but good business, capacity about 1,000 pairs per week and with 40 employees. There were a number of similar shoe factories in the area – Kellet's, Stevenson's, Moore's, NEBCO, Lester, Collins & Green, Leeson's – all now occupied by other trades. Percival's still survives.

We parked our factory keys at the sub police station in the square and thus were friendly with members of the force. They seemed a decent lot of lads to me. I used to be amused to see the number of children who got lost in the area and were kept at the station until claimed, fed on biscuits and tea provided by the staff's own pockets.

I recall one such case. "What do you think of this one?" asked Sergeant. "He looks a nice bright child," I answered. "Oh! He's bright enough. I took him down to the cell at the back to clean it this morning. He started messing about with the door and before I could stop him, the door had slammed, shutting us in with the station unmanned, until the Super came in to release us. Shall be glad when his mother fetches him."

My initiation into clicking was provided with a razor-sharp cutting knife, a tin pattern and a piece of leather to cut. The jump of the knife quickly provided the necessary cut fingers to qualify. The entry into lasting came next. The old hand-lasters kept their sharp tacks in

156

their mouths and these were retrieved one by one as required. The chew of tobacco also featured. What was not explained was that the stock of tacks in the open tin were blown free from dust prior to mouth entry. Thus the newcomer had his mouth full, to the joy of onlookers. Real delight that – taking the boss's son down a peg or two (and a grammar school boy as well). I survived.

On the clerical side my tutor was my father. He explained, demonstrated and made sure of proper attention being paid and then it was all yours. This included costings, invoicing, packing and general dogsbody. Real deep end tactics! His high opinion of some of my school-learnt geography was somewhat dinted when I sent some goods to Shrewsbury – I'd never heard of Dewsbury.

My starting pay for all this was five shillings a week – the usual in most trades, then, for beginners.

What surprised me was the paternal position of the Boss in relation to his employees. Away from factory matters, they came to him with domestic troubles too. We two had a pact never to discuss such matters in our own home. My instructions, when paying wages, to drop a bit extra in some packets were private to the parties concerned.

We had one real character. The only authority he bowed to was the Boss. One day, after a three day breakdown of the engine, which stopped all production, he decided to go on the booze instead of resuming work immediately the "all clear" was sounded. As he was our sole Consol worker, the teams beyond him were without work and had to be laid off.

The Boss left specific instructions. In case the man came in to resume, that would be after he'd seen him personally. And that order was adhered to. At the meeting, his employer told him his fortune, and the condition for restarting was that the offender paid two guineas to the Leicester Royal Infirmary "for leaving work without permission". And the receipt, bearing these words, was positioned at the factory door entrance.

Another case was the pounder up who damaged a hand. The accident was immediately registered, the insurance folk advised and permission granted for half pay forthwith. The casualty had, of course, been accompanied to the Royal for treatment.

After some two weeks, he called in with a packet of documents for the Boss, who had not yet arrived. Telling him to return in an hour or so, I resumed my labours after putting the packet with the in-mail. Later my chief was absorbing the latter's contents, when he suddenly burst out laughing and then I was sternly bade to join him. "What the deuce did I mean by accepting such a document?" I denied any knowledge of the contents of the package. "It's only a summons in its blue colour," said the Boss. "Why not wait until the injured party returns?"

From the subsequent meeting it was found that the man had taken legal advice and had been given the summons form to fill in. As he could not manage this on his own, he'd come to the Boss for help – to summons himself as head of the firm responsible for the accident.

All was sorted out finally. He received his compensation and happily his wound healed satisfactorily and the lawyer used got a guinea fee for his useless advice.

Such are a few sketches – about 1902 to 1917 – of a Leicester boy born and bred, and very proud of it.'

'Early this century there were five factories manufacturing boots and shoes in Earl Shilton. My uncle worked at Eatough's Limited from 1926 until he retired 52 years later.

He started work at 14 years old and lived at the village of Bagworth with his parents and five sisters and two brothers. He cycled to work every day until he was 17 years old when he bought a second-hand motorcycle (an AJS 200 cc which had gas lighting). Later he bought a new Raleigh motorcycle, also with gas lighting, which cost him £58.

If the weather was unsuitable for cycling he went on the Llewellen works bus which was owned by a Mr Wright of Bagworth. During the daytime the vehicle's top was removed from its chassis and another top was put on for the delivery of coal to customers in the area.

My uncle's first job was sticking cotton linings on to vamps for which he was paid twelve shillings a week. After one month his pay went up to 14 shillings per week. After working there for five years and learning many different operations he was able to work on his own time and could earn £2 to £3 per week. Women's pay was always several pounds less than men's pay.

The hours of work were 8 am to 6 pm Monday to Friday and 8 am to 1 pm on Saturday. Lunch time was one hour. There was a canteen where they could eat their packed lunches and boiling water was available for them to make their own drinks. Mid morning and mid afternoon the company provided free cups of tea which were brought to them at their benches.

Only men did the following operations – clicking, punching, bevelling, machining, lasting, eyeleting, welting, lockstitching and heeling. Women did the finishing operations – waxing, touching up with the dye, polishing, examining, wrapping and boxing. Men then packed the boxes into larger boxes (cardboard) for delivery to UK customers and into wooden boxes for export to many different countries.

In the early years they made ladies' felt slippers, brown sandals and sahara sandals (thonged uppers). Many were exported. Later all styles of footwear were made and the company always kept up with fashion and also bought modern machinery as soon as it became available.

Unpaid holidays were one week per year, taken the first week in August, two days at Christmas, one day at Easter and New Year's Day. Occasionally when work was not available my uncle had to cycle to Ratby to sign on the dole.

Employees were able to buy reject shoes cheaply every Friday afternoon at the factory. Every factory had its own football team and cricket team which was taken very seriously. There was a parade every year in Earl Shilton and each factory entered a decorated lorry.

Eatough's motto was "The sun never sets on Eatough's productions".'

OTHER WAYS WE MADE A LIVING

There were, of course, many other ways we made a living, from working in service to hairdressing, teaching to nursing. There were also all the village trades and crafts that were so important when we were self sufficient, from the smith to the milkman, the general store to the tea gardens.

A VILLAGE MISCELLANY

'The period between the turn of the century and 1960 saw great changes in village life in both Shearsby and Arnesby. Much of the earlier self sufficiency was lost. Travel became much easier as the old carrier's cart was replaced by bus services: Miller's at Shearsby and Shirley Snutch at Arnesby – plus the Midland Red, usually referred to simply as the Red Bus. Steam engines brought mechanisation to farm work. Shearsby no longer had a blacksmith by 1928 as fewer horses were used on the land.

Industry first appeared with framework knitting. Sometimes this would be on an outwork basis and one instance used to be recalled where a family of eight children were raised in a two up, two down house, with a "frame" occupying the kitchen. Eventually premises in Arnesby where numbers of people had been employed as framework knitters, were converted to woollen glove manufacture.

Hosiery was manufactured at Arnesby by the firm of Thornton & Mawby until the 1920s. This period also saw the beginnings of both Sidwell & Jackson and the Arnesby branch of J. D. Broughton & Sons Ltd of Wigston. These latter were both "moth-balled" during the Second World War to save fuel, and employees who were not on active service were obliged to travel into either Wigston or Leicester to work. This meant a long day as the Workman's Bus on which they travelled went round a number of the surrounding villages picking up passengers. Both firms reopened after the war.

Shoes were made by Mr Hunt and ice-cream sold in a house near the church at Shearsby, while Mrs Higgs kept a shop in the Square. The local shoe repairer lived at Rose Cottage. Candles were made at Shearsby at The Chandlers Arms. Mr Kirby was still repairing shoes at Arnesby in 1938. Sharp's Garage at the top of Main Street after the Second World War ran a taxi. This was used by the girls on Saturday nights to go to dances in the surrounding villages. The business finally closed during the 1950s.

Elliot's sold meat at Shearsby, as did Langton's at Arnesby. Mrs Kemp took over a small village shop in Arnesby from her mother, Mrs Fowkes. William Henry Walker kept a general store in Arnesby until midway between the wars. The premises were then taken over by Reddell's who kept the shop and provided a weekly service to surrounding villages. In 1947 they were bought out by Wigston Co-op and took over the running of No 3 branch in the village. This shop was during its existence run by three members of the Smith family.

The villages also had their own road man who kept the village tidy, patched and swept roads etc. At Arnesby, Fred Moore came to the village as an evacuee from London and stayed here. He kept his brush and barrow etc in the old Pinfold. The bus shelter now stands on the site.

Arnesby had its own policeman too, years ago. He lived in a house which stood on the corner of Bobby's Lane; just one of many descriptive street names which have gone.

Public houses have disappeared too. By 1960 Arnesby had lost the Bell Inn and both the New Inn and the Crown at Shearsby had disappeared too.

"Taglockit" was made by Read's of Shearsby for many years. This was dried sheep manure and the method of making was as follows:

"Sheep clippings bought (from rear end), placed in a shed and damped down. The clippings heated up naturally. More water added. Heated up naturally again until the wool disintegrated. The 'muck' was left and spread out on the floor to dry. Then it was put through a hammer mill to grind it and it came out like dust and looked rather like soot. With water added it made good feed for tomatoes. Also bought by the London Parks Dept in cwt bags for the London parks and greenhouses."

Read's of Shearsby were actually fellmongers and were in business from around 1900 to some time after the beginning of the Second World War. The business was run by a succession of members of the same family. It is said that on one occasion a man drowned in a vat used to treat the skins.'

A VARIETY OF JOBS

'Mr Long Roberts from North Luffenham was the pig killer for us at South Luffenham. He arrived on foot with his bag of knives. Some of the little girls in the village were frightened of him because of the long knives he carried.

The sweep used to visit from Kings Cliffe and cleaned the chimneys for ninepence. Harry Joyce was the cowman and he would bring the cows up the road twice a day, singing the hymn *Art thou weary, art thou languid*. Mrs Anna Cooper delivered the telegrams on foot to Barrowden and Wakerley from South Luffenham for threepence a time as those villages did not have a telegraph office.

Some men worked at the flour mill or as farm labourers, the average wage being 32 shillings a week.'

'There were always people in every village who could do a variety of odd jobs. They would help out at harvest time or when a pig had to be killed. They were usually strong men capable of doing heavy work and would ask for little payment – just enough for a drink perhaps.

A story told in Medbourne is about a funeral in the village. The local carpenter had made the coffin and an odd-jobbing man was asked to dig the grave. When the relatives came to check that the grave was ready, they found him in the freshly dug hole, fast asleep. Grave digging was thirsty work!'

'Earlier this century at Ketton there were enough small shops and craftsmen for the needs of local people to be supplied within the village itself. Tradesmen included stonemasons, carpenters, joiners, undertaker, slater, boot and shoe makers and repairers, saddle and harness maker, three blacksmiths, barber, chimney sweep, dairymen, three bakers and flour dealers, grocers, drapers, three butchers and dealers in sundries. There were eleven public houses and two breweries. The considerable workforce at the quarries was supplemented by others from surrounding villages, using the various footpaths to get to and from work.'

'Although mainly a farming community, Packington men worked in the mines and brickyards, having to walk four or five miles there. There was a village blacksmith, with his forge worked by hand bellows, where we took the horse for shoeing, and a cobbler's, where we spent many happy hours watching him repair shoes – no pre-cut shoes, but all cut from a sheet of leather. Hobnailed boots

The smithy at Earl Shilton. The work of the blacksmith was as important to the towns and villages of the past as the garage and petrol station is today.

for the heavy workers and always good substantial soles and heels for everyday shoes. His shop was very cluttered but he knew where each knife, hammer and nail was. He used to heat his polishing iron over a candle flame.

Also in the village were the bakery, general stores, butcher, post office and a small general shop which operated from a room in the house. Of course, there was the local public house and an off licence which was run by two sisters. When we fetched beer for harvesting, as we were under age the beer had to be in screw-topped bottles and they were sealed over before we were allowed to bring them out of the shop.'

THE SMITHY

'At the turn of the century Harby was a village of some 600 inhabitants. It contained a brewery, a mill, where farmers brought their flour to be ground, a butcher, baker, blacksmith, saddler, carpenter and undertaker, two shops, three pubs, the parish church of St Mary and a Wesleyan chapel.

Before the coming of the railway the chief means of transport were the horse and cart and the canal. The railway was built in the early 1890s and provided a through service on the LMS from Nottingham to London (Euston) and from Grantham to Leicester by the GNR. The canal was used to bring coal, corn and road stone to the two wharves – one at the mill and one at the brewery.

During the winter when the canal was frozen over the villagers enjoyed skating and sledging, often by the light of lanterns!

The smithy in those days was a very busy place. Agricultural implements were made and repaired and horses shod. During the winter when the roads were icy, the smith, who was also a farrier, would be up at dawn to put "frost nails" – sharpened metal studs – into the horses' shoes. This would enable them to get a grip on the slippery road surface. During the First World War the major part of the smithy's work was making shoes for the army horses. After that war, with the coming of the motor car and mechanisation on farms, the smith turned to making wrought-iron gates, weathervanes and ornamental trivets. One of his customers for the latter was Miss Isabel MacDonald, a daughter of the then Prime Minister.

The smithy at Harby was the first one in the district to make chain gears – before that ropes were used.'

'In 1900 my father was apprenticed, at the age of 15, to Ann Cluer of Burton Lazars, who carried on the business of blacksmith. The apprenticeship lasted until he reached the age of 21 on 19th January 1906. His father paid £6 to Ann Cluer when the indenture was signed, and she agreed to provide sufficient meat, drink and lodging during the time of the apprenticeship. For the last year he was paid three shillings a week.'

WOMEN'S WORK

'The local girls at Newtown Linford did not normally go into service. If someone wanted a live-in maid, they usually had to find someone from an area where there were no factory jobs. Factory work was better paid and when you had done your stated hours your time was your own.

Kit did do some domestic work, at Beech Farm, but from 1925 to 1967 her family ran the village post office from the front room of their cottage. Her father was the official postmaster, but he worked as a carpenter on the Bradgate estate while Kit and her mother looked after the post office and Kit did the deliveries. Her sister worked for the estate office.

Married women had to combine a great many different jobs in addition to home and family, although they didn't go into the factories. There was a good deal of outwork done, such as stocking making on a Griswald machine for Morleys.

A large number of the women catered to visitors to Bradgate Park by serving teas in their front gardens or, if wet, in their parlours. A plain tea of bread, butter, jam and slab cake cost one shilling, while a full tea, which also provided a boiled egg and fruit salad, cost one shilling and sixpence. There was a certain amount of rivalry, with three ladies in the adjoining "Workhouse Row" cottages quarrelling among themselves as they waited at their gates and each trying to drag customers into their own house. Another house had a card in the window stating "Mrs Mee, Hot Water and Tea."

Florrie's mother took in washing, did paperhanging and decorating, and helped with potato picking. She also acted as assistant to Mrs Crooks, the midwife, who also did laying out. (The first trained midwife, Nurse Cousins who cycled over from Groby, arrived around 1930.)

Evelyn's family lived too far out of the village to offer teas, but her mother also took in washing, and Evelyn and her brother had to return it in a wicker basket once it was done. Gwen had a mother who was sent for to help with the washing and housework whenever a new baby was born. Gwen had to do all the family housework while she was away. Many women went out cleaning, or gave special help at spring-cleaning time.'

IN SERVICE

'Before I was married in 1933, I was general maid for Dr Rolleston, who was Health Doctor for schools in Rutland. I started work at 6.30 am and lit the boiler for hot water for eight o'clock for the doctor to bath. He was often out until 9.30 pm, and I had to cook dinner for him, so I was late going to bed, especially when they had visitors. I had to take hot water to the rooms in the mornings for them to wash. While they were down to breakfast I had it all to clean up. They were hard times but they did me no harm. I was treated as one of the family, eating the same as they did.'

GARDENER/COACHMAN

'My grandfather was born in Ashwell and worked for the same family for 47 years as a gardener/coachman (later chauffeur), remaining in the service of the subsequent owner of the house for another ten years. He retired at the age of 78 in 1947.

His longest period of employment was with a Mr F. G. Chattaway, co-founder of the Leicester firm Imperial Typewriters, who originally lived in Ashleigh Road, Leicester but later had Westcotes Lodge built. My grandfather planted many of the trees in the new garden. By the time he retired the trees had come to maturity and he loved them and called them his children. He was the proud possessor of a walking stick made from the wood from one of these trees.

The Chattaway family liked to travel and bought a car in the earliest days of motoring. My grandfather learned to drive it, and must have been one of the first car drivers in Leicester. It was a Cadillac, and he took his employer on touring holidays throughout Britain. Another of his tasks was the care and maintenance of one of the first private generating plants to be installed in a Leicester house. When Mr Chattaway died he left my grandfather £250 in his will, a generous bequest in 1937.'

THE MILK ROUND

'My family were farmers and dairymen and had a retail milk round. I was nine years old when I had to help with the bottling. We had a machine which filled two bottles at a time, operated by a handle at the side of the tank, the action being similar to that of a see-saw, one bottle on and one bottle off. The tops of these bottles were wide and cardboard tops were pressed on by hand. These tops came in long tubes, with the name and address on, and varying designs. (As children we would put two new tops together, press the centre out and wind wool through to make "pompons".)

Later the bottle tops altered and were narrower. We had a new machine, much bigger with a large tank of milk, and underneath we could put a full crate and fill five bottles at a time (a crate held 20 bottles). The tops for these bottles were aluminium, with the name and address on. The tops were pressed on the bottles with a suction gadget.

Milk was delivered in pint and half pint bottles and third of a pint bottles for schools. The latter two were filled by hand from a large jug. We supplied neighbouring village schools and these bottles were taken to a coach garage at night to go out on the school buses the following morning. Milk was also sold from the bucket, ladled out with one eighth and one pint measures into customers' jugs and basins. As a child I used to think people who had their milk in basins must be poor and couldn't afford a jug.

The milk bottles had the name and address on and came in large cardboard boxes which held a gross. They came from the United Glass Bottle Company. We were constantly told to be careful with the bottles because "bottles cost money!".

In a room adjoining the dairy the bottles were washed in big tanks with rotating brushes, rinsed and stacked upside down in crates and sterilized by steam.

The family business went on for 40 years.'

GRANNY'S SHOP

'On 3rd July 1916 my eldest brother was born in a little thatched cottage turned into a general store. My father had volunteered in October 1915 at the Glen Parva barracks, Wigston, so my mother went to Granny's where my brother was born. My grandfather had opened the shop a year or two before the First World War to make a living for his family.

The shop was situated opposite a shoe factory in Almeys Lane, Earl Shilton – it is still in business. It was like most little shops in those days, a bell on the door which tinkled when customers came in and whoever was in the back would shout "Shop!".

The shop window was about six feet square with a chocolate advertisement in bold white letters, which I think was "Fry's Chocolate". Numerous boxes of sweets were on display – dolly mixtures, aniseed balls, marzipan teacakes, fishes, rosebud drops, mushrooms, kali, and dab and suckers. All were a penny for an ounce. There were penny bars of Cadbury's and Fry's chocolate too.

The sugar came in a big strong sack bag, which was weighed up after shop hours, as were the currants, sultanas and raisins. Each item of dried fruit when weighed into half pounds was in a different coloured bag ranging from pale blue to pale pinky mauve. Corned beef was sold by the slice out of a large oblong tin, and York ham on the bone. Nobody could match my granny's cutting of such thin slices of ham. She also used to cut the bread for the Festival Walks, so lovely and thin, and this was placed in a clothes basket lined with a clean tea towel.

She had large scales for weighing potatoes and pot herbs as they were called – swedes, parsnips, carrots and onions. She sold fruit too – oranges, apples and the grapes came in a plywood barrel filled with cork chippings. When the barrel was empty my cousin and brother would wheel it outside at the back of the shop and we would dip our hands in the cork chippings to see if there were any grapes which had dropped off the bunches – we did find some sometimes and shared them.

On certain days, travellers came to sell their wares. I well remember two gentlemen – one was a herbalist and sold Dewitts pills, but on many occasions he would pass on some remedy to my granny for different ailments. The other was a chemist who came from Leicester. He sold Carrs Fever Powders and Express Powders. Both these gentlemen passed many a cure for some ailment or skin disorder to my granny and she passed the information on to customers, family and friends. Very often when she had closed the shop at eight o'clock she would go along the lane to someone who was ill and pass on useful tips. Very few people could afford the doctor in those days.

My mother's eldest sister lived with Granny and they brought up my eldest cousin. His mother had died when he was four. Granny had no widow's pension so she was grateful for Aunt Sally's money at the end of the week. She worked in a shoe factory and helped with machining the sample uppers. A Sunday school teacher and joint leader of the Bible Class, she was kept very busy and later she became a Deacon of the local Nonconformist church. Those were the days when everyone knew everyone else in the village.'

KEEPING THE GENERAL STORE

'Early memories of Leicestershire take me back to Church Farm, Higham on the Hill, hard by St Peter's, at the end of the First World War. My grandfather had lately taken over, having turned his bakery business over to Ernest Pullen, an elder son, who had been demobbed with the accolade of the MC for bravery on the battlefield at Ypres.

Opposite St Peter's, Mrs Fanny Rowley ran the post office until her retirement in about 1950. The Fox Inn in my early days was in the hands of Mr Wells, who went on to become mine host at The Three Pots on the A5 at Hinckley. The Fox was at that time flush with the pavement, while at the rear a little enclave of buildings held a bakery where, in the early mornings, the steamy aroma of

Mr Harrison's bread mingled with that of the hops and malt of real ale. Miss Hammond's sweet shop adjoined the bakery. To pangs of conscience I lashed out some of my holiday cash there.

Pullen's bakery had by then expanded into a typical village store. Ernest added petrol pumps and oil to cater for the emerging motoring/business needs and became a Royal Insurance agent – the eight foot by six foot enamel sign announcing that fact became a notorious landmark, especially for treasure hunts. The old Bowser hand petrol pump served until the 1950s, and when visiting we had to ensure that we arrived with an empty petrol tank to be filled there and keep Uncle Ernest happy.

Uncle Ernest won the rail parcel franchise for deliveries round the area. They were picked up on the early, loaded bread van, the roundsman's mate standing on the running board with the passenger seat full – on the heaviest days some parcels hung by their string from headlamps or wherever. Stoke Golding Constabulary was an early call on the round, where this overloading would provoke no comment from the local bobby. Nor had we any anxiety about leaving the van unlocked for a ten minute cuppa and a chat with a customer. When I took over the business in 1938 the going rate for each parcel was fivepence.

The passage of time since I took over saw the cessation of baking after reorganising the shop to take in the post office, and a complete facelift and extension of the shop to self-service in the 1970s. The old bakery became an attractive cottage, but when opening up the roof space to treat the timber, the mummified body of a cat was found, evidently the victim of the superstitious practice of imprisoning a live cat when topping out to protect the occupants from evil spirits.'

EASOM'S THE GROCER

'During the late 1950s, my mother worked at Easom's grocery emporium at Melton Mowbray, in the market square where Boots now stands. The elegant facade was handsome with its dark green paint and gold lettering. It had a highly-polished wooden-floored interior with long mahogany counters, round-backed cane chairs for the customers, wooden drawers halfway up the walls, with brass labels, and shelving above them.

It was like a treasure-house . . . the drawers contained dried fruits, spices, coffee beans of many varieties, pulses, rice and other exotic dried goods. To open a drawer was to fill your nostrils with evocative perfumes. At the end of each counter were hessian sacks, lined with paper and filled with different types of sugar. On Saturday morning when I went in with my mother, I weighed and packed the sugar in thick blue paper bags.

Tea was stored in tea-chests and then packed into square tins which sat on the shelves behind the assistants. There were at least ten types, Darjeeling was in a red tin, Earl Grey in a grey tin and Easom's blend was in a green one. The assistants would weigh out the tea required on an elegant brass balance and stick a label on the oblong packets. Tinned goods stood on shelves as well . . . and heaven forfend if they were not lined up straight like soldiers, labels to the front.

On the opposite counter were the perishable goods, such as giant crusty Stilton cheeses, cut as required, never pre-wrapped, and sides of bacon which hung from a metal bar above the assistants, usually men on this counter. All this produce, including hams, cold meats, savoury sausages and so on, were never covered and would be cut or sliced as requested, using a gigantic machine with a huge steel wheel, which hissed as it moved.

However, my favourite corner contained the coffee roaster and grinder. The roaster hissed and bubbled, producing a fragrant steam which filled the shop with a burnt perfume, but the grinder was my favourite. I was allowed to pour the coffee beans down through the square funnel, switch on and after a tremendous clatter, collect the brown powder from the little drawer beneath.

The staff on provisions wore white overalls, the men in jackets with wrap-around aprons, tied with long strings, and the grocery staff wore dark green. These overalls were issued, freshly laundered and starched, every week. My mother recalls that it took a quarter of an hour to pull them apart, so stiff were they.

Easom's was "a purveyor of provisions to the gentry" and supplied an extra service that was appreciated by the many large country house owners and farmers' wives . . . they delivered. Orders were phoned in or would be taken down by the counter assistants in little books with pencil attached, adding up the bill with amazing facility, to be presented in a monthly invoice. The customer could then leave the shop with no heavy shopping to weigh her down and expect delivery on the same day. No order was too small but John, the delivery van driver, grew a little cross if someone ordered a packet of tea near closing time. Nevertheless, it was delivered, whatever the time and whatever the distance.

If the customer wanted to take her order, the assistants would trot around to make it up. Usually these customers would bring lists and the assistant could organise her collection but they always dreaded certain ladies who hummed and ha'd and ordered each item as they thought of it. I often wondered how many miles my mother walked on a bad day.

Mr Frank Easom retired during the time my mother worked there and the family sold the business to a new owner who had modern ideas. Within a few months the shop had become a supermarket, deliveries were stopped and my mother gave in her notice. Easom's grocery shop disappeared and a way of life and a very special type of service disappeared with it.'

A LADY ASSISTANT

'In September 1957, when I was 21 years old, I applied for a post at the Leicester City Information Bureau. I still have a copy of the advertisement that attracted my attention.

A lady assistant was required, with a pleasing personality, a good standard of education and a knowledge of typing. The salary at 17 years was £234 2s 2d per annum, which was increased to £301 2s 10d for a 19 year old with certain GCE certificates.

I did obtain the post and worked there for nearly 20 years, eventually becoming the manageress.'

APPRENTICE HAIRDRESSER

'It was 1946 when I started work as an apprentice hairdresser. I was 14 years old.

In those days parents were expected to pay a premium for their daughters to learn to be a hairdresser so mine were delighted when Miss Flora Parker of 14, New Bond Street, Leicester, allowed them to make the decision as to whether I should work one year for nothing, then the next two years for ten shillings a week, or the first year for two shillings and sixpence a week, the second year for seven shillings and sixpence a week and the third year for twelve shillings and sixpence a week. My parents decided to let me do the first year for nothing.

The shop in New Bond Street was a very old building, three storeys high and a horrible cellar where we had to mix the perming solutions. The smell of that was absolutely terrible and we had to dilute .880 ammonia which was used for the Callinam perming machine which at that time was very modern. I only saw the old Eugene machine used a few times – it must have been horrendous for ladies to be attached to.

I had to learn how to do finger waving and marcel waving and woe betide you if the irons got too hot. One lady used to come and have her hair coloured with henna – a very messy business. Miss Parker herself used to do that. The lady, a school teacher with very long hair, liked to have her privacy and had to be enclosed in a cubicle so that no one could see her.

On one floor two sisters had a flat; one taught elocution and the other accompanied singers on the piano, so we got quite used to hearing poetry and music from them. Occasionally Miss Parker had a musical evening to which her friends were invited. The older assistant was asked to attend but I was considered too young, although I did have to help with all the preparations.

Up on the top floor were the bedrooms. It was all very clean and tidy but the ceilings were all bowed. I was always glad I didn't have to sleep there in case it all caved in.

Downstairs on the ground floor, if you went through a green baize door, there was a lovely dining-room leading out onto a tiny yard with a miniature garden full of ferns. It was very pretty.'

BASKET MAKING

'During the 19th and the early part of the 20th centuries Castle Donington was an important centre for basket making.

The industry flourished due to the proximity of the town to the rivers Trent, Derwent and Soar and the canal. This provided flood areas where osiers could be cultivated. The willow rods used for basket making were grown on "stocks" which required skilful attention throughout the year. They were then pollarded annually in the spring and workers came in and cut and bundled the rods ready for transport.

They were carried by horse and cart to various yards in the town ready for peeling and sorting into different lengths. Large bundles of willow rods about three feet in diameter were put into coppers and left to boil during the night before being peeled the next morning. This process gave rods their buff colour. The peel from the rods was used as a mulch for crops such as raspberries. Some rods were peeled "in the green" which left them a white colour and some were left in their natural brown state. They were left to dry on racks before being soaked prior to use.

Much of this preparatory work was done by women and children. The actual craft of basket making was usually done by men, often in family workshops. There was very little "sectional work", the younger men were taught how to produce a properly finished article. A huge variety of baskets was made for many different purposes. Picnic baskets, linen baskets, bakers' baskets, cycle baskets, fishing baskets, dog baskets, pigeon baskets etc, etc including at least 20 different kinds of shopping baskets. Large hampers on wheels were also made for the GPO. The finished articles were collected every day by the railway horse and dray. They were taken to the local station and from there to Derby to be delivered all over England.

The making of a large basket required a unique combination of skill and agility. The worker stood barefoot inside the basket and used his toes as well as his fingers, spending most of the time bending over double and on one leg while making various deft twists and turns. A skilled worker could complete a basket in one hour.

During the First World War the craft had a revival when baskets were required to protect explosive shells in transit. Local craftsmen made these from imported cane. Once again the women and children found useful employment. Children would collect baskets from the yard and take them home to their mothers who stitched two leather pads and a collar onto each one. For this work they were paid about one shilling and threepence each.'

TEACHING

'In June 1935 I was nearing the end of my course at Leicester Domestic Science College and applied for a teaching post in Leicestershire. I was called for interview at the County Education Office, then very conveniently sited in Greyfriars, Leicester. During the interview by Mrs. M. I. Suck, the County Organiser of Domestic Subjects, I was told that, if appointed, I would be required to take single classes, or six-session courses, at any WI in the county. I readily agreed and when she said that I would be paid for these, I was even more enthusiastic!

A few days later, I received a letter offering me a job from 1st August, at a salary of £159 per annum, rising by annual £9 increments! (Had I been, as most teachers were, only two years trained, my starting salary would have been only £150 per annum.) My first pay cheque was paid at the end of August. The final results from the college were not through and I was paid the salary of an uncertificated teacher. This was £11 – I was delighted. I'd never had so much money in my hand at one time! In those days teachers were handed wage packets by the head teacher, to whom they had been delivered by hand from the Education Office.

I started teaching at the old school in South Wigston which was to move a couple of years later to become what is now South Wigston High School. This was only the second school in the country to have a purpose-built dinner kitchen. This brought greater responsibility but no greater pay – this was neither offered or expected. I had Friday afternoons free of teaching to draw up next week's menus, work out quantities to be ordered from the local shops and deliver the orders personally. This worked out very well and created a very good relationship. The dinners cost less than sixpence each!

In 1936 my long association with the WI movement began. I travelled all over the county giving single talks and six-session courses. The tedious part was travelling by at least two buses each way, often with a short car drive at the end. I was teaching from 7 pm to 9 pm but away from home for at least four hours. The pay was ten shillings and sixpence an evening! Those were long, but happy days. Prior to the outbreak of war in 1939, the County Federation held splendid craft and produce shows at the De Montfort Hall. One year I went with the County Organiser to judge the cake competitions. When we arrived at the De Montfort Hall we were confronted with an enormous spread of sponge and fruit cakes. I was to judge the latter. I could not be accurate about the numbers involved, all I know is that having cut slivers out of them all and eaten them I did not touch fruit cake for a long time afterwards!

In 1941 my work scene changed. I was then doing grammar school teaching at the Newarke Girls School. The government had begun to realise that new catering establishments were springing up all over the country – some factories found their canteens very popular; British Restaurants were expanding. Staff were needed in these places. Leicester City Education Committee had been approached by the Ministry of Labour to set up a training centre in the area. The City Organiser of Domestic Subjects found a training kitchen which could easily be adapted to large scale work – this was a former domestic science room on the top floor of the Gateway Boys School.

I was released from teaching schoolgirls for a year. The trainees were immensely interesting. Basically, they had to be over 35 (older than me!) so that they were not of call-up age for the forces. They came from all over the country, twelve at a time, for a very intensive six weeks. They spent four weeks with me – the main meals they cooked were taken over to the nearby "Tech" where all sorts of courses for the forces were being held. The last two weeks of their course was spent in kitchens – in factories, schools or British Restaurants. I remember that several went home to run pit-head canteens in Yorkshire, some to docks in Lincolnshire, some locally. The trainees were paid during the course and stayed in "digs" during the week at government expense. They rushed home on Friday and worked on the family washing, to last them until Mother returned on the following Friday. Over a hundred women were trained this way and all got jobs at the end of the course – a fine hard-working lot.'

NURSING

'I came to Leicester early in 1940 as an immigrant from Liverpool. So many came here for work because Leicester was then a very prosperous city. I had been unemployed for seven months. I worked in the hosiery industry and lived at a women's hostel on Regent Road. It was quite homely, I thought, though the women running it were very stern, and no girls today would tolerate the rules. I found the local people very kind and friendly and soon I was invited to many homes. I was then 18, but my parents were worried that I was alone in the world and with no warning arrived in Leicester to be with me just when I was enjoying life.

Within two years I had decided to do nursing and went to London. By then the blitz was raging but I somehow never felt fear during the

175

raids. I just wanted to help – queer but I can't explain it. I took ill almost immediately and was sent back very ill and later admitted to the infirmary. I was on Fielding Johnson Ward, 40 bedded, almost always in bed. It was very strict, with visiting twice weekly for one hour. I was returned home still very poorly and it was some time before I could return to work.

I got a job at Gerrintons on Market Street. Our clients were the "top people" and they tried still to be very fashionable and so had the top tailors and dressmakers. We had a free cutting-out service. I was in the drapery department and we had to help our clients in every way, so I had to listen to all the latest scandal! We managed our department as though it was our own shop. We were responsible for the buying, keeping a record of sales and ensuring that the profit was adequate. We also did our own window dressing and windows were always well dressed, after all that brought in the clients. We had many eccentric regulars who perhaps came once a year, such as the sisters who came in for Harris tweed to make their knickers. Yes, I tried to discourage the habit but they were only outraged to think that anyone could consider anything but Harris tweed. We had to be always smartly dressed in black. Hours of work were 48 a week. The money was reasonable provided that we made enough on commission.

This was the time all women except mothers with young ones were called up, either to essential service or the forces. Staff were constantly going and my friend and buyer went to be a signalman on the railway at Swannington, most unusual – a very heavy and responsible post. I was exempt from call-up and I had been trying still to return to nursing but with considerable difficulty. Matron at the Infirmary suggested I try Markfield, then a very busy TB and fever hospital.

I was accepted and farewells were such that I might have been going up the Amazon or to the North Pole. Fevers were much feared and no doubt Markfield had difficulty obtaining staff. All fever hospitals were either behind high walls or very isolated in the country – in this case the lovely area of Charnwood. My first day I was shown over the nurses' home. All nurses lived in and we had a comfortable, centrally heated room, a wash basin and plenty of bathrooms with plenty of hot water. Then I was kitted out, surprising how long that took, with three dresses, 21 aprons of the large starched kind, three head squares which we had to pleat into those large angel-type hats, starched collars and cuffs about six inches long, all fastened with studs. I was then taken to my ward, by this time about 4 pm. I was told how to treat pressure areas, given the equipment and turned loose upon the patients, who apparently accepted all this as normal.

Many of the nurses were from Ireland, their first time away from home and naturally they clung together. When on ward duty we took our cuffs off and our sleeves were rolled up. Stockings were black and thick for we could only afford thick ones. We had 15 shillings a week and our hours should have been 48 but we always worked over, plus lectures four or five times weekly. We somehow had to find time and energy to study and write up our notes. We had a very good social life within the home thanks to the sister who was in charge of the home and our well being. It was necessary that our health be watched for we were all vulnerable to infections.

TB was rampant, the wards were full and all patients could expect a stay of at least a year. Many died before a bed was available. We had our own ambulance and we had to go out to bring patients in and very often they died before our arrival. Many of the men were servicemen, young and full of frustration. We also had a small group of children who were evacuated from London and the blitz and many were very ill. The treatment sounds primitive but it did work for many patients. They were in cubicles which opened onto a patio no matter what the weather and the only time the doors were closed was in the evening due to the blackout. The convalescent ones were in cabins, again open to the elements and some mornings snow had to be shaken off the waterproof bed covering.

We not only gave nursing care but did a lot of the cleaning. All soiled linen was sluiced clean before it went to the laundry. Meals were served and we carved joints. If necessary we cooked light meals for the very ill patients. In fact, whatever was required for the well-being of the patients, we did.

The fever wards were full. Diphtheria was rife and whole families were admitted, many to die, for this was prior to immunisation. Scarlet fever was just as bad but the worst was diphtheria with death or later physical complications. Other infections included typhoid and meningitis which was far more prevalent then. Death was often inevitable, though many recovered. Encephalitis and, in young mothers, puerperal fever plus many more – in short every type of deadly disease. We were also on standby for smallpox.

Puerperal fever was a constant threat to new mothers and we were never without a patient. The first antibiotics we had were the sulphonamides, horrible drugs with many side effects. Often at post-mortem it was recognised that the patient had actually died as a result of the drugs. Immunisation was introduced in my second year and the effect was truly dramatic. There were five or six "diph" patients on a ward – then came penicillin towards the end of the second year. It was so momentous that as many as possible were assembled to witness the first injection. It was awful stuff really. It had to be melted first and was given by four-hourly injections. Very painful – no tablets then.

Studying was very difficult, working as we did, and I was thought of as a miracle to achieve my finals in under three years. Our training was for three.

Night duty was for at least three months at a time. I seemed to be always on nights. We were on the ward for twelve hours and alone. We took some prepared food to the ward so we even ate there. We always did a full round of the patients every half hour and we were hectically busy all night. We had to start waking patients from 4.30 am for the night report had to be ready and it took every moment then to complete our duties: all patients washed, half the beds made, treatments, medicines done and, of course, the inevitable sluicing, plus the ward report to be given to sister at 7.30.

We were expected to eat a full dinner when going off duty, followed then by putting on a clean apron and sitting through a lecture taking notes that were all too often unreadable. Night off-duty was two breaks in five weeks, a two nights and a three nights. It was very hard and it was not unusual for some to run away after two weeks. I was not eligible for a staff post until my three years was complete and I left then to take my first post at Groby Road Hospital. I left shortly to return to London until 1947 when I returned to marry. Married nurses were unable to continue nursing and it was 1949, after my first born, that I was the first ever married part-time district nurse.'

CHEESEMAKING

'Stilton cheese was first made in the early 18th century by a farmer's wife who lived near Melton Mowbray, and it continued to be made in farmhouses in the area for the next 200 years. In the early 1900s, however, commercial production of the cheese was given a boost by the formation of the Stilton Manufacturers Association, who continue to safeguard the character of this famous delicacy.

In 1911 the Long Clawson Dairy Farmers Co-operative was founded by twelve local farmers from the Vale of Belvoir, and started to make blue and white Stilton in the former village inn, The Royal

Oak. The company prospered, with another dairy opening at Hose, until the First World War caused milk to be diverted away from cheese production to supply milk to London. The Hose dairy was temporarily closed and Long Clawson dairy concentrated production on hard, pressed cheeses. In 1914 Jack Clark, a water diviner, was called in to find a site for a well. His fee was one Stilton cheese.

After the war, Long Clawson was able to purchase its first delivery vehicle and post-war recovery began. A long hot summer in 1921 with a severe drought led to the dairy purchasing the water rights of Brickyard Field and a 20,000 gallon reservoir was constructed; an electricity generator to provide power for lights and fans in the main cheese room was also a must. Milk testing began by 1927 to ensure clean, good quality milk.

The 1930s depression hit agriculture in general and the dairy hard, sales fell and employees were forced to take a pay cut. However, with the formation of the Milk Marketing Board conditions improved, with 150 cheeses a day being produced at the height of the season. Then the war came, and Stilton production stopped entirely "for the duration". Cheddar was still made, but it was not until 1949 that Stilton production began once more. In 1953 Long Clawson won the Perpetual Challenge Cup for the best Stilton at the London Dairy Show. Today, Long Clawson is the UK's largest Stilton producer.

Tuxford & Tebbutt is another long-established firm producing our most famous cheese. In 1867, and probably for many years before that, William Thorpe Tuxford was trading as a cheese factor buying Stilton from numerous farmhouse makers in the Vale of Belvoir and Melton Mowbray area. The Tuxfords went into partnership with a firm called Tebbutt & Crosher, who specialised in Melton Mowbray pork pies and other pork products, and they traded from Thorpe End at Melton Mowbray. They never looked back, and in the 1960s decided to concentrate their efforts on Stilton and Leicester cheeses.

Today true Stilton can only be made within the county boundaries of Leicestershire, Derbyshire and Nottinghamshire and has to conform to strict standards. Leicester cheese, our other famous cheese, is easily recognised by its bright russet colour, which is obtained by adding the natural food colour, annatto.'

'I used to make cream cheese for my own use on my farm at Wymeswold. The cream was skimmed off, and drained, and allowed to sour. Sometimes I added rennet to luke-warm milk (as it was, straight from the cow). When curds formed, the product was put to drain in a cheese tin, which had holes in the base, and which was lined with muslin. The curds were about one and a half inches thick. It formed a soft cheese rather like Brie, and it was made in the summer and at harvest time, for home use. This was about 50 years ago.

I can remember that my grandmother made Stilton for her own use. My grandmother died about 40 years ago at the age of 94, so the time when she made her own Stilton must have been pre-1914.

Wymeswold had a central dairy which made Stilton commercially. All the milk went there until the last war. But Stilton was a luxury cheese and so production stopped, while manufacture went over to producing "hard soap", as the wartime cheese was known.'

WAR AND PEACE

THE GREAT WAR 1914–1918

Though the fighting went on far away, for the first time attacks by Zeppelins brought war to a civilian population. Recuperating soldiers in their blue uniform, refugees and prisoners of war became familiar to us all, and we shared the hardships and food shortages – and the suffering that did not stop in 1918.

BOMBS AND HOSPITALS

'We were on holiday in Hunstanton when the war began and had to come home as soon as we could get a train, as it was felt the East Coast would be raided immediately. I remember some of the raids and we heard bombs dropping on Loughborough one night. I believe a Zeppelin was brought down. At first we used to get up every time there was an air raid warning and come downstairs. The lady next door was very nervous and she used to come into our house with her little boy as her husband was a policeman and had to go out every time there was a warning. My father went too, as a member of the Cycling Corps. Rough, our dog, had a keen sense of hearing and barked every time a bomb dropped, but there weren't any very close to us.

A hospital for wounded soldiers opened where the Wyggeston Boys School is. There were numerous other hospitals but I remember this one particularly because my parents arranged for some of the men in blue to come to tea with us on Sundays and quite a number of them turned up. They were so pleased to have invitations out and we children loved having them'

REFUGEES AND CONSCIENTIOUS OBJECTORS

'I can remember the Belgian refugees coming to Blaby and being given bedsteads from Yew Tree House, where we lived at the time. A little Austrian girl also came to the village and seemed to be much loved by everyone. I can also remember the blackouts and being able to see the searchlights when the Zeppelins flew overhead with a frightening "zooming" sound. We would go under the stairs or under the table whenever they were about.

A number of young men from Blaby did not think it right to be fighting this war and so stood out as conscientious objectors. Many of those who did so in the county and were not prepared to join non-combatant units were imprisoned for their beliefs, at Leicester prison.

After the war, the Duke of York came through the village to unveil the Countesthorpe war memorial and the schoolchildren all lined up at the bottom of School Lane waving flags. He never looked our way, though.'

FOOD WAS SCARCE

'It was 1915 when my parents, brother and five year old self came to Anstey. My home for many years was to be a rather nice farmhouse standing in five acres of ground, some three quarters of a mile from the village centre.

Food was very scarce during the war as it took time to get the rationing system working. We were not too badly off, having our own vegetables, eggs and goat's milk. Occasionally there was a pig to slaughter, but butcher's meat, sugar and butter were often unobtainable. I often had my play-time sandwich snatched by some hungry infant.

Children could leave school at twelve providing they had reached a certain standard and my brother, who had reached this stage, unbeknown to my mother applied for work on the City Farms. He was so proud to give his first wages to our mother – six shillings was the amount. My father drove a lorry for a wholesale food firm. He was paid 28 shillings, rising to £2 by the end of the war.'

'THERE'S A MAN COMING!'

'I remember the airship coming over Newtown Linford around 1917, on its way to bomb Loughborough. All the children ran out of school to see it.

When my father came home on leave, my brother and I saw a man in khaki coming towards the house and, not recognising him, ran in, shouting, "Mum, there's a man coming!"

On Armistice Day the schoolchildren at Newtown were given a half day holiday. I was too young to be at school but I walked along too, waving a little flag.'

'The lord of the manor of Heather lived at Highfield House and owned two brickyards, one in Mill Lane trading as "Wains" and the other in Pisca Lane trading as the "Heather Brick and Terra Cotta Co". Men earned a living carrying bricks from drying sheds into kilns (setting) or from kilns to the railway tracks for despatch (known as drawings). Men's wages for this would be in the range of fivepence farthing to sixpence halfpenny an hour, paid in farthing stages according to their particular work. A village lad commenced office work at Wains in October 1914 just after leaving school; he was paid four shillings a week, increased to five shillings a week after a three month trial period.

In 1917 the Pisca Lane yard was taken over by the Ministry of Munitions for use as an explosives store, known as HM Magazine Heather. The superintendent appointed was the lord of the manor, Mr H J Ford, and the office lad mentioned above was his clerk.

This munitions store was barricaded with a high, barbed wire perimeter fence and patrolled day and night by armed guards. In addition guard dogs were stationed at intervals alongside the fence by chains and a sliding ring affixed to steel wire. Soldiers and army personnel lodged at the brookside cottage, known locally as "Waterloo", a stone's throw from their work at HM Magazine (the cottage exists today).

When the Ministry of Munitions had finished, the yard returned to normal and produced bricks again until its final closure in June 1941, when men were again called for the 1939/45 war.

Five village lads were killed in action in the war; they are listed on the Roll of Honour in Heather church. Tragedy struck the village again at the end of the war when another local lad, the son of the stationmaster, returned home with shell-shock as a result of fighting in France. Sadly, his convalescence was short lived for one Saturday evening after supper he went out for a breath of fresh air and never returned.

An organised search party worked through the night, but with no result. His mother felt sure he would be found in the Long Mill Dam; the lord of the manor owned the water mill and gave his permission for the drainage operation to be put into action. As the mill dam water level drained into the river Sence, the body was found face down. Another demobbed soldier, who was convalescing on his return from France, went into the water, pulled the corpse to the bank, grasped him by the hand and said "Goodbye old friend". He then set off for home to dry out.'

THE SECOND WORLD WAR
1939–1945

When war came again, we faced danger and bombing on a day
to day basis. It did not seem possible to many on that day in
September 1939 that we could be at war again, but the reality soon
made itself felt.

FROM FIRST TO LAST

'The day war was declared it didn't seem possible, despite the
warnings. Was the first air-raid siren at Bitteswell real or just a
practice, and what did we do? Later I remember my father telling
me to buy some sugar! Then there were the evacuees, poor things. I
had Joan, with adenoids, the clothes she stood up in and a gas mask.
She went to the village school and was happy there. Army convoys
were all around the parish and even up our drive. I worked at the
army canteen in Lutterworth and in the Park and used to cycle up
and back. On the night before D-Day the green was packed with
lorries and troops. I lived on the green and was challenged – who
goes there? I replied, "The Queen of Sheba". The sentry was not
amused and told me what a fool I was, as I could have been shot.
    Bitteswell aerodrome was a training station for bomber crews and
as I had a cousin there (later killed) I often had a sitting-room full of
young RAF lads.
    As my father was in charge of the Home Guard in the Lutterworth
area and my husband was also involved (he wasn't in the forces as
he manufactured elastic for gas masks and parachute cord) and we
were on the phone, it was my job to wake up the local men when
they were called out in the night. I used to go round the village
throwing stones at their bedroom windows. One night, while the
German bombers flew overhead, I did wonder who was looking
after me.
    I remember hiding under the dining-room table when the
incendiaries dropped on the airfield. This was war at first hand and
I was very frightened. Once a plane came in low, machine-gunning
across the village, and some bombs came much too close. On the

night of the Coventry raid we went into the neighbouring farm's cellar. I got very restless and went home to make some tea – the farmer's wife was very cross with me but did appreciate the tea. I could see the sky all aflame and hear the continual roar of planes.

Food was short but we managed really quite well. Being in the country we had plenty of vegetables and fruit, and (hush-hush) a pig. Frequently, strange pieces of meat appeared, which at first I didn't know what to do with, but I soon learned. We were also allowed a pie – I think once a month, and of course the ration coupons everyone had, including clothing coupons and sweets.

On the Sunday the church bells rang we really thought the invasion had come. I was playing tennis – yes, we did have some amusements – and one of the party was RN and I've never seen anyone move so quickly. He was gone before we had got our breath.

A jelly was a real treat and one Christmas we had a party at the golf club and my husband and I walked across the fields to the club (two miles) carrying this treasure.

I remember on D-Day looking out of the bedroom window and seeing the sky full of planes towing gliders and wondering where they were going. We made a pretty good guess and had our fingers crossed for all the lads involved.

VE Day – as it happened I wasn't at home, but I went into Lichfield cathedral to say Thank God.'

'During the war the village hall at Husbands Bosworth was taken over by the army. There were two regiments based here – the Worcesters and the Hussars; one camped in Bosworth Park and the other in the Highfield House park.

Dances were still held in the village hall, but another of its uses was as a mortuary for any army personnel who died, with soldiers standing guard all night. The side room of The Bell Inn was taken over as a tea room for the forces, run by Toc H and manned by volunteers from the village.

The RAF was also based at what is now Coventry Gliding Club airfield, adjacent to the village. Evacuees came, and several stayed and settled here. POWs were also sent to work on the land, and again some of them stayed on.

To celebrate the end of the war a bonfire was held on the school green.'

A VILLAGE AT WAR

'During the Second World War, queueing became a normal part of life; it was said "Any two, form a queue". People would walk the two miles from Newtown Linford to Anstey, queue for hours at the butcher's and then finding nothing left. It was easier in the country than in the town, though, as people not only had gardens and allotments, but often fowls and pigs. A good deal of swapping went on: eggs from the family hens for somebody else's cheese ration. The acquaintance of useful shop assistants was carefully cultivated.

As far as fuel was concerned, Florrie and her family would go into the woods with a sack, wooding, and her father would saw up logs on his bench. Everybody who worked on the Park was allowed one horse-dray load of wood per year. Coal, of course, was on ration.

Evacuees were boarded in the village. Gwen's main memory of them was of impetigo, which many of them suffered from. One child's vest was stuck to her body with impetigo. About a dozen children came from London and filled the school to overflowing.

During the bombing, people from Leicester would come out to the village to sleep. Evelyn, who was newly married, put up several of her workmates who would come from Leicester for a break.

There was a first aid point in the Sunday school and army huts in Main Street. When the soldiers who had been billeted in them were sent to France, they were occupied by Scottish miners who were working at Desford or Bagworth. There was a searchlight in a field in Markfield Lane, and munition huts all round Charnwood Forest. Local lads would sometimes break in and play "fireworks" with them. Police tried to stop them, but nobody heard of anyone coming to any harm.

The only local bomb fell noisily but harmlessly in Cropston reservoir in September 1941, during the evening. Evelyn was living close by and was so startled she fell over.

A busload of women was transported one evening each week to South Charnwood school to prepare vegetables and make puddings for the next day's school dinners – unpaid, of course. When the Home Guard went on manoeuvres on Sunday mornings, some of the women prepared breakfast at the village school, and the Girls' Training Corps packed up their lunches. One of the girls put a poem she had written into a lunch box, chosen at random. The recipient sent a reply and a romance and eventually marriage followed.

The tin hut at the back of the British Legion club was brought into use by Dunlop as a factory for the assembly of aircraft parts.'

GERMANS AND GIs

'A prisoner of war camp for Germans was set up at the Sir John Moore School at Appleby Magna. They are remembered as being good looking, pleasant young men with a talent for making wooden toys which found their way into many homes in the village.

Dances were held to raise money for the Red Cross, and these were very grand affairs with people making the most of what little finery they had during the days of clothes rationing.

There are vivid memories of the bomb that dropped about a mile from the centre of the village, and of the GIs who were sent to deal with it – this was the first time many of the villagers had seen a black person.'

'I was sometimes scared when I was out walking. I used to think, "Suppose I see parachutes?"

One day I looked up and there was this German pilot in full view, in a swastika-marked plane. I was as terrified of him as if he was the worst person on earth. I don't suppose he was at all, but that's how he seemed to me at the time.'

THAT SINKING FEELING

'The outside air raid shelters became filled with water and had to be pumped out, and under the stairs at home was warmer. I remember with horror the sinking feeling when the air raid siren went and the relief of the all clear. I walked to school (no trains) the morning after the Victoria Park pavilion had been hit at Leicester and remember clearly the devastation.'

'Shortly after the big Coventry air raid, I was working, as a land girl, on a farm not many miles away as the crow flies. Sure enough the sirens went one night and the drone of enemy planes could be heard overhead. I had no intention of being buried under debris if a stray bomb was jettisoned so, leaving my bed and donning my dressing gown, I crept downstairs, let the sheepdog out of the stable and we crept into an old empty water tank lying on its side on the lawn. Putting my arm around Glen and holding him close, we listened to the thuds and bumps as Coventry endured another raid and we shivered and shook for two or three hours. When all was quiet we crept out just as the boss came to look for us. He'd found my bedroom door open and me departed. He really had a good laugh as Glen and I were covered in flakes of rust from the tank – and of what use an old water tank would have been if a bomb had dropped nearby I can't imagine!'

PRACTICE AND REALITY

'I did a secretarial course at the Underwood School of Commerce when I left school in 1925 and my second job was at Wadkin Limited in the general typing office. The chairman was Mr J Holland Goddard who was a member of a well known Leicester family, two of his brothers being directors of the plate powder manufacturing business. In addition to being chairman of Wadkin he was also chairman of The Imperial Typewriter Co Ltd and had outside interests including being secretary of the Rotary Club Service Committee, so when I was made his secretary my work was very varied and interesting. In wartime in the early 1940s he undertook to work out plans to get important firms going again if they had been bombed out of their buildings. A committee was formed and I did a lot of the correspondence and clerical work involved.

The government department to whom we were responsible planned an exercise for one Sunday and all those involved arranged to meet at the Grand Hotel and we were given details of where bombs had been dropped and where help was needed. We couldn't understand where Mr Goddard could be as he was the head of all our activities. Anyway, we carried out our duties as well as we could with many comings and goings as our members visited the "destroyed" premises and the premises where help had been promised if necessary. We were supposed to finish about midday and have a meal at the Grand Hotel before dispersing. Much to our surprise Mr Goddard arrived and it was only then that we learned he had been made a "casualty" and had not been allowed to come to the exercise. It was a very clever ruse by the department concerned who had realized he was the brains behind the scheme, but he was not amused, and it certainly gave the committee more headaches than if he had been in command. Mr Goddard was knighted by the Queen some time later for his services to the Machine Tool Trades Association and other wartime activities.

There were several incidents near to Oadby and we saw a bomb drop just off the Wigston Road on an allotment, but the only casualties were some hens and their house. The Leicester raids, however, affected us all. Working on Green Lane Road in Leicester I had to use two buses to get to the office, one from Oadby to the

189

Victoria Park, and one from there to Green Lane Road. One morning we managed to get on a bus in Oadby which was very late coming, and we soon learned why. We went down Ratcliffe Road from the London Road and along all sorts of small roads until we reached Welford Road. We then went down University Road back to the London Road. The reason was that a number of land mines had dropped in Stoneygate and one on the Victoria Park which demolished the pavilion and cafe. When I eventually reached my office there were no windows intact as a land mine had dropped on St Saviour's Road and the blast had damaged our premises. Fortunately there was netting on the windows which saved at least some of the glass coming into the offices, but it was dirty and cold and we worked in our coats for several days.'

'Swinford, in keeping with elsewhere, was protected by the Home Guard, who held parades every week and were "armed" with broomsticks and members' own shotguns. A local major was armed with a horse pistol that he had used in the Boer War – but he only had one round of ammunition for it. Rifles were not issued to the Home Guard until later in the war.

One day a local farmer spotted parachutists descending and alerted the Home Guard who searched Shawell Woods. No trace of the parachutists was found but it was later discovered they were part of a Polish group taking part in an exercise mounted to mark the opening of Bitteswell aerodrome, in the presence of George VI. Thus ended the invasion of Swinford!

On a more serious note, bombs did fall around the village on several occasions and at the time of the Coventry air raids German planes were spotted over Swinford.'

BOMBS AND MUNITIONS

'We had an Anderson shelter in the garden which we went down into when the sirens went, and sat in until the all clear. We had tea and sandwiches, and a bucket in the corner in case anyone took short. One night in 1941, my friend and I had gone to a cinema in Belgrave. We had only been there a little while when the siren went. I wanted to go home, but they would not let us out of the cinema. We could hear bombs dropping. At the end of the film at 10.30 pm, they emptied the cinema and we were turned out into the street. Everywhere was lit up red, with fires going. A land mine dropped on Abbey Lane, and everywhere shook. We were making for a friend's house when a string of bombs dropped, and an air raid warden was shouting to us to get down, so we lay on the ground. He came to us and said, "Oh goodness, it's two girls! Come with me!" and he took us into a lady's home. It sounded as though the bombs were dropping street by street nearer to us. In reality it was the Highfields area. The lady gave us tea and biscuits, and we were there until 4.30 am, when the all clear went and we finally got to bed.

I went into munitions and worked a capstan lathe. We worked two weeks days and two weeks nights. When the sirens went, we had to be ready to evacuate but carried on working until the red light came on. When I was expecting, I went on to examining and at six months stayed home. After my son was born, children were being evacuated from the doodlebugs, and I was brought a boy from Ipswich who I had for 18 months, then his parents fetched him home. My husband was in North Africa, and Italy. He came home in December 1945, and we then settled down to a peaceful life again.'

IT'S OVER!

'After the announcement on radio on 8th May at four o'clock that the war was over in Europe, everyone became highly excited. The village hall at Great Easton was opened for a dance in the evening which carried on through the night. The Sun Inn also remained open and all drinks were free as the landlord's only son, who had been in Stalag 18B prison camp, would soon be released. Everyone was wild with excitement.

As a wartime teenager I certainly thought there was something to celebrate.'

'As an eight year old living in Leicester, I celebrated VE Day in May 1945 dressed as a daffodil in a crepe paper dress.

Surely pre-war, these unlikely garments could be bought from a warehouse-cum-shop in Narborough Road? They came in a variety of pretty flower styles and I had already owned two or three of them before but being paper they had only a very short life and my mother, thinking no doubt they were a waste of money, refused to buy any more.

As VE Day was such a special occasion, I begged to have a new one and this was allowed. So I ended up pirouetting about on the corner of Fosse Road where convoys of US troops passed by on their way to camp on Braunstone Park. As far as I can remember that was all that happened that day. It was all a bit of an anti-climax really. There were no street parties in our neighbourhood.'

'One of my most vivid memories is of the sports and party held to celebrate VE Day at Huncote. In the obstacle race for ladies, they had to get through a large tyre suspended from a rope. Unfortunately, one rather large lady got wedged, head and shoulders hanging on one side and legs in the air on the other. It took quite some time to extricate her.'

A CHILD'S WAR

As children, we soon regarded war as part of our lives – sometimes it even seemed like fun! We did our bit towards the war effort when we could, and we accepted into our lives those less fortunate children evacuated from the cities, who came to fill our schools and our homes.

LUCKY ESCAPE

'I had a lucky escape one afternoon at Barrowden. I was going home from playing with a friend and I heard a plane coming very low overhead. It was firing its guns and I ducked down by a wall. I was very frightened.

Trenches were cut on the village greens and a large pipe was sunk into the village pond for fire hoses. If there was an alert while we were at school we were to go down to the rectory garden where they had a high wall with a row of trees, and go in between them. Thank goodness we never had to do it.

There were a few local raids. One night the Germans bombed the railway line near the tunnel. There was a cattle train on the line and the police fetched my father, who was in the Home Guard, to go and put some of the animals out of pain. I hid under the stairs. Another time a land mine dropped near the station, and many windows were broken that night.'

IT SEEMED LIKE FUN

'We had an Anderson shelter in the back garden and one particular night the Germans dropped bombs on Leicester. The noise was terrific. We had lovely neighbours who had eight children and that night their air raid shelter was flooded so they joined us in ours. There were 15 of us in total and we were packed in like sardines, but to keep us children calm my dad organised a sing-song to shut out the noise of the bombs until the all clear sounded in the early hours of the morning. It seemed like great fun to us and it wasn't until years later that we realised how serious the situation had been and how close the bombs were.'

HARDLY TOUCHED

'Fresh vegetables being in short supply, our diet was supplemented by nettle tops and tops from wild hops. There was great excitement one day when my father managed to acquire a tin of Penguin-type biscuits. These were shared out one at a time over many weeks.

On the land at harvest time my parents would get permission from a local farmer to glean wheat to feed our chickens. I also had to help with this task. Two close friends and I used to help another farmer with getting the harvest in. We also liked helping him to take his sheep down to the washbrook. At sheep shearing time we would jump up and down in the woolpack, which was suspended between two apple trees, to press down the fleeces. I also vividly remember going potato picking from school on cold, frosty, foggy mornings. Pocket money used to be earned by picking rose hips for the making of syrup. I believe we were paid sixpence a stone.

On the outskirts of Whissendine there was a searchlight battery. One day the school was invited to look around the unit. Following this the school helped by threading strips of canvas through the camouflage nets.

I belonged to the Girl Guides and towards the end of the war it was felt safe to hold a Guide camp in a spinney at Ashwell, belonging to our captain. The American air force were based at Cottesmore and rumour went round the camp that they were going to invade the camp one night. After dark we "battened down the hatches" of our bell tents and had mallets and other such weapons at the ready. One night at about ten o'clock we heard twigs cracking in the spinney so we all armed ourselves. The noises got nearer so we decided to lift the canvas and beam the torch in that direction – cows from the adjoining field had broken into the spinney!

Another night we had a tremendous storm that flooded our tent. Our captain had an empty chicken hut in the field so she put us in it to sleep. In the middle of the night one of us wanted to spend a penny, and that was when we found the door would not open from the inside. Several more were now desperate to go, so we had to get a small Guide to struggle through the loop-hole to open the door. The next day the tent pole went through the top of the tent. Quite a memorable camp.'

NATIONAL SAVINGS

'During the war there was a constant drive for National Savings at my primary school. We had special weeks when our savings went to help different parts of the armed services – War Weapons Week for the Army, Wings for Victory Week for the Air Force and Warships Week for the Navy.

During Warships Week a giant model of a warship toured the villages hoping to increase war efforts. When it reached Bitteswell my headmistress thrust a printed poem into my hand and, clambering on to the ship's deck, I recited this:

> "From over the ocean beyond our ken,
> Where the ghostly frigates stir again,
> Where Nelson sailed and Howe and Drake,
> And all who passed for freedom's sake.
> I heard the call of our younger dead,
> Shipbuilders ho! full speed ahead,
> *Rawalpindi* is sunk and *Hood*.
> Go make those losses doubly good.
> By the guns that blaze on Jervis Bay,
> Give us the ships we need today:
> Build them, we need them, down the slips,
> The fighting ships, the cargo ships,
> A thousand ships, and a thousand more,
> We shall need them all to win this war."'

LIFE AT KIRKBY MALLORY

'Early on in the war we welcomed child evacuees from the city of Birmingham. They were accompanied by a Mrs Lloyd and her helpers. Some carried little suitcases and others had their clothes tied in bundles. All had their gas masks and identity bracelets and a favourite toy. The village parents who could accommodate children were issued with mattresses, sheets and blankets and helped financially. We went home with a brother and sister, Kenned six years old and June five years old. My sister and I slept in one double bed and Ken and June in the other in the rear bedroom.

Their mother visited them as often as she could and brought with her extra clothes and goodies for them. She left Birmingham in the early morning by train, then travelled by bus to Earl Shilton, and walked the final two miles. She spent a few hours with them, enjoyed a meal and then started the long trek back.

We all attended the village school which had two classrooms and was heated by coal fires. We sat at wooden desks and wrote with pen and ink. Cooked dinners were provided daily, always ending with raw carrot and turnip sticks. Once a week our teacher took us for a nature walk. Some of the evacuees hadn't seen cows and sheep grazing before. She also accompanied us to see the meet of the Atherstone Hunt regularly on the village green.

Every May Day we had a parade through the village starting at the school. The May Queen was at the head of the procession riding in an old cane bathchair which was decorated with bluebells, hawthorn blossom and beech leaves. She and her attendants wore long white dresses. The following children walked in pairs holding decorated hoops.

In the autumn we picked blackberries and rosehips during school hours and the children of farmers had time off to help with the harvesting. We also picked potatoes and gleaned corn.

One job we enjoyed was to walk to a farm at Peckleton and come home with baskets full of whiteheart cherries, all of us adorned with fruit hanging from our ears and singing at the tops of our voices.

Clothing for school was varied. Most girls wore gymslips, blouses and jumpers and the boys wore short grey trousers, shirts and jumpers. Most of the clothes were handed down from family to family. Anything thrown away was used to make peg rugs. Every Tuesday the WRVS ladies met after school was out to distribute orange juice, cod liver oil, pork pies and small Swiss rolls to the villagers.

My father was an ARP warden and went nightly with his torch, whistle and rattle to check for any illegal lights showing from houses. If enemy aircraft were flying we slept under the dining-room table, which we thought was fun. No air raid shelters were provided in our village.

Every evening after tea (which was usually bread and jam and cake) all four of us shared the newspaper round in Kirkby and my mother cycled to Peckleton. All the large fields surrounding the village had tall poles erected in them to deter enemy aircraft from landing and every morning before school we looked for strips of tin foil which had been dropped by aircraft. We used this foil in many ways including making decorations for our Christmas tree (which was usually holly).

Kirkby Hall was taken over by the army for several years. Tanks and other army vehicles were always on the move and soldiers marched along the lanes on exercises. Later on we saw German prisoners of war marching through to their place of work. They were billeted at Peckleton.

We enjoyed delivering papers nightly to the soldiers in their rooms throughout the Hall. The *Leicester Mercury* and *Evening Mail* were priced at a penny halfpenny each and usually we were given sixpence each for them. We also had lots of sweets and chocolate given to us from the stores.'

WARTIME SCHOOLDAYS

'At the outbreak of war, Holygirt School for Girls was evacuated to Billesdon. The headmistress, Miss Stafford, was concerned that Nottingham might be a target for German bombers so offered parents the chance to send their daughters as boarders to the safety of the Leicestershire countryside. And so it was that a coachload of girls and teachers arrived in the village to take up residence in the manor house and to occupy various other buildings and parts of houses as dormitories or classrooms.

I joined the school later and spent several happy years there, returning to Nottingham with the school on the cessation of hostilities. These are some of my memories of those times.

Although some girls slept elsewhere, the manor house was the focus of our lives. It was here in the dining-room each day began with breakfast, followed by morning assembly. Then off to lessons for all, carting gas masks with us wherever we went. The youngest children, some as young as three years old, stayed in the morning room looked after by the headmistress's sister, Miss Ethel, whose duties also included those of housekeeper and matron. All the teachers taught more than one subject and in today's terms our curriculum was restricted, lacking facilities for most sciences and physical activities. However, we were taught English, maths, geography, history, scripture, biology, needlework and French by the four teachers and a local resident who had been a professional singer taught us music and dance. Sometimes we would go to the village school playground for games.

There was very little by way of domestic help so we all kept our dormitories and bathrooms clean and took it in turns to wash up and tidy other rooms. Some of us would help to look after the "little ones" who included a few boys of up to six years old.

Food was short as everywhere at that time. We always felt hungry but my mother always said that I was fed better at school than she could have done at home. Our diet included nettles and dandelions as well as the vegetables and fruit grown in the manor garden by Miss Bennett assisted by a part-time gardener. I well remember the excitement when the first spring onions appeared on the tea table accompanied by bread and margarine. Sometimes we had jam, at others we had a bun each, but never both at the same meal!

The coming of the postman was eagerly awaited each morning. Would anyone get a parcel from home? Would there be any food in it? Would there be enough for a Midnight Feast? Most of us received a weekly parcel and many mothers must have used a great deal of ingenuity to ensure that there was always something edible in them . . . many adults in the family went without their sweet rations for the duration of the war and helped to provide ingredients for cakes and biscuits for us.

At the weekends, there were long walks in crocodile under the watchful eye of Miss Bennett. She ensured that the older girls did not fraternize with the local boys, or with the young Italians from the prisoner of war camp. In spring we collected sheep's wool from fences to wash and dye and make into powderpuffs for mothers and aunts. Later in the year we scoured the hedgerows for wild fruits to eat and nuts to roast in the evenings.

On Sunday mornings we went to church and many of the girls were confirmed there. In the afternoon, we had to write our letters home and do such things as darning socks or knitting shapeless articles destined for "our boys overseas". These were sent to France by Mademoiselle who had escaped to England just before Dunkirk and taught us French and needlework.

About once a month, we would entertain the teachers and younger children with plays and concerts in Miss Stafford's study. Much of our spare time was taken with rehearsing little plays, often based on fairy stories, Enid Blyton books or stories from *Girls' Crystal*. Piano and recorder solos and duets and recitations also required much practice. Other activities in our leisure time included reading, playing board games, raffia work and embroidery, twisting brightly coloured wire to make bracelets and frightening each other with ghost stories. Or we played practical jokes on one of the teachers; making an apple-pie bed, sewing up the sleeves and hem of her nightdress and putting a hedgehog in her bed or Andrews' Liver Salts in her chamberpot! Outdoors we played tic, rounders, hopscotch, whip and top or with hoops. I cannot remember being bored in spite of the absence of television or radio.

War touched us occasionally. One father was lost at sea and another badly wounded in action. The air raid warning would send us scuttling for the cellar where we spent the time waiting for the all clear telling stories or munching apples which were stored there. And we saw men and women in uniform on leave in the village or observers going to and from the Observer Corps post, but the realities of war were kept from us.'

THE EVACUEES ARRIVED

'I was eight when the war started and I can recall going to our local market when the evacuees were billeted out to people who could accommodate them. They all had gas masks, a few belongings and luggage labels with their names on. They had been in Market Harborough a while before Mum was asked to take a young girl in until another home could be found for her. Later we were to take another lady, Annie, who eventually asked if we could put up her sister in law and young nephew. Mum agreed to take them and we children slept on mattresses on the floor, which we thought was great fun. When they went back to London, because things seemed to have quietened down, the Germans started sending over the V2 rockets and we never heard what became of our evacuees.'

ESCAPING THE BOMBS

'In the summer of 1944 I set out with my mother from our home in Surrey to escape for a while from the "doodlebugs", the V1 pilotless planes, to stay in Billesdon. Even as we sat in our steam train on London's Marylebone station bound for Leicester Central, the siren sounded and we feared for my father who had come to wave us off.

Having found the correct bus in Leicester we had to break our journey at Thurnby to have our ration books specially stamped.

When eventually we arrived at our destination we were directed across the village square to one of the village stores whose kind occupant had agreed to take us in, having been approached by a colleague of my father whose family were also taking a respite. We were warmly welcomed and shown to her spare bedroom, where stood a massive brass bedstead for Mum and me to share. For a wash and brush-up we were given some cold greenish water – drawn from the pump in the yard and placed in the pretty china bowl on the washstand. After my urgent request to use the toilet, Mum explained to me that there was an outside chemical toilet across the yard! This I could not believe as I had never come across one before. Somehow the urgency had disappeared. However, we became used to this and even became accustomed to using newspaper when there was nothing else! As time went by and I was befriended by our kindly lady's granddaughter and her friends, I learnt to hold my nose, once a week, with the best of them, when the "stink cart" did the rounds to empty the buckets!

To round off our long day, we joined the younger members of the family up in the fields to do some stooking. This involved picking up a sheath of corn, which was tied with string in the centre by the harvester, and leaning it with four or five others on its end to form a stook, where they stood to dry. After being assured by everyone that yes, it was safe to remove our underwear before going to bed, we retired for the night. (Down in Surrey we had kept some underwear on at all times in case we had to exit quickly at night from under our Morrison shelter.)

These were very happy days, and I have very clear memories of the living rooms behind the shop. The rag rug, home-made of course, and the black range, with the kettle always in place, surrounded by a large brass fireguard, with a shiny patch in the centre where our friend always perched to chat to us between serving customers coming into the shop. Although electricity was installed the old gas lamps were still in place. All water had to be boiled, and enough cooled each day for cleaning teeth and drinking. Several years later when the "town" water was piped to the premises, there was great excitement, likewise when the first WC was brought and installed in the house of my friend. What quarrelling there was as to who would be the first to use it!

The weeks went quickly by and my father joined us for his annual holiday. He arrived looking quite pale and strained but soon relaxed and enjoyed the rest. The time came for my friend to return to her school, this was in a temporary home in the manor house of the village, as they had been evacuated out of Nottingham. I was allowed to join too, and thoroughly enjoyed the experience.

We seemed to be able to roam quite freely around the village and fields without any fears; about the only place that was "out of bounds" was the prisoner of war camp on the edge of the village. It was quite common to see the POWs around the village, mostly Italian.

One of the many good things that came out of our evacuation was my interest in church bellringing. Of the family where we were staying my friend, her father and her uncle were keen ringers. When I went home I asked at our local church if they would teach me to ring. This of course had to wait until the late 1940s as no bellringing was allowed during the war – only as a warning had we been invaded.'

'I am a Londoner by birth and my early memories of Leicestershire are confined to a period of about nine months when I was evacuated to Wigston in 1944/5. I was ten years old.

My memories are of things which were different from what I was used to at home and include the toilet being out the back – what on earth did one do in the middle of the night? The house didn't have a bathroom but a galvanised bath was used in front of the fire once a week. I had a special privilege, being the only girl in a family of boys, in that I was allowed to go to their aunt's house a few doors away to have a bath in her proper bathroom.

I don't remember anyone going to work but I suppose the men, and there were plenty of them around in spite of the war, must have done. I do remember my mother's friend's husband working in his orchard and myself and other children being paid twopence per skip to pick plums.

I barely remember shopping but I do remember Wigston had a post office where I went every week to cash the two shilling postal order my mother sent. There was a park on Aylestone Lane and we children spent a lot of time there and kite-making and flying was one of our pastimes – we'd not been allowed to fly kites in London during the war so this was all new to me.

My school was Long Street. I was put in the B stream for about a day but then moved into the A stream. The evacuees sat together at the back and did more advanced work than the local children as we had to take the eleven-plus exams for our home areas. My mother brought books from my old school to my new teacher for me to work on. I know the new teacher was surprised I could already do long division.

We spent a good part of Sunday, it seemed, plus some evenings at the local Congregational church and it was here I first began to understand the gospel message, although I had always been to Sunday school at home. We also went to the local cinema quite often, not only the children's Saturday clubs but also midweek evenings. The midweek films seemed to be all-singing, all-dancing, all-glamour, as far as I can recall and often starred Rita Hayworth or Betty Grable.

One evening I had been playing in the snow and came home with raging earache. Only my foster father was at home and he made me put my feet in a bowl of hot water. I kept telling him it was my ear that hurt, not my feet, and could never understand how my earache was relieved!

For breakfast we had white bread spread with margarine and sprinkled with sugar. On Sundays we had a cooked breakfast and a laxative pill.'

DOING OUR BIT

For all of us, life had to go on and we grew adept at 'make do and mend' and making the most of our rations.

I WAS IN THE WI

'During the war I was in the WI at Kirby Muxloe. I had two children at school. We did a lot of jam making and bottling and canning so we took turns at meeting the children from school while the rest continued bottling etc. I also worked for the Infirmary in Leicester. We used to mend sheets – turned the side to the middle (by machine) – this was the Linen League section of the WI. We also put tapes on gowns, made layettes for babies, and knitted, too. I visited a nephew and saw him kitted out in beautiful things but I was shocked to see those things we made were washed and dried on radiators – they went as hard as buckram! We also made slippers for the hospital. I went round with a friend collecting felt hats in a pram. We had a marvellous collection of felt hats. We had to cut slippers out of them – not easy.

I also collected money for the Red Cross. They took meals to the elderly round the village. I collected all up Gullet Lane and in the rest of the village. I still have a letter from the Duke of Gloucester thanking me for all the collecting, and a certificate. There was a lot of money; I started by taking just one afternoon but in the end it took three days because the others went to do ambulance work or went in to the hospital.

We had different WI demonstrations in the afternoon – in the Co-op or in the schools, anywhere we could meet. Ladies used to come and tell us how to make do with raw potato instead of lard in a pie crust, how to make starch, and toffee with no sugar or condensed milk. I made some toffee and took it to the next WI meeting: I gave everyone a piece. We stood up to sing *Jerusalem* and everybody's teeth had stuck together. The gentleman who'd come to teach us how to use gas masks said it was the quietest WI meeting he'd ever been to! We were also taught how to make starch with a candle. I made mine in a pudding basin and left it on top of the mangle (a table-top mangle) while I went to do the collecting. My husband thought it was blancmange and didn't think much of it.'

FAVOURITE CUSTOMERS

'Our shopping was done on market days at Melton Mowbray. When we used the ration books at the grocer's, one assistant would hide goodies under the counter for her favourite customers. She might not like the next person in the queue and would say no to them!'

WE TRIED TO LOOK SMART

'The war years were of necessity very austere but we always made a good effort to look smart. Stockings were few and not of good quality so we painted our legs and took great care doing so. Shoes were a problem and we tried to keep a best pair even if otherwise we were shabby at times. I had extra coupons for stockings because I was a nurse, but only black ones. I used lisle stockings on duty in the hope they would last longer. Then there were the things we did with available army blankets – I had a very nice suit and a warm dressing gown. Parachute silk became French knickers and "camies", now called teddies. We all made most of our own clothes if possible.'

'Make do and mend was the order of the day. Any coat my family had no more use for was never discarded. I unpicked all the seams and washed all the pieces and made up a smart double breasted coat with cap to match for my three year old son. I also made a coat for myself out of an army blanket and put on a velvet collar so it wasn't rough round the neck. An extra bonus was obtaining a parachute!'

'They used to steal blankets from the depot (Belgrave area). Everyone around our way had these grey coats made out of RAF blankets.'

WE DIDN'T GO HUNGRY

'My mother's profession was a cook and my father was a baker so we. didn't go hungry. Mother used to concoct some lovely dishes out of our meagre rations, especially on meatless days. She had a large yellow mixing bowl and into this went vast quantities of mashed potatoes, to which she added one chopped hard boiled egg (one person's egg ration for a week) and chopped spring onions. If it was a day when meat was available, she left the egg out and added four ounces of corned beef. She then made rissoles, rolled them in breadcrumbs and fried them. They were absolutely delicious and until the day she died, when she was 85 years old, we used to request them when she invited us to lunch.

On Mondays, the bone from the small Sunday joint was put in a saucepan with onions and carrots and simmered all morning whilst Mother was out at work and when I arrived home at lunch time it was my job to add the sliced potatoes. It was then served up after half an hour when Mother came home and we all had steaming soup bowls full of "Irish stew". Mother, being Welsh, had a Welsh name for it; I can say it but I can't spell it! HP sauce added a certain piquancy to the stew.

The only meal I could not bear was lentil soup. Mother used to try and coax me to eat it because she said it was full of much-needed nourishment, but to this day I can't touch it.

Dad being a baker, he used to deliver bread and he had two bread rounds in the rural areas. When I was on school holidays, he used to collect me mid-morning and take me with him for the day. I used to think the villages had wonderful names, one such being Barton in the Beans. Most of the customers became like old friends and I loved delivering to the outlying farms.

One day Dad bought a raffle ticket for sixpence from a farmer and won a pig. As city dwellers it was impossible for us to keep

ON HIS MAJESTY'S SERVICE

Your
Ration Book

OFFICIAL PAID

Issued to safeguard your food supply

HOLDER'S NAME AND REGISTERED ADDRESS

COMPARE WITH YOUR IDENTITY CARD AND REPORT ANY DIFFERENCE TO YOUR FOOD OFFICE DO NOT ALTER

Surname *HARRIS*

Other Names *JUNE*

Address *Mill Bank*

Whissendine - Oakham

NAT. REG. NO.	*TUBA*	*138*	*3*

Date of Issue **7 JUL 1941**   Serial Number of Book

If found, please return to   NQ 109728

OAKHAM RURAL DISTRICT

FOOD OFFICE.   R.B.1 [General] 4

R.B.10 ISSUED. N.M.91.

Many foodstuffs quickly became scarce and ration books part of our lives for several years after the war had ended.

it and because money was tight Dad couldn't afford to pay for it to be looked after, so he struck a deal with the farmer that if he looked after the pig he could have half when it was slaughtered. Dad had to acquire a licence to have the pig killed and also had to given up his bacon ration for a year. The pig was slaughtered and Dad arrived home with half of it. Mother laid down clean sheets in the dining-room and she and I set to work with saltpetre to cure the side of bacon and a whole ham. The ham was hung up in the kitchen and the side of bacon was hung from a picture rail in the dining-room (covered in a clean white sheet of course). Mother rendered down all the fat and we had a bucket of pure white lard, an absolute treasure trove in those days. She made brawn out of the head and we ate all the offal.

Dad knew where all the most likely fields were for mushrooms and he would suddenly stop the van and out we would get with the bread basket and go picking mushrooms. When we arrived home, Mother would make a mushroom suet pudding. The field mushrooms were big, black and juicy and when the pudding was cooked all the juices soaked into the suet.

Everybody in those days kept fowls in the back garden and usually a cockerel to fatten up for Christmas. It fell to Dad's lot to be the official "cockerel killer". How it came about I don't know, because he was the gentlest of men. At Christmas time neighbours used to call at the house and ask if Dad could go round and kill the bird. He then brought it home and Mother and I plucked and dressed it. Mother did all the hard parts, such as the tail feathers and wings but, although I wasn't very old, I was expected to do the rest.

Mother was also a confectioner and made wedding cakes for all the brides in the district. Ingredients used to have to be saved up for months and by the time Mother received them the icing sugar, which came in a blue bag, would be solid. Again, I was expected to do the labouring. I used to peel the bag away from the sugar and it looked just like a sculpture. I hammered at it with the rolling pin and used to roll and sieve for hours. All the fruit had to be washed in those days and again I had to do my bit and put it to dry on a large baker's tray and keep turning the fruit, as it would sink to the bottom of the cake if it was not completely dry.

Ground almonds were unobtainable for the marzipan and Mother hated soya flour, which most cooks used as an alternative, so she concocted marzipan out of semolina, heavily laced with almond essence. It was so good you could hardly tell it from the real thing.

Rationing ended in 1954, the year I was married, so food was rationed to some degree for all my early youth but in spite of that everyone I knew grew up healthily and although money was scarce our lives were simple and full of fun and I look back on my childhood with love and affection.'

THE WOMEN'S LAND ARMY

When the time came for young women to be called up, they had a choice between the services, factory work and the Land Army. Many, experienced country girls and those who were 'green as grass', chose the latter, and despite the hard work and often primitive conditions very few regretted their choice.

I JOINED THE LAND ARMY

'The time was October 1939, the place Sutton Bonington Agricultural College. I was underneath an Ayrshire cow vainly trying to extract a modicum of liquid.

This seemed to be the scenario for my month at the college, training to be a land girl. Over a hundred girls from very different backgrounds assembled there, requisitioned by the "Min of Ag and Fish", for a month's training, after which time we were allocated to various farms as "competent". We, who were as green as grass at the outset, were not much better at the finish.

I opted for the dairy course and that is how I found myself seated precariously on the obligatory three-legged stool. But the number of would-be dairymaids outstripped the number of available cows so we had to double up, one milker on each side, each clutching a teat left and right!

I never did achieve a frothy pail of milk. That came later when I had to hand-milk ten cows before breakfast.'

PLENTY OF HARD WORK

'During the 1940s I joined the Land Army and worked at Carlton Curlieu. We had electricity but no piped water. There was a soft

Land girls Sylvia, Jessie and Sybil, taking a break from a hard days work.

water pump outside the cottage but drinking water had to be fetched about 100 yards from the farm opposite.

We did hand-milking and some butter churning. I worked with horses but War Agricultural Committee employees did tractor work. When picking potatoes we had schoolchildren from Leicester bussed out daily to help. Corn was cut with binders and stooked, then loaded up on wagons pulled by horse and then stacked. We were not allowed to use the elevator because too much corn was knocked out, so it was thrown on to the stack by hand. On occasions we worked till dark on double summer time.

Haymaking was a little more mechanised but we did most of it the hard way, cocking and cobbing, then sweeping to the stack with a horse, usually hand-pitching again. On one occasion in an inclement summer we actually turned a whole field of hay by hand using wooden rakes – really primitive. The 300 acre farm had four men and myself, then one was called up and he was replaced by two Italian POWs. We had to take horses to the blacksmith in Kibworth to be shod, a walk of about two miles. I later moved to Sapcote with more milking, machine this time, and definitely more mechanisation though still plenty of hand work.'

I WOULDN'T HAVE CHANGED IT FOR ANYTHING

'Being born and bred in the country, it was a foregone conclusion that my wartime job would be in the Women's Land Army. I couldn't have imagined doing anything else.

I was lucky to be able to try my hand at several different land jobs, from gardening and tomato growing to general farm work, and even a short while in a timber yard. This involved moving tree trunks around with an antiquated hand-turned crane, and sawing logs with a huge circular saw, for children to fetch on Saturday mornings at sixpence a pram-load. Luckily all my fingers were still intact when I left.

My fondest memories are of the farm where I worked. The cowshed was a lovely warm spot at seven o'clock on a cold winter's morning, and very welcome after riding a mile from the Land Army hostel. Muck spreading with a fork was very healthy exercise, though cutting the tops off sugar beet was very cold on the hands. Potato picking meant going as fast as possible, to have time to sit on my upturned bucket before the tractor got the next row up.

In summer we spent a great deal of time scything down thistles, then haymaking and harvesting corn. We set the sheaves upright in stooks to dry (and got stookers' rash all down our arms), then pitched the stooks onto the cart to be taken to the barn for threshing.

On threshing day, when the huge steam engine rolled into the yard pulling the threshing box behind, I had to do one of the jobs I detested. That was raking the chaff, and carrying it away – a filthy, dusty job.

We were a lot of weary girls when we wended our way back to the hostel after a hard day's work. But I spent six and a half years in the Women's Land Army, and I wouldn't have changed it for anything.'

WE CARRIED ON

'I lived in Blaby and was 17. In December 1944 I was working in the NAAFI offices. In the New Year of 1945 I went to sign on for the Land Army and about March I was sent to Hathern to do two weeks of training.

On Easter Monday 1945 I was sent to a farm at Twyford. There was two inches of snow on the ground. I didn't live at the farm at first, I lived in a small cottage with another Land Army girl, but the old couple there couldn't cope with us so after six months the other girl was sent somewhere else and I went to live at the farm.

It wasn't very homely. I was only allowed in the kitchen and my bedroom. I was allowed to eat my meals with the family but that was all. In the evening I had to sit in the kitchen alone and wasn't allowed to make the fire up. Once it had gone out that was it. In the end I took a book and went to the pub that was close by, just so I could have a warm and meet some people to talk to.

Some mornings while at work a lorry would drop two German POWs off and pick them up again in the evening. I was told not to talk to them. One was quite young and tried to communicate but the other was older and used to tell him off if he tried to talk to me.

When VE Day came I was allowed home for the day to celebrate, but when VJ Day came I couldn't go home because it was harvest time and we were busy.

The Land Army was still needed even though the war was over and after leaving Twyford I went to the market garden at Blaby, so I lived at home which was much better. They grew tomatoes and I used to stand on Leicester market. I met my husband while working there, he had just been demobbed from the Navy. I had to leave there after the season because there was nothing for me to do. After that I went to work for Peppers at Oadby. I learnt to drive and I used to deliver milk in a lorry. I wanted to leave there because I had to bike from Blaby every morning and back every night, so I was sent to a hostel for Land Army girls at Stathern. I finally left the Land Army in November 1947.'

ENTERTAINING THE TROOPS

'I was 17 when war was declared, and working in a large store (Grice's) in High Street, Leicester. It was strange getting used to everywhere blacked out and young men going into the forces. We had to do incendiary duty on the roof of the store, with our gas masks and buckets of sand. We had a card which was a pass to show to those on duty to allow us through and up onto the roof of the store. At 17 years old, it was exciting but scary.

My friend and I knew we would have to join the forces or work in the factories or munitions. We didn't think much of that and wanted to stay together so we joined the Land Army in April 1942. We were sent to a farm in Nailstone near Ibstock. We were thrown in at the deep end, having to learn to drive a tractor, work with horses (haymaking etc), milking cows by hand, after fetching them in at 5.30 am on cold, foggy mornings. It was hard work. I even milked cows in my sleep!

The summer that year was hot, and we were very sunburnt working in the fields, and blistered handling sheaves.

We left Nailstone in November and were sent to Cotesbach near Lutterworth. We worked for the War Agricultural Committee, so didn't stay in the hostel. We were given a very basic bicycle which I had until the end of the war. That cycle was our only means of getting to work, which could have been anything from twelve miles to 50 miles a day. Of course there wasn't the traffic on the roads then, but lots of troop movement.

I auditioned with Ted Foster to sing with other artistes in a concert in Rugby called *Ship Ahoy!* I sang with a dance band at the Palais in Leicester when it was broadcast over the radio and I was singing quite often at the aerodromes around Lutterworth with the dance band. I had a free drink and food for this, which was good in the days of rationing.

I did a double act with Alec Layton, who used to be in ENSA.

A guard of honour formed by her land girls friends for Lily. Everyone pulled together to make wartime weddings as enjoyable as possible. (Huncote member Vera Primmer is 2nd from left)

He taught me to tap dance. We used to rehearse in the pub at Bitteswell, The Royal Oak. Then we travelled round the clubs at weekends when work was finished. My friend used to go with us as a chaperone. In July 1943, I was in a concert entertaining the troops in Rugby Park. There was an audience of over a thousand of the forces and I was paid ten shillings for the performance.

We worked hard in the daytime. After hoeing, ploughing, haymaking etc in all weathers, very often soaked to the skin, we then had to cycle back to the digs, where our landlady had a meal waiting. It was amazing how she conjured up a meal with dried egg, ration meat from the butcher, potatoes and basic rations. We would have extra rations for harvest-time in the field. The farmer gave us eggs, potatoes and vegetables. We had bread and jam sandwiches for our lunch. The jam soaked into the bread (I've never enjoyed jam sandwiches since). We also had a lemonade screw-top bottle full of cold tea which we put in the radiator of the tractor to heat up. This was all we had until our evening meal when we finished.

211

I was given the job of taking the fuel to all those working in the fields on various farms all around Lutterworth. I drove my Fordson tractor with a trailer behind holding the fuel. I also had to move caterpillar tractors and other tractors on trailers and take them to the next farm where we would be working. I was known as "The Singing Land-Girl".

I remember the activity and gathering of American troops and tanks etc in the staging-camp at Lutterworth in 1944. We knew something big was going to happen, but no one knew what it would be. The town was alive with troops. We talked to them and danced with them at the dances. They gave us candy-gum, which we thought was wonderful, as we were on rations. I wondered many times if those boys we met had ever made it back home.

Friday night was bath night. We had to get the old tin bath in and put it in front of the fire in the living-room. It was filled with hot water from the copper in the kitchen. We both had to bath in it, then it was emptied by buckets carried outside again. No bubble bath; cheap soap. The Land Army girls were a happy, hard-working crowd. We were doing men's work but we enjoyed it.

I enjoyed working with tractors more than with horses. They had a mind of their own! I remember sitting on the cold iron seat of the raking implement with the cart horse pulling it. When I wanted him to go, he would stand still, then suddenly he took off, galloping like mad across the field with me hanging on the reins for dear life, until eventually he tried to get through the gate and got stuck. I tried to move him, still trembling, but had to get the farmer to help me. I was made to get back on the seat and finish the rest of the field, trying to look as if I knew what I was doing.

I loved it when we were threshing, although keeping up on the drum wasn't my idea of fun. I do not like heights, and the sheaves were thrown up on pitchforks by those below and there used to be quite a few rats and mice in them, so we kept our dungarees tucked tightly in our wellington boots.

The Land Army was a happy time of my life. Although there was a war on, everyone was cheerful, helping one another. There seemed to be more camaraderie than there is today. We had very little money: 25 shillings a week, out of which we paid board.

I remember one night hearing a clattering in the streets. The men had tied tin cans together in strings and were dragging them down the road, to wake everyone up and get them outside. It was the end of the war! Everyone ran out and joined in the celebration.'

GROWING UP THROUGH THE WAR

**For those who were children when the war began and young
adults when it ended five years later, the war seemed to occupy
a particularly large part of their lives.**

FROM DEPRESSION TO POST WAR

'During the 1930s my mother and father moved from Birmingham
because my father was unemployed. He got a job at the Midland
Red bus depot and a council house at Braunstone went with the job
at ten shillings a week.

About a year after moving my five year old brother died of
whooping cough and my baby sister died of the vaccination. Years
later, in 1944, my mother had to go to court because she wouldn't
have the new baby brother vaccinated. In 1944 it was against the law
not to have your babies vaccinated but the judge ruled that this was
an exception.

I had rickets so I spent hours at the infirmary having sunray
treatment. We paid the doctor sixpence a week but seemed to get
our money's worth.

When I was at junior school (Braunstone Hall in the middle of the
park) the war was on and overnight the park seemed to be covered
with Nissen huts and the US army moved in. They made a big impact
on the area, with lots of sweets and nylons.

Every week we seemed to have new teachers as one by one they
were called up for duty. We all had to dig for victory, growing most
of our own fruit and vegetables which we bottled in Kilner jars. We
had hens in the back garden and we sold some of the eggs to pay
for the fowl food, and some of the eggs were put into waterglass to
preserve them.

We loved "playing out" after school and spent hours playing at
snobs (marbles), skipping, ball games, hide and seek and "poddy
1-2-3". I don't know why, but there were seasons for games. We
only played marbles in the spring and hide and seek in the winter.

We would sit on the step eating rhubarb and sugar or go to the corner shop and buy a pennyworth of cocoa and sugar, then go home to toast and dripping for tea.

We were all bussed to local farms to go potato picking. We thought it was better than lessons and if we worked hard all week we could earn 30 shillings.

When father was allowed home on leave he would take us to see the prisoner of war camp on Shady Lane. The Italians were there first and it was a really dirty, scruffy place but when the Germans were imprisoned there they kept the place immaculate.

I hated being woken up in the middle of the night to go down to the air raid shelter. It was an Anderson which was a concrete square hole with corrugated iron on top with bunk beds inside and it was always wet, cold and dark.

Father was on leave when Coventry was bombed. He let us stand on the doorstep and watch the planes go overhead and the sky full of bright orange fire – a sight I'll never forget. You could see it easily from 25 miles away.

In 1947 Leicester Education Committee wanted to start to mix boys and girls in senior schools – something that had never been done before. So they sent about 200 of us, half boys, half girls, to Shooting Butts, Rugeley, Staffordshire. We were from all walks of life. They just wanted to see if twelve and 13 year olds would get on with their lessons or would we be giggly etc. We stayed there for a term and treated each other as brothers and sisters. I loved every minute there. I remember seeing the Royal Wedding on the school TV.

It was always my job to queue for bread etc. Rationing didn't seem to bother us because you had to have money to go with the coupons. There weren't any street lights and we all went to the cinema to keep warm when the coal ration ran out.

When I was 14 I was old enough to go to night school. I learned to type on Mondays and Wednesdays and to write shorthand on Tuesdays and Thursdays. Friday night was always speedway night when we would go to Blackbird Road Stadium in our red and yellow scarves and support the Hunters. It was the place where the boys met the girls.

We also had really good youth clubs, such as The League of Youth belonging to the Labour Party, the Conservative Club etc. There was a Youth Parliament in town where we debated all sorts of things. We got the council to allow us to play games on the park on Sunday – something that was against the law before.

The Germans from Shady Lane were made to dig up our air raid shelters after the war. They seemed very nice; they made toys for the local children out of bits of wood. The English soldier with the gun guarding them was really mad and couldn't understand why the mums were giving the Germans cups of tea.'

SCHOOLWORK AND FARMING

'The day before war broke out we were on holiday at Sutton on Sea; we came home and I remember listening to Mr Chamberlain on the wireless telling us in a very sad and grave voice how he had not been able to make Hitler stop his troops advancing into Poland; and if they were not withdrawn by 11 am on 2nd September 1939 then war would be declared between Great Britain and Germany. My birthday was on 7th September and this would make me 15 years old.

We had been issued with gas masks earlier in the year which we were told to carry with us everywhere; we expected German aeroplanes to start dropping bombs straight away. Those who could dug shelters in their back gardens, and we had to put black material up at the windows. As we had been away we found the shops had sold out, but our dining-room table had a large black chenille cloth, which was tacked to the kitchen window, and luckily the sitting-room did have black velvet curtains, but for several nights we had to get undressed downstairs and feel our way to bed. Any light showing would soon have the air raid warden shouting, "Put that light out!" Street lights were painted black and special headlamps for cars and bicycles were installed.

The Collegiate School did not have shelters so while they were being built we used the Wyggeston Girls School from 8 am to 1 pm and they went in from 1 pm to 6 pm. The senior girls at the beginning were all helping to dig out the shelters, during break. In due course we moved back to Collegiate School, where volunteers were asked to fire watch. This entailed six pupils and one teacher, stopping at night. If there was an air raid we were expected to put out any fires. We were instructed how to use the stirrup pump; working in pairs one could keep the bucket full of water and direct the water on to the fire, while the other pumped madly. We took sleeping bags and slept on the floor in the headmistress's study; the teacher, sleeping in the staff room, must have wondered what we were talking and giggling about so late at night. We were never called out, although Highfield Street, which was very close to Prebend Street, did get bombed.

We were also asked to help plant potatoes on the city farm at the top of Mowmacre Hill, around the sewage works. My friend and I used to cycle all the way through Leicester by the clock tower, do a day's work and then cycle back again. The potatoes had been chitted, but my row would be a bit small because I pushed off all the chits. The next job we had was to pull up the rhubarb, then to hoe the potatoes; it was such a long field we only got three rows completed in a day, even with the foreman working with us, to set the pace.

We were paid so much an hour according to our age and had to collect our wages on a Saturday morning from the town hall in the centre of Leicester. This must have been during the Easter holidays, because after we had taken our exams in late June, a Mr Burrows from Cropston whose daughter was at Collegiate School asked for people to pick peas. Once again my friend and I biked to and fro, picking between eight and ten hessian sacks a day, which were weighed and we were paid one shilling and fourpence. I was very disgusted to see some of the old hands putting stones into the sacks as well as the peas.

Mr Burrows asked me to continue working for him and the next job was to help stack the hay on the wagons. I stood on the wagon whilst the men put the hay in the right place with their long-handled hay forks. All I had to do was move the hay into the middle of the cart and hang on when the horse moved to the next cob of hay. It was a bit frightening sliding down when the hay wagon was loaded. When the hay was all in the next job was to gather up and burn the hedge trimmings. That was a very hot job and I was pleased when some soldiers who had been detailed to farmwork joined me. They had actually come to help with the stooking. That means standing light sheaves of corn up to finish off ripening, before they were loaded on to the horse-drawn wagons and transported to the edge of the field or the rick yard and built into ricks where they would be threshed at a later date.

I carried on working on that farm until the end of the summer and will never forget the wonderful harvest supper held in the farm kitchen that I was invited to, also the egg and bacon and fried potatoes that we had for breakfast, before going to school the next morning. During this time I was studying for my school certificate. I was also confirmed and went every Sunday to Knighton church or St Guthlaxton church with my Granny. I joined the St Mary's youth group and we used to put on reviews or plays to try and raise money for the church.

One evening when I was at the Knighton cinema, the siren went, the cinema was closed, and I started to walk home. I will never forget hearing the whine of the bombs coming down, or the huge explosions of a string of bombs landing very close by. I dived into a hedge bottom and then ran very quickly home, where my father was anxiously looking out for me. The next morning when I biked to school I saw a bomb crater at the top of Carisbrook Road, Knighton Road, on the London Road, with an abandoned car up-ended in the hole. The Victoria Park pavilion had been flattened by a land mine. This was a type of bomb that came down slowly with a parachute and as soon as it touched something in the air it exploded, causing wide devastation. During this time I think the bombs were dropped on Highfield Street and St Peters Road. Eventually I arrived at school to be told it had been closed for the day.

My granny asked me if I would help at a NAAFI canteen at the church rooms at the bottom of Holbrook Road for soldiers who were billeted in the racecourse buildings. This meant making beans and sardines on toast and huge piles of sandwiches, washing-up and making cups of tea. I made friends with three of the soldiers who used to walk home with me, where usually my father would be waiting at the gate. Feeling sorry for the soldiers, he invited them to come on Sunday afternoons to take a bath and have tea. Those early days of war everyone was digging for victory and knitting, the iron railings round the parks and the houses had been removed and people gave their aluminium saucepans to be melted down and made into Spitfire aeroplanes.

My brother Tom volunteered for the army and was stationed at Rennes in France, so you see how anxious my father was when the Germans bypassed the Maginot Line and advanced into France at great speed. We heard on the news how the French refugees were being bombed and shot at, and the French and British armies, until eventually many of the British soldiers escaped from Dunkirk. Once again I was amazed to see the Victoria Park full of sleeping soldiers, resting after their terrible ordeal. A day or so later my Uncle Jack, Uncle Gaston, Uncle Roy and their wives arrived from France where they were born. Somehow or other we all squashed into our home, including a blind aunt and her maid from London who was fed up with the bombing. We had to have two sittings for the evening dinner and then they all played Vingt-et-un. The French aunts did not speak much English and what they did was with a terrible accent. I remember one aunt when playing cards saying, "She would put her arse on the table." No one could explain to her what she had said for laughing.

Eventually my brother arrived home from France and the uncles and aunts found other accommodation. My French improved, which came in useful on many occasions. I remember going with my aunt to the Bishop's house on the London Road to help pack Red Cross parcels for the British prisoners of war in Germany. I had always wanted to train as a nurse, which I hoped to do when I had taken my school certificate, but Matron Hughes at the Royal Infirmary told me to find a job and she would let me know.

That day at dinner I was grumbling to my father and he said a farming friend of his wanted a worker. So on the Monday we visited Mr Benford and his wife at Broughton Astley and it was agreed that I would start work on Wednesday, living in at their house. When I arrived I was received with a big welcome, as poor Mrs Benford had fallen down the stairs breaking her wrist, which was in plaster, and was badly shaken. My first job was to pump up some water, put the kettle on and make a pot of tea.

As she got better Mr Benford wanted me to help outside on the farm. I helped him drive the cattle to Ullesthorpe Market, me walking, him on his bike. I then rode his bike home.

It was not worth teaching me to milk as it was all done by hand and they had four people to do it. I used to carry the buckets across the yard and put the milk through the cooler, which took gallons of water. It was my job to pump the water up morning and night. I also fed about twelve young calves on a type of gruel from a bucket. One day Mr Benford and I went to get willow sticks which he showed me how to make into thatching pegs.

I had half the day off on Saturdays and Sundays, when I would visit my friends in Leicester. Coming back one dark night on the train I opened the door of the carriage on the wrong side and stepped on to the line instead of the platform. The people in the carriage were concerned but I could hear the whistle blowing and told them to leave me and that I would shout to the porter when the train had gone. I thought I had broken my ankle. The porter was very surprised to see me and helped me to The Station Arms pub where I surprised everyone by only wanting a drink of water!

I stopped farming when I received a letter from Matron Hughes to say I could start nursing at the Swithland Convalescent Home on Boxing Day. I went to say goodbye to Mr and Mrs Benford and he gave me a £5 note and said I could always work for him again and he would give me good references. I was 17 and at last going to start nursing.'

PARTY FROCKS TO WEDDING DRESS

'I had been at grammar school for just one year when war was declared and had enjoyed a Christmas party in 1938. I had been half promised a new party dress but it didn't materialise and for a time the disappointment was quite devastating. I had a pale green frilly affair made of cheap net. It was about three years old and had been used for playing weddings with cow parsley for bouquets and daisy chains for head dresses. It now reached just below the knee having started out as ankle length and it was grubby and slightly torn, due, I think to an over-zealous and possibly jealous bridesmaid wanting to be the bride. After a wash and a few stitches it didn't look too bad and once at the party I forgot all about it and thoroughly enjoyed myself.

The few parties I had attended had been childish affairs with pass the parcel, musical chairs and so on. We had been staying behind after school to learn the lancers, palais glide, valeta, barn dance etc to the music of *The Merry Widow* and *Pirates of Penzance*, nevertheless I was not sure what to expect. A few days before the party I was rather disconcerted to be asked by one of the boys in my form if he could take me in to supper at the party. I was in a group of giggling girls at the time and they giggled all the more at this request. I didn't want to decide there and then so I said I would think about it. I didn't want to hurt his feelings but I had read *Little Women* and I felt Laurie's timing would have been better.

The party was a dance, quite grown up in fact, with normally straight-haired girls appearing all curly, but with no signs of any make-up. I danced every dance with boys, no girls dancing together on this occasion and I was asked by a different boy to accompany him in to supper. I didn't even know his first name because at our school boys were always called by their surname. I am not surprised that the first boy didn't ask again. Later in the evening the parents arrived and watched the dancing from a balcony and I finally cycled home with my father. We were not allowed home until parents arrived. In the war to come, other people lost loved ones, homes, their children were evacuated. I was lucky. I lost no one close, but I missed out on school parties. That one in 1938 was my one and only. It all sounds rather 19th century now.

The war didn't affect me greatly. I was sent home from school on more than one occasion for my gas mask. They had to accompany us everywhere. There was quite a fashion in fetching gas mask cases. They became an accessory, like gloves and handbags. Occasionally we had to sit in class in our masks for a few minutes to make sure they were in working order. The black rubber smelt ghastly. My baby sister's mask was a Mickey Mouse pink one and I remember my mother shedding a few tears when we fitted it on her.

We were never hungry as I believe they were in the First World War as rationing was introduced early. We were always short of sugar, fats, cheese, meat and bacon. We had plenty of tea and when sweet rationing was introduced the ration was far more than we in our family were used to. My father was a very energetic man with a good appetite. He was foreman on a colliery bank, responsible for coal from the pit coming safely to the surface and its disposal. Until nationalisation of the mines he worked most weekends without extra pay, and even then I believe it took some time to get it. He dug a large garden, helped out at my uncle's farm and went on Home Guard manoeuvres, all on basic rations.

Manual workers were allowed extra cheese and also meat, I believe, but he was regarded as staff so didn't qualify for extra. Luckily he kept chickens and rabbits and we had plenty of vegetables. One year onions were like gold dust in the shops nationally but we were eating them with everything after we'd had a bumper crop. We occasionally had rabbit pie or stew (this was before myxomatosis), and we had plenty of eggs although we had to supply the Egg Marketing Board with some. These last had to be cleaned with a damp cloth before collection. With fats so scarce there is a limit to what could be done with eggs and while we had them fried, boiled and scrambled we never had an omelette. I don't think my mother had heard of them and I certainly had not.

My father acquired a duckling which grew into a fine white drake. He was rough and tough with a decidedly off-hand manner so we called him William after Richmal Crompton's William Brown. We then acquired a brown duck which followed William everywhere. She was a petulant little thing but adored her lord and master so she became Violet Elizabeth. You could imagine her saying, "If I can't come with you I'll quack and quack till I'm thick." Sadly, William ended up on a dish at Christmas, with apple sauce, tough no longer but as tender and tasty as you could wish. Looking back I don't know how I managed to eat him but he smelt so good. My younger sister couldn't face a thing: she was inconsolable – and so was Violet Elizabeth.

During the school holidays I went potato picking and one year a group from school went flax pulling. It was pulled so that all the plant including the root could be used for oil, glue and linen. This was grown in a field between Swannington and Ravenstone.

Women and girls knitted for the forces in drab shades of khaki, navy and air force blue. We knitted scarves, gloves and helmets mostly. I seemed to do this for years. A schoolfriend and I would spend our holidays and evenings knitting and playing board games. Halma and draughts were my favourites. We listened to ITMA, Arthur Askey and Charlie Chester. Eventually we seemed to be the only two left in the village knitting for the troops and I'm afraid that avarice overcame patriotism and we began knitting for a local shop. We knitted toddlers' suits and dresses in fine wool and for these we received three shillings. Gloves were one and sixpence but were fiddly things done on four needles. I remember being in this friend's garden one evening when her older sister came out very upset. She didn't normally notice us, as is the habit of older sisters, but she had just heard that Glenn Miller was reported missing. We were quite overcome as we enjoyed dancing to his music at the weekly local hop when we could afford to go – it cost half a romper suit or a pair of gloves.

Another time we were asked at school for volunteers to write ration books at the council offices in Coalville. We were not paid but how we enjoyed it – no lessons, no pork pie hat or "lumpy Latimer" tunic but lots of lipstick and no thought that exams might suffer. Several teachers were called up and replacements were not always very good. Lessons had to be abandoned when the siren went and we trooped to our designated supposedly safe areas. My place was near the boys' cloakroom, not a very choice spot, redolent of sweaty sports gear and dirty shoes. Some went under the stage and this seemed a much better proposition. What they did amongst the old stage props and scenery I don't know but they often came back late, laughing and giggling and saying they hadn't heard the all clear.

We were not allowed out of the school gates during the midday break unless we went home for a meal. Hats must be worn at all times outside the school gates, and food must not be eaten in the street. When the weather was too bad to be out at midday we danced, usually only the girls though, if we could pressure someone into playing the piano. We had to wear plimsolls in school to protect the parquet flooring until it was discovered that some of us had flat feet, then we had to have house shoes with heels. We played hockey and rounders and the boys played football and cricket. The tennis courts were abandoned as the groundsman was called up.

I left school at 16½ years of age, regrettably with very little in the way of qualifications but having enjoyed every minute of it.

Before I left school I already had a job lined up. It was so easy then – you applied and were offered it. My first and only job until I married and moved away was as a clerk in the wages office at a colliery. My boss didn't like women employees and I understand did not suffer them before the war. My job was to replace a young man who was waiting to go into the Navy. Until he went I worked in several offices to get a smattering of knowledge. In the sales office where I learnt about Derbyshire Brights and Nutty Slack we sat on high stools at sloping desks, used round batons for rulers and pen and ink for fountain pens. Quill pens would have been more in keeping. Biros were not yet in common use. As could be expected, all the offices had coal fires, enormous things that you drew back from rather than up to. The best coal was used. Even so, when I eventually started work in the wages office with the fire at one end you either melted or froze. We used to stop to warm up and change places.

I loved the work and the camaraderie and I was treated as an equal. I also loved the sulphuric smell of the pit bank which smouldered day and night. These fires never went out and people said they never would. Attempts were made as it was feared that the flames would attract enemy aircraft. On the site of the old colliery there is now a large supermarket, DIY stores and petrol station so I assume the fires were quenched effectively.

When I started work clothes were, to me, a problem. I could hardly wear school uniform but I had very little else. When I left I was over five feet ten inches. I grew out of things overnight. Most of my friends stopped growing at 13, except perhaps outwards, so they could normally find something to wear. My hems were let down, belts inserted into waists, false hems were added and then, when they became impossible to wear, they were passed on to my sister. When friends were still wearing children's shoes I was having to find extra coupons for adults' shoes. Stockings were another problem. Trousers were not in vogue and fully fashioned stockings (ie shaped stockings) were three coupons a pair and were longer than the others, also dearer, but even fully fashioned stockings were not long enough for me. I used to unpick the double welt at the top of the stockings and reinforce it with a welt from an old pair, which gave me a few more inches. Suspenders were always stretched to pinging point like a tight violin string and I blame my later back problems on wartime stockings. Of course in summer we went bare legged.

My mother went to night school to learn dressmaking and tailoring. She made me a pleated skirt out of my school tunic.

When I had coupons and cash she tailored for me a beautiful grey striped pleated suit, called a costume in those days. She also made a pink satin bra and French knickers with a scalloped edge. What a change from the barrage balloons we had worn at school. A friend and I shared a cotton parachute and I made underwear – some people managed to get silk ones. I managed to get some Air Force lilac long-johns and even though they were machine-made I managed to unpick them and knitted a ribbed polo necked jumper.

My great-uncle, an old seaman, taught me how to do netting using a spool and the back of a chair. He made string shopping bags for Christmas presents. My attempt at a snood ended up as a dishcloth. Even combs and hair grips were difficult to get but not as difficult as it was for people living in London. I used to send my cousin any extras that I could. She was in charge of the House of Commons switchboard where the scramblers had to be used to prevent conversations being overheard. She would tell us which MPs she had met and was quite a fan of Winston Churchill. Her mother came to stay for a few days – she was desperate for a bath, not daring to get into the bath in London because of the raids.

I hadn't been at work very long before PAYE came into force. This caused quite an upheaval in the wages department as everyone came into the system, even if they didn't earn enough to pay tax. Before that only a few people paid and then I believe it was the same amount each week. An extension was built, central heating installed and new machines were bought. I was sent to Felt and Tarrant's Comptometer School in Leicester and I was able to meet up with a schoolfriend for lunch. In 1945 a Labour Government came into power and the nationalisation of the coal mines quickly followed. Being a wages office we had notices and advertisements for National Savings pinned up, but after nationalisation they were taken down. When I asked why I was told, "I have no intention of giving this Government any help." This was my first experience of the deviousness of politics. Naively, I had thought the good of the country should be the priority.

Other changes were made. We received no Christmas presents but our wages went up slightly. We were told we would be paid for any overtime – previously we had worked overtime during Bank Holiday weeks so that we could have a day off and also at the end of the year but had received no extra pay in lieu. This overtime pay did not materialise, however, as staff from other offices were sent in to help. Apart from these irritations I found working conditions good provided you kept good time and worked hard. On one occasion I was told I was wearing too much lipstick but I ignored this as I felt that this was my concern and didn't affect my work.

Friday was the culmination of the week's work. In the morning when the banks were open the cashier would take one or two of us with him in the chauffeur-driven car to pick up the cash for the wages. Sometimes I would go – security was tight even then and sometimes we would have a coal lorry as an escort. When the cash was ready we would go to the post office for the stamps, two sorts – insurance and unemployment. We then returned to the office when all hell was let loose. The cashier and head clerk would each take a table, a pile of money and pay slips. They would count out the notes and silver and slap it on the table where it would be checked. There would be six of us and we had to be finished and balanced by midday, ready to pay out to the men. The money, not very much, four or five one pound notes plus silver and maybe a ten shilling note for the ordinary miner, was stuffed into a little metal can and placed on a narrow shelf over a number. The miner had to collect a numbered tally which had to be presented to the wages office before he received his wages. After the frenzy of the morning, we generally relaxed in the afternoon, stuck stamps on the cards and answered any queries relating to pay and stoppages. On Saturday mornings we started on the next week's work, getting information from time-keepers, but Saturday afternoons we had off.

My friend and I wanted to go down the mine and permission was granted but it had to be a Sunday so that we wouldn't hold up production! This colliery had two mines, one deep and below the shallower one. My friend's father was working on maintenance and was standing in several feet of water. He often had time off because of rheumatism, I began to see why. We walked to the pit face, bumping our heads as the roof got lower and lower. It got very hot and behind us we heard a small fall. Of course there were no toilets or washing facilities and it was quite a long walk. Men were working at the coal face in very cramped conditions. We showered on reaching the surface and I spent the rest of the day blowing my nose to remove the dust.

I was engaged to be married by this time and whilst underground a miner noticed my engagement ring and offered me some clothing coupons, but at a price – two shillings and sixpence each. I couldn't beat him down at all but I bought enough for material for my wedding dress. This was unpatriotic, undesirable and quite despicable but I told myself you only marry once – well, you did in those days.

Just before I left to get married a colleague gave me my first pair of nylons, incredibly sheer but still short. Getting a trousseau together was difficult as things were still in short supply. Shoes for my mother were also a problem as she took size eight. We tried Coalville, Ashby, Nottingham and Loughborough and finally found a pair to fit her in Leicester. They were hardly suitable for a wedding, being sturdy, flat-heeled tan-coloured suede. My fiancé had introduced us to peanut butter and we were close to being addicted to it. Imagine our delight when we found a shop selling it in Leicester on the same day that we found the shoes. The peanut butter was not in jars but sold loose in greaseproof paper and then a bag. Our delight turned to despair upon reaching home when we found the peanut butter had leaked all over the shoes. We were near to tears but the stain wasn't too noticeable. The day was moist and the confetti, which I think had been made from bus ticket clippings, left a yellow stain on my face and dress, but apart from that the wedding went off quite well!'

FROM SCHOOL TO JET ENGINES

'1939 and the outbreak of war. It was a sunny Sunday and we children were not worried at all, but then at ten years old the full significance of war thankfully does not register. In some ways it was quite exciting. There was the arrival of evacuees. The school was closed for a day and used as a reception centre for them. We children all gathered there with great curiosity waiting for them to arrive. It must have been awful for them, tired and bewildered, to alight from the buses to a crowd of gazing children. They were billeted with anyone who had room to house them.

At the same time every day the granite works at Croft would do the blasting, which was clearly heard here in Cosby. The first time the evacuee children heard it they ran indoors, shocked and frightened, thinking that it was bombs.

Several empty houses were taken over and given to whole families where the mothers came with the children. A group of volunteers went round the village, collecting anything people could spare to furnish and equip these houses. People were generous and gave chairs, tables, beds and loads of linen, pots and pans and cutlery. Almost every household was moved to give a little something and this at a time when there were shortages of everything. The empty houses each had at least a table, chairs, beds and bedding, towels and basic pots and pans. Most of them were so grateful and thanked

225

the ladies profusely for what they had done. They were just thankful to be away from London and Ipswich. Only a couple of families complained at the sparseness of their new homes – complaints which were not received very favourably by the ladies who had spent many hours collecting, cleaning and polishing for their arrival.

Right at the beginning of the war we were issued with gas masks which we had to carry with us at all times. The school advised us to put a bar of chocolate or something in our gas mask holders in case we were ever holed up for any length of time because of an air raid. We were told one dinner time to run home as fast as we could and check how long it took. When the times were reported, everybody was so eager to outdo each other on how fast they had run that there were very few accurate times given. It was then decided that if an air raid warning was given, we would run down the longish school drive, across the road and into the hedge bottoms of the meadows. I do not think that idea was taken up either after one practice.

The next August I went to senior school. My mother went on the Comforts Fund Committee which worked hard to raise funds for our village lads in the services. She also became a fire spotter. All lights had to be completely blocked out with heavy blackout curtains or shutters. There were no street lamps – no signposts either. Even bicycle lamps had to be hooded and only showed a small strip of light. Air raid wardens kept a close eye on all of this.

My dad tried to join the Navy, in which he had served during the First World War, but was too old. He became a sergeant in the Home Guard for a while, then joined the SRS. The Special Repair Service was composed of men from the building trade who would in turn travel in a lorry to Coventry every day to do quick repair jobs on buildings. He was there the morning after the blitz. Such sad sights he saw. He moved to Birmingham where he lodged all week. Later he moved to the South Coast and came home every few weeks. Every night the Germans bombed the coastal reinforcements and every day the men built them up. After that, he was transferred to London where he stayed for the rest of his time. He was there when the first buzz bombs dropped. I first heard news of them at work. One of the women rushed into the office to say that the BBC had announced that the Germans were now sending over pilotless planes. There had been a lull in the bombing and a lot of the Londoners had taken their families home by the time the flying bombs started. They were all right while you could hear them but as soon as the engine cut out, they zoomed down and exploded, causing a great deal of damage.

My father was caught in the blast from one and was lifted bodily and blown along the street. His hearing was affected for a long time.

At 14 in 1943 I left school and started work at the Power Jets. One day we were all summoned to the works canteen. Group Captain Whittle was there (later to become Sir Frank Whittle) to talk to us. He told us that his invention of the jet engine had been perfected and was successful and ready for production, and that the next morning we would read the announcement in all the newspapers. He was a very quiet, polite and modest sort of man. He thanked the directors who had backed him and many others, including workers who had been with him through all the trials and tribulations of the early days where sometimes during the earlier tests, they had to run for it when things got out of control. There had been a great deal of frustration over the years but also many laughs along the way. He had never thought of his engine being used in war. His original dream was to perfect the engine to speed up mail planes.

A number of RAF personnel worked at "The Jets" where engines were tested. Sometimes test pilots would come over the works in a plane and swoop down so low that all the RAF men and others who went up on to the roof to watch, would instinctively duck. One summer the Sports Entertainment Committee organised a gala which crowds of people attended. A test pilot flew a plane overhead and performed a little show of stunt flying. He dropped down into another steep dive but that time he did not come up – instead a column of thick black smoke spread out across the sky. It was a very dramatic moment. There was complete silence while the crowds watched in shocked horror then men started to run across the fields to that billowing smoke. The young pilot, of course, was killed. His wife was expecting their first baby.

In the early 1940s, although I mostly cycled to work, the bus fare each way to Whetstone was twopence. The fare to Leicester was sevenpence single and ninepence return.

There were great celebrations when the war ended. We all collected at the Bunning Hall where music was relayed to the street by loudspeakers. The street was packed with singing, dancing, laughing people, all very happy and relieved. The church bells, which had been silent throughout the war, now rang out again and there were lights blazing everywhere. For weeks I stood at my bedroom window every night for the sheer joy of looking at all the lights.'

HIGH DAYS & HOLIDAYS

MAKING OUR OWN ENTERTAINMENT

Cricket matches, whist drives, clubs for men and for women, plays in the village hall, dance bands and singers – and even, sadly, dancing bears. We made our own entertainment in the days before TV and cinema, and even before radio! Every village could produce a wealth of talent and enthusiasm to fill our few leisure hours.

THE DANCING BEAR

'Dancing bears, poor things, were once a form of entertainment. They were attached by a chain to a long pole, stood on their hind legs and shuffled a few steps, and people put pennies in the owner's cap.

My grandfather told a story, which took place in about 1860. He offered, one Sunday morning, to go and fodder his girlfriend's father's cattle which were in a field on the Langham to Oakham road on the outskirts of the village. It was a late winter morning and barely daylight. There was (and still is) a red brick barn in the field in which the hay was stored. Luckily my grandfather put his hand over the lower half of the door and grabbed the pitchfork before going inside for he was not alone. A figure raised itself up from the manger. Grandfather thought it was a tramp on his own, but then discovered there was also a large bear chained to the standing post.

The man was very reluctant to leave his cosy bed and the bear added several threatening growls as well, but the pitchfork was a welcome defence. Man and bear eventually ambled off towards Melton and the cattle got their hay.'

WHIST DRIVES

'As the long winter evenings began, so a little social life emerged at Knossington. Whist drives were popular ways to raise money for various charities, such as the Leicester Royal Infirmary. You could buy £2 vouchers to help poor families needing hospital treatment. A whist drive would yield about £10.

Dances were more sixpenny hops, with local musicians providing the music – a piano, drums and a violin being the most common trio. You were lucky if there were more.'

'For many years from the late 1920s there was an annual Boxing Day whist drive and dance at Newtown Linford, organised by Mrs Warrilow. Everybody went, whatever their age. The whist drive was from 7.30 to 9 pm, then everyone helped to clear away the tables and chairs and there was dancing until about 11.30, with music by Sid Partner and the Boys from Stanton under Bardon. There were refreshments at half time, made by the village ladies. Hundreds of pounds were sent to the Leicester Royal Infirmary from these events.

There were also a couple or so whist drives during the year, one being a Fur and Feather Drive.'

'The village reading room was situated in Sapcotts Yard at South Luffenham and whist drives were regularly held there, admission sixpence. One old lady would sell eggs and vegetables to ensure she had enough money to attend the whist drives.'

ONE ACT PLAYS

'Thanks to the good stage in the village hall, the Lockington and Hemington Amateur Dramatic Society was formed by Miss Valerie Hasard. Many one act plays were performed to the delight of the parish, despite the fact that the leading (and only) man had a cleft palate, which was apt to make his soft murmurings of love a little hard to hear.'

MEN'S AND WOMEN'S INSTITUTES

'The Men's Institute at Arnesby was formed in 1923. A committee was chosen in July and the first meeting held in late September. Members met upstairs in a building in Mr Grant's yard (Mr Grant lived at the manor house and was sub-postmaster at that time). The room was heated by a coal burning stove and lit by oil lamps. For a small charge the young men of the village played billiards, skittles, solo, "slippery Anne" etc. Whist drives and socials also provided income.

During the first three years of its existence an annual "Children's Christmas Treat" was organised. Carol singing on Christmas Eve helped to fund it. After a meat tea, Santa Claus gave each child a present and the evening ended with an entertainment by the children themselves.

The Institute moved to their own premises in 1932/3, built on land donated by Mr R. P. Freer, a local farmer. The building was also rented out for other village functions and by 1960 arrangements were being made to hand over the "Institute" to a committee for use as a village hall.'

'Until the formation of the Women's Institute in November 1927, the women of Buckminster and Sewstern scarcely knew one another. There were very few cars in those days and only the regular churchgoers from Sewstern who came to Buckminster to worship in the parish church were known to Buckminster people. In those days Sewstern church was only opened once or twice a year.

Then in 1927 along came the WI and this feeling of "us and them" was done away with to a certain extent, although monthly meetings had to be held in the school, so that neither village could complain of favouritism!

Strangely enough, the Buckminster and Sewstern Mothers' Union also began in November 1927, and these two events must have had a great impact on the lives of the women of both villages.

Early meetings of the WI were somewhat staid affairs. The first official meeting in February 1928 had a demonstration on slipper making, followed by the social half hour, which was made up of "games and dancing" (so the programme records). The following meeting had a lantern lecture, and was followed by a roll call on "My favourite kind of housework"!'

'In the mid 1920s the men of Newtown Linford got annoyed that when they went to the public house, The Bradgate, on a Sunday lunchtime, they would be pushed out by friends of the landlord, who had been publican of the Midland Hotel in Leicester. So in 1926 they started their own British Legion Club. They bought an old wooden, tin roofed hut which had been a tea room in the garden behind Beech Farm, and transported it onto land bought from Zaddy Harrison by Mr Pettifor of Anstey Brewery. The money was later repaid as they could afford it. Zaddy became steward and my mother was paid a shilling to hold Mr Pettifor's horse when he went in for a drink.'

THE SINGING MINER

'When I was very small my father worked for Balfour Beatty as a labourer, digging the trenches for the electricity cables which were being introduced to the area at that time. My father was part of a team carrying out the work and they left home on a Monday morning, returning the following Saturday lunchtime. They were all too poor to be able to pay for accommodation so the big wooden spools which held the cable, like giant cotton reels, were used at the ends and tarpaulins were stretched over them to form a large tent-like area in which they slept and ate their meals, cooking over open fires.

This work, of course, was very hard and his hobby was to sing. He had never had a singing lesson in his life but sang ballad-type songs similar to the ones sung by Richard Tauber, such as *The white dove* (my favourite), *Bless this house*, *The Holy City*, *Six feet of earth*, and many others.

During his period of work in the Anstey-Shilton-Wolvey area near to Coventry he, along with his pals, went to a local church social and while there he gave them a song or two. The next day a lady came along to their working area asking for the man who had sung, and Father went to meet her.

The lady, unfortunately I do not know her name, was a local singing teacher who thought that my Dad had a lot of potential. Through her my father went to Birmingham to another teacher for an audition and after that the "lady" wanted him to take professional lessons and she would pay all his expenses, but because he had three small daughters at that time he would not take the chance, although the "lady" said that he would soon be able to repay her. Life for the family could have been so changed as at that time he was earning about tenpence an hour and having to work all hours to make ends meet. Still, we all had a good life with lots of love and that can be more important than money.

Father kept on with his singing and he carried on until well after the war. In fact he was singing until his breathing became too bad for him to carry on.

Father was known as "The Singing Miner" because he changed his job about the time of the outset of World War Two and went to work at Whitwick Colliery. Even as early as this Whitwick had pithead baths, therefore he was able to come home clean instead of having to be scrubbed in front of the fire as many men were.

During the war my father belonged to several concert parties but the main one was "The Ace" in which I joined him as a singer. The concert party was made up of singers (men, women and children), dancers, comedians, pianists, a compère etc. All very amateur but putting in a lot of practice so that they gave enjoyment to many people.

As you can appreciate, most of our work was done for charity and we used to go along to hospitals such as Bretby Hall Orthopaedic where there were many young men who had been badly wounded. When they were a little better they were transferred to Thorpe Hall and Gopsel Hall and they would then be transported to Ibstock Working Men's Club where we fed them and provided the entertainment for the evening.

Mother at this time used to make most of the costumes which we all wore. The ladies were all dressed in red pleated skirts and white mandarin blouses and the men had white trousers with red mandarin shirts – all made in satin. This was our uniform but we all had others for our "turn", as your performance was called.

Father had several changes of job over the years: from mining he went to be a steward at Bardon Working Men's Club and at this time the whole family was able to help him as he had had several accidents at the colliery which made it almost impossible for him to do heavy work. He then became landlord of the Boot Inn at Ibstock and in both of these he was ably supported by my dear mother.

His last job was as a needle polisher for the Grieve Needle Co at Coalville, from which he retired at the age of 65.

Always a fine husband and father, he worked tirelessly for the good of his family. He was not always well paid but a man who made sure we were all well shod, well fed and given lots of love.'

FRANK WATSON AND HIS ORCHESTRA

'My father, a man of intelligence and independent spirit, trained as an engineer in Leicester, but did not relish the working life pursued by most men between the wars. As he stood well over six foot, he joined the City of London police (who at that time recruited only tall men) and he served there for two years before returning to Leicester to run a small hosiery factory with my mother.

In the 1930s he and a friend formed a band called Morrell's Melody Makers which became very successful and won many awards. Later he started his own band and, although perhaps not really musical, he had a good sense of rhythm so he became the drummer.

In due course he became the resident dance band leader at the Bell

Frank Watson and his orchestra were well known as regular performers at the Bell Hotel, Leicester.

Hotel in Humberstone Gate, Leicester, for the regular Saturday night dances, and many older local people will remember Frank Watson and his orchestra. Eventually this led him to the formation of an agency for booking bands and entertainers. It was a lifestyle which suited him very well but, like so many others, was disrupted by the Second World War.'

CRICKET TO SIX

'In the past Cossington had a football and a cricket team. The captain of the cricket team was the Rev Mr Mathias and as they played on a Sunday afternoon the game had to finish before the bells rang at six for evening service.'

SPORTS DAY

'For a few years in the early 1920s, my mother and eldest sister arranged a sports day for the children of the locality. It was the highlight of the summer holiday and looked forward to eagerly by all the children. A book was hung outside our yard gate with a list of races to be run, and a space for names to be entered. The local children walked up and down the road outside waiting for the book to appear, they could not wait to put their names down. The event took place in a field at the back of our house. There were egg-and-spoon, three-legged, sack, wheelbarrow, and sprint races.

The parents sat on a bench to watch, and Mother supplied tea and cakes. The prizes were presented by Mr Rippin of Desford, who thoroughly enjoyed it. He was very fond of children. I never remember a rainy day, I think the sun always shone for this event.'

A VERY SPECIAL DAY

'In 1921 my great grandmother was 100 years old. The day was declared a public holiday at Castle Donington. The children from the school went in a procession to her house on Bondgate with the parish councillors preceding them. The factory workers were given one hour's leave to watch the procession. The children sang *Abide with me*, *Art thou weary* and *O God our help in ages past*. I was four and a half years old and chosen to present her with a bouquet, nearly as big as myself.

She had been bedfast since the age of 95 but still read the Bible very day and could sew without the aid of spectacles. She had been a marvellous dressmaker. There were a great many relations and friends there that day. She had four children, 33 grandchildren, 62 great grandchildren and three great great grandchildren.'

ROYAL OCCASIONS

Leicestershire's splendid hunting country brought royalty to the county on many occasions, formal and informal. We also celebrated national royal occasions with enthusiasm.

THE HUNT

'Between the wars the Prince of Wales (later Edward VIII) and the Duke of York (later George VI), hunted in Leicestershire with the Fernie. On this particular occasion they had arranged to be met by their "man" at Arnesby. While waiting for him they took shelter in The Old Cock public house for warmth and refreshment. Unfortunately the Prince of Wales got too close to the fire, with the result that his trousers scorched.

A local farmer used to recall opening a gate for them and being shocked at their language as they touched their caps and passed through. In his words they were "swearing like troopers".'

'I remember seeing the Prince of Wales and his brothers, the Dukes of Kent and Gloucester, on many occasions with the Cottesmore Hunt. Once a year the meet was held at our farm and Mother allowed the ladies toilet facilities in the bedrooms (chamber pots).

The Prince schooled his horses in our home field. He arrived in his Rolls Royce and the grooms brought his horses from Craven Lodge in Melton.

My father once attended a dinner at the De Montfort Hall in Leicester, given by the Prince for all the farmers whose land he hunted over. We were rewarded with pennies when opening gates for the riders. I remember one occasion when my poor mother had been taken by Father to the dentist and my sister and I were left to do various chores, including washing the kitchen floor. When the hunt arrived we simply tipped up the buckets of water and followed. I can only imagine the dressing down we got.'

'The Hunt Ball at Witherley always provided a spectacle and also work for the villagers. Indeed, the Hunt itself was a great employer for there were over 15 members of staff besides the kennelmen who

The Prince of Wales was a regular visitor to the county in the 1930s, seen here at the Leicester Show.

looked after the dogs and the huntsmen in the cottages. The head huntsman, Mr Pavitt, lived where the dairy stands in the village today. One thing that stands out in my mind as a child was when the Master of the Hunt, Luke Lillington, landed in the cottagers' piece in his private aircraft. This was amazing to us children who barely ever saw a motor car, let alone an aeroplane.'

ROYAL JUBILEES

'Queen Victoria's Diamond Jubilee in 1897 was recorded by Mrs Edith Shilcock in 1977 when she was 91 years old.

"The day's events started with a united service in Swepstone church at eleven o'clock. We children at Newton Burgoland met at the school and walked in twos with our day and Sunday school teacher to the service. Mr Evans kindly lent a field and the wagon hovel for the day. At midday the men, and youths over school age, had a dinner of beef and plum pudding. Later, the women and children had high tea. There were sports for all; we had two violins and piano to give us music. My father and his friend, Mr Insley, played the violins. It was a lovely summer's day. In the evening there was dancing. It was a day to be enjoyed and remembered by all.

Later in the year we had a gala day at Swepstone to raise some money for the clock on the church, which gives many people the time of day."'

'For the Silver Jubilee on 6th May 1935, the parish council at Castle Donington called a public meeting to discuss the celebrations. A "parish tea" was suggested and my mother was asked to organise it. The council allowed her £40 to pay for the food. Bread and cakes were bought and joints of beef, ham and tongue were cooked in the local baker's oven. My mother bought a bolt of red, white and blue material (40 yards) and gave a piece to each helper to make herself a "pinny". In all, 1,000 adults sat down to a meat tea in different halls around the parish. Schoolchildren were presented with a Jubilee mug. The weather eventually put a stop to the festivities as it rained heavily in the evening, but all those who helped with the catering were very glad to get home and put their feet up. My mother kept detailed accounts and discovered she had overspent by £2.'

The winner of the second prize in the George V Coronation Procession at Wigston in 1911, posing outside The Royal Oak.

'The Jubilee Day in 1935 began at Cossington with a special service in the church. It was conducted by the Revd Mr Mathias and the whole service was marked by a great enthusiasm and loyalty. The service was followed by races in Mr Astill's field for the children. A marquee almost filled the orchard by Mr Astill's house where dinner was served to everyone attending. Those who could not come had dinner taken to them. In the evening races were held for the adults and prizes and mugs were handed out by Mrs Abel-Smith.

As it was not dark enough yet to light the bonfire, the drama group put on two plays in the school – *The Lustre Jug* and *House Full*, and the house was indeed full to overflowing. Then came the bonfire, a magnificent blaze to end a perfect day.'

CELEBRATIONS THROUGH THE YEAR

Every year brought its regular celebrations and festivities.

THE VILLAGE YEAR

'Plough Monday was on the second Monday in the New Year when Cossington men and youths dressed in fanciful attire and played primitive instruments. They paraded neighbouring villages where they received tips and hospitality. They then returned and paraded their own village during the evening. Their cry was "Please to remember the plough".

At Candlemas all the Christmas decorations were taken down and carefully burnt before noon. On no account was anything removed before 2nd February.

Numbers of the village women assembled on Shrove Tuesday and, having chosen a leader, proceeded to visit the chief houses in Cossington. A formula was repeated and money was handed out to them. At the farmhouse eggs and milk were given and flour at the mill. Thus the women were able to provide their families with the time honoured pancakes.

On May Day the cows were turned out of their quarters. There was maypole dancing on the green.

Royal Oak Day, 29th May, was specially observed in Cossington. Each child wore a sprig of oak in memory of King Charles who hid in an oak tree. No child would dare to appear without his oak leaf. If they did they were promptly stung by nettles wielded by other children.

The school holidays were arranged to fit in with the harvest so that every child should be free to spend all his time in the fields. They gleaned the corn which was carefully garnered and afterwards threshed and ground into flour at the mill. This was made into bread by the mothers and baked at the public bakehouse each Friday. There was formerly a barn called Sunhill on Mr Astill's farm where the gleaners used to gather for their midday meal.

The Feast was a great day both at the church and in the village. The first Sunday after All Saints Day was Feast Sunday and all the

The first May Queen at Oadby Gartree School in 1937, part of the Silver Jubilee celebrations for George V.

members of the family would assemble and come to church together, as a family. Peals were rung on the bells and there was a general rejoicing. For the only time in the year joints of meat were cooked at the bakehouse and a plum cake was made. This was known as Cossington Wakes weekend and roundabouts were put up on the green.'

'May 1st was "Maypole Day". The maypole was made with a wooden hoop attached to a broomstick. The hoop was decorated with flowers picked from the meadows, marsh marigolds, lady's smocks and buttercups. There would be several groups going round Newton Burgoland village. We sang *Come lasses and lads* which we learned at school and our local song which ran as follows:

"The first of May is a very fine day
Please remember the maypole
Around the maypole we can trot
See what a maypole we have got
Dressed in ribbons tied in bows
See what a maypole we can show
A jig and a jag, and a very fine flag
Please remember the maypole
If you haven't got a penny, a ha'penny will do
If you haven't got a ha'penny, God bless you."

May 24th was Empire Day. We celebrated by standing around the Union Jack in the playground singing patriotic songs. As we marched back into school, we saluted the flag.

On May 29th, Oak Leaf or Oak Apple Day, we wore a spray of oak leaves. Any girl seen without one would be chased by the boys with a stinging nettle.'

'On Plough Monday, which is the second Monday in the New Year, the boys of Rothley would put on a white smock and an old felt hat and go round the village singing:

"Teagle eagle on pom pom,
I'll sing you a song which isn't very long,
But I think it as good as any,
Put your hand in your pocket,
And pull out a penny,
And give it to the poor plough boy."

On Royal Oak Day (29th May) we all wore a sprig of oak or we were stung by someone with stinging nettles, up to twelve noon.

On Shrove Tuesday, we would get our shuttlecocks and battle-dores out to play with – that was traditional. Also on Shrove Tuesday we used to sing at playtime in the school playground:

"Pancake Day, a very fine day,
If you don't give us a holiday
We'll all run away"

knowing all the while we would have the afternoon off. We would then go to the Court House (a building on the village green) when halfpennies would be thrown which we would scramble for.

There was Rothley Wakes week. The fair would come and on the Saturday all the family would go and have a wonderful time. The fairs were much nicer than they are now – not so crowded and noisy. The people who ran the fair lived in wooden caravans which were painted in bright colours. On Wake Sunday families would get together – this was called "Feast Sunday".

August Monday was another bank holiday family day. We would gather on the village green where people in fancy dress and beautifully decorated horses and drays would be judged for prizes. They would then go round the village headed by Mountsorrel Brass Band and finish at a field where there would be stalls of various kinds, games and races for the children and skittling for a pig for the men – we thoroughly enjoyed ourselves.

Each Christmas Eve – and it nearly always snowed – the Mountsorrel Brass Band would come round and play carols, which sounded really lovely. We would creep out of bed and look out of the window to listen to them, then on Boxing Day they would come round with the collecting boxes. Rothley, at one time, had a male voice choir and they too would go round the village singing carols.'

PLOUGH MONDAY AND SHROVE TUESDAY

'The first Monday in January was celebrated as Plough Monday at Newtown Linford, when the children dressed up and went round the houses singing. In the 1930s one of the songs we sang went as follows (to the tune of *The ash grove*):

"Plough Monday, Plough Monday, when men go to plough,
Doll Durden, Doll Durden makes pancakes so new,

She burns them, she turns them, she makes them coal black,
She covers them with hen shit and poisons poor Jack."

A very similar song was sung at Shepshed on Shrove Tuesday:

"Shrove Tuesday, Ash Wednesday, when men go to plough,
Poor Polly makes pancakes she didn't know how,
She baked them, she boiled them and fried them in fat,
She rolled them in hen muck and poisoned poor Jack."

The church bell was rung at noon to tell people it was time to start making pancakes and we children used to run home singing the song.'

'At my first school at Oadby we always had a half day for Shrove Tuesday when, after our pancakes, out came the battledores and shuttlecocks and the boys' tops.'

LUTTERWORTH AGRICULTURAL SHOW

'Lutterworth Agricultural Show was held annually in the 1920s and 1930s in Bitteswell Hall Park, and attracted visitors and exhibitors from all over the country and beyond. Prize cattle, horses, pigs and sheep were arriving for days before the show and their carers would stay with them, preparing them for the judging on the morning of the show.

I well remember the heavy bull carts trundling along the lanes, with their man in charge walking alongside the horse-drawn vehicle. Each bull had its own cart and he could just see over the top, which was open. Often they were blinkered.

At the show itself there was always a top brass or silver band, and displays of horse jumping and pony trotting. Local firms had display stands, and huge marquees housed flower displays, dairy products, fruit and home-made provisions. There were refreshment tents and ice-cream stalls.

On one occasion the Duke and Duchess of York, the future George VI and the present Queen Mother, visited this show and had lunch there. There was a great demand for tickets on that occasion.'

THE CARNIVAL PRIZE

'In the 1950s the carnival procession finished its tour of Market Harborough in the Little Bowden recreation ground. There were many attractions and activities, one being a competition to find the biggest family of children. Consequently the six boys and girls of a local family lined up to collect the prize. They were full of hope. What would it be? Sweets, chocolate or a toy maybe? But oh dear, how their little faces fell when they were presented with a tea towel – to help Mummy with the washing-up. I wonder if the person responsible for such a thoughtless gift had any idea it would still be remembered in Little Bowden today, so many years later?'

COTTESMORE FEAST

'Cottesmore Feast was the event of the year. It was fixed to fall on the Feast of St James, which is 25th July.

It was a great family gathering. Girls and boys who had married or had gone into service and left the village always tried to get home for the Feast, and it *was* a feast.

The children had a holiday from school and on Friday the preparations began. The bakehouse was open all day and the people had a great baking of pastries, plum cakes and plain cakes and delicious curd cheese cakes, which were a Feast speciality. Most of the cottagers kept a pig and a ham was always saved and cooked.

Then the fair arrived. There were all kinds of stalls on the village green – Grantham gingerbread, lovely brown and white rock, fancy stalls, etc. In the field adjoining were roundabouts, swingboats, coconut shies, a shooting gallery and all the fun of the fair, lit up at night by flares. There was a hurdy gurdy which played the same tune all the time.

On Saturday there was always a cricket match and the village inn did a roaring trade.

On Sunday most people took their dinners to the bakehouse – huge joints of beef and Yorkshire pudding – and then went to church.

In the evening the church was packed. Greetham Brass Band played for the hymns and the singing was very hearty. The Methodists held a camp meeting on the village green which was well attended. After church the band played on the green and people walked in from other villages to call on their friends. All were very

The band leading Oadby's fancy dress parade in about 1930. Each year money was raised for the Leicester Royal Infirmary.

welcome. The tables were set out with ham, cheesecakes and plenty of home-made wines and beer.

On Monday there were sports, such as running after a greasy pig, which were great fun. A cricket match was played in the evening and a dance held in which everyone joined, both old and young. The fair kept open until very late and was well patronized.

On Tuesday money was getting a bit short and on Wednesday the fair moved on, the children went back to school, and the Feast was over for another year.'

HINCKLEY HORSE FAIR

'The Horse Fair held at the end of August in Hinckley saw horses standing in certain streets and being trotted to show their paces to customers, but this custom was slowly dying when I was a girl.

The fun fair held at the same time, was, of course, worked by steam engines with the lovely steam organs providing the music. I remember the "gallopers", horses going up and down as well as round, and the "Dragon and Serpents", each holding perhaps six people and revolving on an undulating track but very sedately. Going in from the entrance would be an avenue of booths selling candy floss, toffee apples, balls made of sawdust and coloured tissue paper on an elastic, and "singing" birds made of moulded cotton wool and feathers on a string mounted on a stick which one swished through the air. These stalls were all lit with naphtha flares – very exciting. I also remember the swingboats, small ones holding two with ropes with a fluffy part to hold, and the "King and Queen" boats – two very large ones, steam driven and netted round the sides to prevent people from falling out.'

BROUGHTON ASTLEY WAKES

'As a child in the 1930s, at Broughton Astley, I think the highlight of the year was the Wakes (never called the Fair in those days). Feast Sunday always followed the 26th of August and the Wakes always arrived ready for that weekend – Friday to Tuesday.

On the previous Wednesday word would get around that the traction engines were on the way and gangs of children would hurry along to meet them and escort them to the fairground. This made quite a procession through the village with often three great steam traction engines, the ornate horse-drawn caravans and large vans carrying the various amusements. The field was almost in the centre of the village and the brook running alongside provided water to keep the engines working. It was also just at the rear of The Bull's Head public house, which no doubt kept everyone well lubricated.

Some of the older boys would be allowed to help erect the various rides and the fairground men would often give them free tickets for rides in return. On the Friday night we children could hardly wait to get there, clutching our precious pennies which we had been saving for weeks past. Galloping horses, chairoplanes, cakewalk, swing boats and even donkeys were all waiting to delight us. As we approached the coloured lights would twinkle in welcome and the sound of the engines and the music from the fair organs all added to the atmosphere. Brandy snap was always on sale just inside the gate – always very tempting but not often any pennies left for that luxury.

Saturday and Monday were the main nights when families and friends all assembled and the ground was absolutely crowded. Tuesday was usually a little bit cheaper as they were beginning to dismantle and pack up ready to move on the Wednesday. Once again the procession would trundle through the village to their next port of call.

We would settle down and await the arrival again the next year. What excitement and fun we had even without much money.'

FEAST WEEK

'One of my most happy and vivid recollections of my childhood was when the celebration of Feast Week took place each year at Kibworth at the beginning of October.

Two fields adjacent to the A6 motorway were taken over for this week by the fair people who had booked it for that year. The main ones in name were Collins, Holland and Thurston, well known travelling showmen of their day. I wonder if any of their descendants are still around today. The power to drive the roundabouts, ferris wheels, cakewalks and other whirling delights came from huge traction engines fed by coal. These can be seen at collectors' and steam fairs today. (There were no electric cables in those days.)

Music from the various organs, the lights' glitter, plus the lovely polished brass-work was so magical I can still remember it as if it was happening today. Among the sideshows were shooting galleries, coconut shies, Aunt Sallys, goldfish stalls and fortune tellers who all seemed, or were reputed, to be related to Gipsy Rose Lee! If I could bribe a penny or two from my mother or auntie I would visit the fair during the week but the highlight was on Saturday night when my Dad, mother, my brother and I would go together. Dad would give us half a crown – a princely sum in those days. This he could afford as he had worked hard bringing in the harvest in the evenings after his full time job on the railway!

After a wonderful evening on the various merry-go-rounds we used to keep enough money to buy a bag of home-made brandy snaps or Grantham's flat ginger-type cakes – these were my favourites.

As we walked home very tired and happy at the end of a truly magical evening, to finalise Feast Week on the Sunday evening a service was held with the organ playing the hymns and the vicar taking the service. A lovely end to a special week in my life. Simple pleasures are still the best.'

CHRISTMAS PAST

Christmas had a unique magic all of its own, with that very special excitement that built up when the first cakes and puddings were mixed. We had little money in those days, so presents were simple and few, but we knew how to enjoy ourselves.

CHRISTMAS IS COMING

'Excitement built up in the weeks before Christmas. One evening was devoted to making mincemeat. My mother gathered us children round the kitchen table and we were given our allotted tasks. My eldest sister bagged the coveted job of using the mincer. Suet came in blocks and had to be cut and minced, together with the apples.

I was given a cup of hot water in which to dip the almonds to make them easier to skin.

There would be complaints from whoever was stoning the raisins about sore fingers, but Mother assured us we were really enjoying ourselves! It was certainly the build-up to the excitement of Christmas.

The Christmas party was the highlight, and much preparation went into it. Invitations were sent out and replies anxiously awaited. Games were thought out and prepared.

Mother cooked a whole ham; it was covered in flour and water paste and baked in the oven. The night before the party my small sister and I were too excited to go to bed, and as a special treat we had a ham sandwich, the first delicious cut from the joint.

The room we called the hall had a large table in it, and this was covered with a white damask cloth and laden with food – ham, home-made pork pie, bananas in jelly, trifles, chocolate log cake and other cakes, mince pies and home-made lemon curd tarts.

Above the table was a large cracker and the individual crackers were pushed in each end with a streamer attached ending at each plate. When the time came to pull them down they went everywhere amid much laughter.'

FUDDLIN AND CHARITY

'Preparations for Christmas began six weeks beforehand when everyone helped to stir the Christmas puddings for luck. The puddings were then boiled in a big copper. We used a copper which belonged to someone in Junior Street, Leicester. Anyone who had a copper would let you borrow it; there was another one in Sanvey Gate.

We all went window shopping – known as "fuddlin". We gazed at the box of trains in the window of Crowes, a draper's shop on the corner of Bond Street and Eastgate Street. Below the shop, in what was called the "Bear Pit", we watched the model trains.

In those days, at the beginning of the century, Cohen's, the Penny Bazaar in Eastgates, sold things like hat-pins and slides for one penny which we gave away for presents. We also bought tins of coloured sweets for a penny which went in the stockings.

After Christmas Cordells sold penny bags of pins and lace oddments etc. There was always a big queue. I remember in some shops like Giles', how the money was taken and change dispatched from the shop's office in a box attached to a wire which ran across the shop above the customers' heads.

We made paper chains out of coloured paper to decorate the house a month before Christmas. Also we took the hoops from apple barrels from the market, covered them with cut-up tissue paper and hung four penny-oranges from them. These were then hung around the house. During the First World War, my father sent us threepence each for Christmas. It was all he could afford. We sent him money and my mother sent him a cake as often as possible. (I remember she once forgot to add the sugar to the mixture and put it in while it was cooking – it turned out all right though!)

There was a Christmas Dinner Charity Fund from which you could get a piece of fat meat, potatoes turned black and Christmas pudding free – if you had nothing else. Also you could get a pair of boots from the *Leicester Mail* and a toy from the Corn Exchange. (My saddest memory of Christmas was of being given a boy doll and wanting my sister, Elsie's, girl doll – all dressed in pink!)

Before Christmas the "Sally Army" sang in the town and round the houses. One of their songs went,

"Christmas is coming
And the geese are getting fat,
Please put a penny
In the old man's hat."

For two shillings and sixpence you could hire the "Town Waits". They had singers and buglers in their band and would come round on a dray after midnight on Christmas Eve and play and sing carols. They also played at the bottom of Bond Street by the factory, Inks & Saunders.'

CHRISTMAS AT GRAN'S

'Though my sister and I had our own home with our parents, we moved to Gran's at Bitteswell, lock, stock and barrel for the Christmas festivities. For several days before Christmas Eve there was evidence of the coming season, biscuits in the cut glass barrel, decanters filled with spirits and glasses ready on a tray for any visitors and family. The evergreens were not brought in until Christmas Eve, because it was considered bad luck to do so.

Grandmother's house had been three cottages, so there was a back scullery, a kitchen, a front kitchen and a lounge. To add to these delights there were two staircases, and dark passages connected the downstairs rooms, lending themselves to much fun and excitement.

On Christmas Eve, Mum, Dad, my sister and I moved in with Gran and two maiden aunts, to be joined by more relatives for Christmas Day. Mum and Dad went carol singing and the aunts were left to bath us and put us to bed. How well I remember that evening, a good soak in the coffin-shaped bath by the jet black range. On the range the kettle was always on the boil, and at this season there would be ham bubbling too. Gas lighting was used downstairs only, and the pewter tankards twinkled on the high mantelpiece, and the willow-pattern china shone on the dresser.

The bath finished, we went up the front staircase to our bedroom lit by a candle. My aunt had already used the copper warming pan in our bed, and I can still remember the smell of the hot coals. Excited and beautifully warm, we watched the candle burn low, making shadows on the ceiling, before going reluctantly to sleep.

On Christmas morning I enjoyed the atmosphere as much as the gifts. We all sat down to breakfast of a locally made pork pie, and then it was time for morning service. Following Christmas dinner, when my father always set the pudding alight, we settled down to table games in the front kitchen. We played "Strip Jack naked", "ludo", "Happy families" and "lexicon". In later years our favourite was a horse racing game called "escalado". During the war years Grandma entertained Air Force men from the local aerodrome on Christmas Day, and they joined in this game with great gusto. When

Grandma had had a little rest in the lounge we all moved in there to play charades. My Aunt Lil was a great entertainer and she would persuade us all to do our party piece. My cousin played the piano, which had two candlesticks with candles lit for the festive season, and we sang carols and well known songs. My sister and I would always ask Auntie Lil to sing *The Mistletoe Bough*, a saga of a young bride trapped in an old oak chest whilst playing hide-and-seek on her wedding day.

All too soon it was tea time: bread and butter, jelly, trifle, blancmange and of course Christmas cake. How could we have been so hungry! Now was the time for crackers and we did enjoy the mottoes and novelties inside. Then the adults retired to the sitting-room for cards, and the aunts in turn read or told us stories until it was time for bed.

On Boxing Day the hunt met on the village green, making a colourful sight when followers came from miles around. On this night my mother and father went out for dinner, and so it was time for more games and stories with the aunts before having "proper supper" and staying up late.

It has always been the custom to go carol singing in our village. In the early 1900s the church choir were the participants and they were accompanied by the vicar and took a piano on a cart. In 1926 the new vicar organised a party of children to sing round the village, and this went on throughout my childhood.

I recall we waited until after the general festivities to begin our carol singing and it was naturally undertaken in daylight hours. We sang all round the village first. In those days it always seemed to snow for the festive season, and after singing round the village we moved to the outlying farms. We set out with our kindly vicar, who was not so sure footed and walked with a stick. He suffered terribly with chilblains very much in evidence on his mitten-clad hands. He was extremely tolerant for we tried him sorely. Out for an enjoyable afternoon in the snow, we were not always too concerned about the carol singing itself. Warmly clad against the elements (and the wind could blow over those fields) we tramped through the drifts, making sure snow went over the tops of our wellies! We ran on ahead, or lagged behind the vicar, who would patiently call us to order at the front door of the houses. All the parishioners seemed to appreciate our visit and we would often be treated to drinks, biscuits and mince pies. At times we would hide from our dear vicar, and employ many delaying tactics to extend the afternoon and return home in the dusk.'

Index

Anstey   25, 30, 41–42, 130, 132, 140, 143, 183, 187, 233
Appleby Magna   89, 188
Arnesby   34, 71–72, 108, 139, 160, 161, 236
Ashby-de-la-Zouch   150
Ashwell   166
Ayston   79

Bagworth   187
Bardon Hill   43
Barwell   144, 147
Barrow on Soar   133
Barrowden   192
Basket making   173
Belgrave   24, 35, 59, 84, 124, 190, 203
Billesdon   196, 198
Birstall   48, 120
Biscuit manufacture   150–151
Bitteswell   35, 75, 87, 185, 190, 194, 211, 251
Blaby   70, 81, 182–183, 209
Blacksmith   162–164
Boot and shoe manufacture   64, 156–159
Bradgate   25, 42, 63, 142
Braunston-in-Rutland   22–24
Braunstone   14, 213–215
Brooke   23
Broughton Astley   31, 51, 218, 247
Bruntingthorpe   29, 32, 64
Buckminster   232
Burton Overy   51

Carlton Curlieu   206
Castle Donington   74, 85, 114–115, 173, 236
Chamberlain, Neville   215
Charnwood   175
Cheese manufacture   148, 178–180
Childbirth   89–90
Childhood   100–108
Church and Chapel   17, 23, 37–52
Churchill, Winston   11, 223

Christmas   29, 38–39, 40, 42–43, 84, 230, 243, 249–252
Coalville   137, 221
Coleorton   146
Collieries   143, 146–147
Copt Oak   140
Cosby   42–43, 82, 111, 116, 117, 132–133
Cossington   86, 96, 235, 240–242
Cotesbach   210
Cottesmore   192, 245–246
Cottingham   51
Countesthorpe   31–33, 106, 183
Cropston   30–31, 142, 187, 216

Dancing bear   230
Daleacre   114–115
Debdale   44
Desford   45, 143, 187, 236
Domestic service   164, 165
'Dummy Town' (Belgrave)   24

Earl Shilton   144, 148, 158, 167
Edward VIII (Duke of Windsor)   20, 113, 236
Elephant Man, The   18
Ellistown   143
Elmesthorpe   43, 144, 149
Empingham   77, 85, 136
Enderby   144, 145
Evacuees   185, 186, 187, 191, 194–201 passim, 225–226
Evington   152, 156

Farming   136–142
Fashion   14, 31, 37–38, 41, 42, 53, 64, 109, 202–203, 222–223
Fernie Hunt   66
First World War   11, 182–184
Fleckney   106
Food   84–89
Funerals   23, 58, 96–98, 162

Games and Pastimes   55, 105, 107, 109, 115, 117–124

George V 23
George VI 21, 107, 236, 244
Gilmorton 32
Gipsies 33, 35–36, 46, 93
Glenfield 45, 143
Glooston 41
Great Easton 50, 51, 73, 91, 191
Great Glen 17, 50
Groby 25, 78, 142, 143
Guy Fawkes night 31–32, 113

Hairdressing 172
Harby 39–40, 67–68, 81–82, 91, 96, 163
Heather 67, 184
Hemington 127
Higham on the Hill 91, 140, 168
Hinckley 36, 79, 129, 144, 147, 149, 168, 246–247
Holidays and treats 110–116
Home remedies 90–91
Hose 109
Hosiery and underwear manufacture 143, 144, 147, 151–156
House and Home 54–69
Huncote 144, 192
Husbands Bosworth 186

Ibstock 143, 210

Jarrow marchers 16

Ketton 162
Kilby 108, 111
Kilworth, North and South 103, 113, 138, 248
Kings Cliffe 162
Kirby Muxloe 46, 75, 201
Kirkby Mallory 194–196
Knighton 216–218
Knossington 85, 141, 230

Leicester 10–19, 44–45, 78, 79, 82, 103–105, 115–116, 118, 122–124, 125–127, 138–139, 153, 166, 171–176, 187, 191, 210, 235, 258
Leire Halt 51
Lindley 91, 93
Little Bowden 245
Little Dalby 86
Lockington 127
Loughborough 49, 100–102, 182, 183

Lubenham 27
Lutterworth 32, 36, 110, 132, 137, 185, 210, 212, 244

Mablethorpe 31, 111
Market Bosworth 92
Market Harborough 26–29, 82, 121, 198, 245
Markfield 12, 25, 176–178
May Day 23–24, 25–26, 30, 113, 242
Medbourne 134, 162
Melton Mowbray 20–22, 49, 170, 178–179, 202
Merrick, John ('Elephant Man') 18
Mount Sorrel 144
Mowmacre Hill 61, 216
'Mushroom Special' 47–48

Nailstone 210
Nanpantan 41, 142
Narborough 145
Newton Burgoland 121, 238
Newtown Linford 24–25, 38–39, 62–64, 127, 130, 139, 140, 141–142, 143, 164, 183, 187, 232
North Luffenham 162
Nursing 175–178

Oadby 50, 112, 128, 189–190, 244
Oakham 23

Packington 162
Pancake day 240, 243, 244
Peatling Magna 32, 33, 78, 136
Peatling Parva 29–30, 64–66
Peckleton 196
Pig-killing 65, 68, 86–89, 204–205
Police 16, 24, 34, 105, 156
Preston 78–79
Prisoners of war 28–29, 186, 188, 214–5
Privies, outside 15, 56, 62–73 passim

Quarries 143, 144–146, 149
Queen Victoria 238

Rationing 19, 61, 183, 186, 203–205
Ridlington 78–79
'Right to Work' march 11
Rothley 34–35, 83, 117, 126, 144

Sanvey Gate   12, 13, 118, 250
Sapcote   144, 147–149, 150
Sargent, Malcolm   22
Scalford   49
Schooldays   14, 19, 24, 28, 30, 32,
   58–59, 106, 125–134
School teaching   174–175
Seagrave   48–49
Second World War   14, 28–29, 185–227
Sewstern   232
Shacklewell   86
Shearsby   160, 161
Sheepy Magna   96–97
Shepshed   25–26
Shilton   149, 233
Shopping   77–83
Sileby   49
Snibston   143
Soar, river   16, 24
South Charnwood   187
South Luffenham   85, 89, 162
Sproxton   93
Stamford   77
Stanton under Bardon   12
Stoke Golding   169
Stoney Stanton   88, 144, 147, 148, 150
Sunday school   38–43 *passim*, 101
Superstitions   93–95
Sutton Bonington   206

Swepstone   238–239
Swinford   47–48, 72–73, 190
Swithland   43
Syston   133

Thurcaston   30
Thurnby   68
Tradesmen   77–83
Tramps   36
Transport   18, 44–52

Ulverscroft   24, 130, 140
Uppingham   23, 78

Water and washday   63, 68, 70–77
Welland Valley   27
Whetstone   71, 227
Whissendine   193
Whittle, Frank   32
Whitwick   234
Wicksteed Park   40, 46
Wigston   80, 104, 132, 153, 167, 200
Witherley   93, 112, 122, 130, 237
Women's Institutes   40, 201–202, 232
Women's Land Army   28, 206–212
Wyggeston   48, 128, 182, 215
Wymeswold   180

Yelvertoft   48

255